A PRACTICAL GUIDE TO TRA
PRIMARY MATHEMATICS

A Practical Guide to Transforming Primary Mathematics offers inspiration and ideas for all training and practising teachers committed to making mathematics enjoyable, inclusive, engaging and successful. The companion to Mike Askew's bestselling book, *Transforming Primary Mathematics*, this practical guide focuses on showing you how to unlock the powerful potential of a small set of consistent principles and practices, known as the teaching tripod, to develop a coherent approach to teaching mathematics.

Organised around the major strands of the curriculum – number, calculations, shape and space, measures and data handling – it offers an accessible introduction to the teaching tripod, a careful choice of tasks, supported by a range of tools that extend our natural abilities and held together by careful attention to classroom talk. A range of classroom tasks, each including key learning outcomes, clear links to the tripod, links to relevant research and suggestions for making the tasks easier or harder, are offered for every topic, helping you plan units of work for meaningful learning.

A Practical Guide to Transforming Primary Mathematics offers all teachers a vision, rationale and ideas for how teaching can support better learning of mathematics. It also suggests how to encourage learners to see themselves as being capable of – and enthusiastic about – learning mathematics.

Mike Askew is Professor of Mathematics Education at the University of the Witwatersrand, South Africa.

A PRACTICAL GUIDE TO TRANSFORMING PRIMARY MATHEMATICS

Activities and tasks that really work

Mike Askew

Routledge
Taylor & Francis Group

LONDON AND NEW YORK

First published 2016
by Routledge
2 Park Square, Milton Park, Abingdon, Oxon OX14 4RN

and by Routledge
711 Third Avenue, New York, NY 10017

Routledge is an imprint of the Taylor & Francis Group, an informa business

British Library Cataloguing in Publication Data
A catalogue record for this book is available from the British Library

Library of Congress Cataloging-in-Publication Data
Askew, Mike.
A practical guide to transforming primary mathematics : activities and tasks
that really work / Mike Askew.
pages cm
Mathematics—Study and teaching (Primary) 2. Mathematics—Study and
teaching (Primary)—Activity programs. I. Title.
QA135.6.A84 2015
372.7—dc23
2015008562

ISBN: 978-0-415-73844-6 (hbk)
ISBN: 978-0-415-73845-3 (pbk)
ISBN: 978-1-315-81731-6 (ebk)

Typeset in Interstate
by Swales & Willis Ltd, Exeter, Devon, UK

Printed in Great Britain by Ashford Colour Press Ltd

TABLE OF CONTENTS

Acknowledgements		vi
Introduction		1
1	**Tasks**	2
2	**Tools**	12
3	**Talk**	18
4	**The number system**	23
5	**Additive reasoning**	56
6	**Multiplicative reasoning**	81
7	**Geometry**	109
8	**Measures**	130
9	**Data handling and statistics**	161
	References	172
	Index	174

ACKNOWLEDGEMENTS

Since writing the companion volume to this book (*Transforming Primary Mathematics*) I have been privileged to spend time working with terrific teachers and researchers in Australia and my thinking has been greatly influenced by them. A particular thanks to Peter Sullivan, whose work on challenging tasks and building learner resilience is exemplary. Of the many teachers, a particular thank you to Rhys Coulson, Robert Smart and Angie McKail, and their colleagues, for giving me access to classrooms and for trying out many of the ideas here.

As always, my UK colleagues continue to inspire me. Thanks as ever to Margaret Brown, Jeremy Hodgen, Lynne McClure and Rob Eastaway. My dear colleagues in South Africa, especially Hamsa Venkat and Jill Adler, continue to convince me what a wonderful discipline mathematics education is and I'm grateful to them for the continuing collaboration.

Thanks to Joe Carter for permission to adapt for inclusion some activities originally published in *Teach Primary*.

Thanks to Helen Pritt at Taylor and Francis for suggesting I write this follow-up volume, and to her, and Sarah Tuckwell, for being so understanding over those pesky things called deadlines. And thanks to Charlotte Howard for her support.

Last, but of course not least, thanks to my 'boys': to Max for distracting me and to Russell for putting up with me being distracted.

To everyone else that I've forgotten, my apologies – it is not intentional (and I hope it's not old age!).

Introduction

And they all lived happily ever after

Having married a princess, defeated a giant or rescued granny from the wolf, classic fairy tales end with the homily that life then proceeds free of difficulties. Steven Sondheim's musical *Into the Woods* ends its first act with the characters' wishes coming true. So strong is our collective memory of that being the end of the story that apparently, at early performances of the show, many members of the audience thought that was the end of the entire show and not just the interval. The second act reminds us that happily ever after is, well, fiction. Having got your wish, the hard work may only just be starting.

In a sense this book is a second act, following on from my previous book *Transforming Primary Mathematics*. In that book I set out my vision for what the quest for mathematics teaching that might be engaging, empowering and enabling might look like, but that was only the beginning of the story. There was still the challenge of what that vision looked like in more detail and the implications for teaching particular content, and it is this that this book turns to.

Each book is written to stand alone – you do not need to have read *Transforming Primary Mathematics* to enter into this practical guide, but for those readers who have not yet read the companion volume a small reprise of some of the first act themes is needed.

Transforming Primary Mathematics (or *TPM* as I'll henceforth refer to it) ended with a model for thinking about mathematics classrooms – the teaching tripod of tasks, tools and talk. There I suggested that preparing for and enacting teaching was more secure when based upon careful choice of tasks, supported by a range of tools that extend our 'natural' abilities and held together by careful attention to classroom talk. The first three chapters in this volume take up this tripod of ideas. There is a small overlap with what I had to say about these in *TPM* but here I go beyond the initial discussion of these to look at each in more depth.

The remaining chapters then look at the core content of the primary mathematics curriculum and its teaching. The sections in each of these chapters are structured similarly. For each topic I note the key learnings in terms of big ideas and mathematical connections and then set out an overview of the issues involved both in coming to understand that topic and in teaching to help pupils understand. A number of classroom tasks are then presented in some detail. Note that these are not meant to be lesson plans, although they do read a little like they are. They are, rather, intended to give a feel of how a task could play out over time, and that time might be only part of a lesson or it may run over more than one lesson. My hope is that these examples embody and put flesh on the more general arguments made in the first three chapters and in *TPM*.

As I note in Chapter 1, my aim is not to be comprehensive and supply everything you might ever need to teach every topic! There is an abundance of resources available and the challenge, I think, is in choosing between what is available and, having chosen, making the best use of these resources with learners. Through the combination of the general (*TPM* and Chapters 1, 2 and 3) and the particular (Chapters 4–9) I hope the reader might get a sense of how mathematics teaching and learning need not be a diet of worksheets.

This volume need not be read in the order presented. You may want to turn immediately to look at ideas for particular topics. If you do, however, I would encourage you to return to the first three chapters at some point as the later ideas will, I think, then be clearer. Occasionally I have made reference to where ideas are also explored in *TPM*, but I have kept these to a minimum as this volume does stand on its own.

1   Tasks

Tasks lie at the centre of learning and teaching mathematics. Tasks bring mathematical activity into lessons, by which I mean mental activity, not just physical activity. Tasks have to meet the needs of specific pupils, so some writers encourage teachers to design their own tasks. As a former primary school teacher I know that time demands make this a high expectation, and having devoted my time teaching in higher education exclusively to mathematics education, I've also come to appreciate just how difficult task design is. Besides, there is such a plethora of tasks now available on the Internet I am not sure any more need creating. But not all tasks are created equal. I think it is a more reasonable expectation that teachers need to make good choices between tasks and a primary aim of this book is to support that decision making.

I do this in two ways. In this overview chapter I set out some ideas and principles about choosing tasks. Then, in the chapters devoted to specific curriculum topics I provide a number of elaborated examples. These examples are not meant to be an exhaustive list of all the tasks needed to develop understanding of and proficiency in the primary mathematics curriculum. My aim is to provide a sufficient number of examples to illustrate the general principles set out here, so that when subsequently faced with choosing tasks you, the reader, have some sense of what might make one choice better than another.

This chapter examines two general aspects of selecting tasks. It's Sunday afternoon, Monday's topic is subtraction and a search on the Internet has brought up a range of tasks: how to choose between them? The first part of this chapter examines what might influence choice making at such a moment in time.

Taking a longer-term view, introducing a mathematical topic to a class, then the type of task needs to change over time. Tasks offered to learners at the beginning of a unit of work on subtraction, when many of the ideas to be worked on may be relatively new, need to be different from the tasks offered towards the end of the unit when the ideas are beginning to bed down for learners. In the second part of this chapter I present a model for a cycle of tasks over time.

Choosing tasks with aims in mind

There is growing acceptance that learning mathematics is not a simple set of skills, but a complex interplay of a number of 'proficiencies', one model of which is set out in a major U.S. review of research into primary (elementary) mathematics – *Adding It Up: Helping Chlidren Learn Mathematics* (National Research Council, 2001). The authors of that report identify five proficiencies: conceptual understanding, procedural fluency, adaptive reasoning, strategic competence and productive dispositions.

Various versions of these proficiencies have found their way into National Curricula around the world and at the time of writing England's new National Curriculum highlights three of them:

- fluency
- problem solving
- reasoning.

Taken together, these provide a balanced set of aims for teaching and learning that can lead not only to mathematical competence but also to understanding. When selecting a teaching and learning task we therefore need to be clear about which of the proficiencies of fluency, problem solving or reasoning the task is most likely to encourage learners to engage in and 'good' tasks will invoke more than one proficiency.

It's a popularly held view that, in primary mathematics, fluency needs to be addressed first: that problem solving and reasoning have to follow on from some 'basic' proficiencies in core skills. However, research suggests otherwise. Not only are all three proficiencies inter-related, there is also increasing evidence that reasoning is the most important, so let us look at these in reverse order.

Tasks with a focus on reasoning

A recent major longitudinal research project looked at the mathematics of 8- and 9-year-olds and what understandings correlated with later attainment. The primary finding was that, 'Mathematical reasoning, even more so than children's knowledge of arithmetic, is important for children's later achievement in mathematics' (Nunes, Bryant, Sylva, & Barros, 2009, p. 1).

Correlation, of course, does not imply causation – it could be that pupils who have a talent or taste for mathematics reveal this through being able to reason, but over a wide range of studies it is becoming clear that reasoning in mathematics – asking why or how an answer is correct, not simply focusing on getting it right – is as important, if not more so, as arithmetical fluency.

Yet there is also evidence that the aim of developing mathematical reasoning is the least attended to in many mathematics lessons and that is not because primary pupils are not capable of mathematical reasoning – they most certainly are. I think this aim is neglected partly because reasoning is the most difficult proficiency to identify when selecting tasks. For example, the majority of mathematical tasks that come in a written form – pages in a textbook or worksheets – rarely address reasoning as it is hard to convey reasoning on the printed page. Taking music as an analogy, no piece of sheet music can present tone or a sense of rhythm – it is only in the playing of the music that such things emerge. A mathematics worksheet might provide a prompt to activity, but as with music, mathematical reasoning emerges in the playing, the doing, of mathematics.

Mathematical reasoning cannot be 'done' in isolation of mathematical content. You cannot simply go into a classroom and announce that the lesson is about reasoning and invite pupils to think! Pupils have to have something to reason about, say, subtraction or capacities of containers. Yet as soon as the content – the direct object of learning – comes into focus, attention to that content can take over and eclipse the reasoning. The lesson ends up focusing on whether or not the subtractions are correct, rather than whether it makes sense to use the same calculation method for 146 – 23 and 257 – 248. Or the focus is on how to record litres and millilitres rather than reasoning about the multiplicative relationship of a litre being 1000 times as big as a millimetre. It is not a question of focusing on reasoning or on content, but on developing both in tandem. In the extended examples in the content chapters I provide advice on how to enact this. I also suggest that a key way of bringing more reasoning into mathematics lessons is by making problem solving an integral part of all lessons.

Tasks focusing on problem solving

There are two ways to think about problem solving in the mathematics classroom: teaching *for* problem solving and teaching *through* problem solving.

Teaching for problem solving is probably the most common approach – problem solving is treated as the application of ideas previously learned. Pupils are taught how to, say, add or subtract, and then given problems that require addition or subtraction to solve them. While, obviously, pupils do need to use the mathematics that they have learned, the issue with much teaching for problem solving is that what is offered to pupils are not genuine problems, in that the learner is initially stumped and has to think deeply about what to do, but that problems are often just exercises practising what has been taught but 'wrapped up' in an often spurious context.

The 'flipping' of this approach – teaching through problem solving – rests on two assumptions. First, that mathematics is, at heart, a problem solving discipline and learners can come, through problem solving, not only to understand mathematics but also to appreciate its power. Second, that pupils come to school already skilled as problem solvers. Given a suitable problem to solve, the mathematical learning comes about through looking at ways to refine their informal solutions, to express them in mathematical terms. To distinguish problems chosen to help learners engage with new mathematical ideas, I call these foundational inquiries, and go on to discuss them in detail later.

Tasks focusing on fluency

Fluency is primarily (but not exclusively) about skills and procedures. It is the mathematical equivalent of working on scales when learning to play a musical instrument and, like scales, mathematical fluencies are a means to an end, not ends in themselves. Practising pages of, say, long division just for the sake of becoming fluent in the algorithm is not mathematically valuable if the pupil cannot appreciate when a problem may need to involve long division.

There are two aspects to becoming fluent in mathematical skills such as being able to use a ruler accurately or carry out the algorithm for long multiplication. First, having a clear sense of what expertise in the skill looks like: many skills can be modelled by the teacher or other pupils through direct instruction that shows how to set up a ruler to measure a line segment or demonstrates how to set out the digits for a long multiplication of a three-digit number by a two-digit number. Second, pupils then need to practise!

Objects of learning: direct and indirect

The language here, taken from variation theory (see *TPM*), of 'objects of learning' (rather than learning intentions or objectives) carries the connotation that pupils are supposed to take something – an object of sorts – as a result of the tasks they engage in. When choosing tasks for lessons, the focus is most often on the direct object of learning – the explicit mathematical content, for example, subtraction or fractions or 3D shapes. The direct object of learning is what pupils would say in response to the question, 'What did you do in mathematics today?'

As the researcher Ference Marton points out, however, every lesson (and not just mathematics lessons) engages learners in indirect objects of learning (Marton, Runesson, & Tsui, 2004). Reasoning, problem solving and fluency are examples of indirect objects of learning. Pupils have to reason about something, a lesson cannot be directly about reasoning – there has to be some direct content to reason about. Similarly, problem solving has to involve problems that address some particular content and learners become fluent in some particular mathematics.

When choosing tasks we need to bear in mind different possible indirect objects of learning – reasoning, problem solving and fluency – that might be provoked. Whenever possible, we need to choose tasks likely to provoke indirect learning that helps pupils learn more about mathematics and the nature of mathematical activity, such as the importance of looking for patterns or seeking generalisations as well as helping them master some particular content.

Tasks with multiple indirect objects of learning

Although a task might focus on only one or two direct objects of learning, it is possible for tasks to serve several different indirect objects. Let us look at this through the example of a game, *Say ten*.

Say ten

A game for two players. The player to go first can start either by counting 'one' or counting 'one, two'. Partners then take it in turns to count on from the last number, always counting on one or two. The player to say 'ten' is the winner. For example, play might go:

P1: *One*
P2: *Two, three*
P1: *Four*
P2: *Five*
P1: *Six*
P2: *Seven*
P1: *Eight, nine*
P2: *Ten. I win.*

The direct object of learning is for learners to play a counting game, but *Say ten* can address all three aims of fluency, problem solving and reasoning. At a basic level the game provides pupils with the opportunity to practise fluently counting on in ones or twos. With that object of learning in mind the task can be adapted to provide further practice in similar counting fluencies. The game might, for example, be changed to start at 30 and the winner is the person to say '50'. Or it might start at fifty and players count on in ones, twos, or threes. Or they might play the game counting backwards and win if they say 'one'.

Another indirect object of learning of the game is being able to solve the problem of what a winning strategy might be. Playing *Say ten*, pupils soon come to realise that saying 'seven' is a winning move – whether their partner then says 'eight' or 'nine' they are certain to be able to say 'ten'. Using this task in school, I find it interesting that many players stop at that point: having solved the problem of what number before ten ensures you win, learners stop there and do not look for further winning moves. Despite realising that saying 'seven' is a winning move, they do not go on to look at whether there is a strategy that ensures getting to say seven. The mathematician would expect there to be other winning positions, and learners closing down after finding seven is, I suspect, the result of most mathematics teaching that presents pupils with situations with only one answer to find.

A little reflection reveals that saying 'four' ensures that you can say 'seven' and saying 'one' then ensures you get to say 'four'. The game effectively becomes one of 'go first'. Encouraging pupils to go deeper into the problem of finding winning strategies thus introduces the indirect object of mathematical reasoning.

A big part of mathematical reasoning is looking for generalisations and a mathematician would expect that if saying 'seven' is a winning move, then this must generalise to there being other winning moves in variations of the game. The question then is, is whether there being a set of winning numbers is unique to this particular game, or whether all versions of the game have winning strategies. Thus, reasoning and generalising can be pushed further by altering the game to, say, being able to count on one, two or three and winning by being the first person to say 'fifteen'. Pupils can be challenged to come up with a new rule that works for this variation (in this instance, counting back in fours from 15 produces the 'unbeatable' numbers). They can then be encouraged to conjecture (the mathematical term for coming up with a 'theory' that is not yet proved) as to whether there is a general rule that can be applied to any target number and any choice of steps to count on. Once they have explored different versions of the game, pupils can often articulate a generalisation along the lines of 'count back from the target number in jumps one more than the highest number you can add'. That can be further explored to see whether it always holds true – what if you can count on two, three or four? Thinking can be provoked to go deeper: what if the game was to count on by 1/4 or 1/2 and the goal is to say 'three'?

Say ten thus has the potential to provide rich dialogue about mathematical reasoning and to extend learners' thinking. Such potential has to be considered when selecting tasks but it may remain only as potential depending on how the task is enacted. *Say ten* can remain at the level of a time-filling game unless pupils are expected to engage in thinking more deeply about it and challenges and extensions are provided. No task in itself can be 'rich', but tasks can be worked on in rich ways.

Even a task as seemingly mundane as working through a page of examples from a textbook can be 'played' with to make it more 'rich' and to encourage pupils to go beyond simply practising some fluency. For example, in pairs, one pupil could do the even numbered examples and their partner the odd numbered ones. After a time they could swap and check each other's work. Or, rather than working through the page from question one, pupils could spend a minute or two to select what they think are the five most interesting examples on the page (or the easiest, or most challenging), share these with a partner and agree on two examples to discuss with the class. Good choice of tasks is important, but the way they are enacted makes the difference in bringing mathematics to life.

The tasks cycle

At any given moment in planning for teaching we have to choose between possible tasks and this has to be balanced against tasks addressing different aspects of teaching and learning over time. If a unit of work is going to be for, say, three weeks, then the tasks learners need to engage with at the beginning of this time need to be different from those that they meet in the middle of the unit and then again at the end of the three weeks. I suggest thinking about this in terms of a tasks cycle where pupils move through foundational inquiries to practice and consolidation and then on to extension challenges.

Foundational inquiries

Foundational inquiries provide pupils with problems that they do not yet have the necessary formal mathematics to draw on in finding a solution but that they can solve informally. The teaching then comes through helping the pupils refine their methods to be more mathematical. The key to this lies in choosing problems carefully, with the following in mind:

1   They exemplify the mathematical ideas that pupils are going to go on to learn within a unit of work, but with which they are not yet familiar.
2   The problems would be easy to solve if the learners already knew the maths.
3   The problems are chosen with the expectation that they are not so difficult that learners are overwhelmed but not so easy that there is no challenge. Having the problem set in a simple narrative helps here, as pupils can then draw on their everyday understandings in finding a solution.
4   Pupils are expected to, and do, solve the problems with improvised, informal methods. In doing so they begin to get a sense of the underlying mathematical ideas that the problems exemplify.

Another important point to bear in mind is that the pupils' informal methods of solution will vary. By careful selection of which solutions to share and examine with the class, the teacher can introduce the mathematics that will help pupils refine their initial solutions (Ashlock, Johnson, Wilson, & Jones, 1983, p. 26).

For example, suppose a unit of work on fractions was being started with a class of 6-year-olds. Although seemingly simple (and this problem would be for older pupils) a problem like *Four hungry children* provides pupils of this age with a rich mathematical experience. They will have had enough everyday experience of solving things fairly to be able to solve the problem, even if they have not yet learnt very much about fractions. Their solutions could involve drawing pictures or cutting up pieces of paper, and two solution approaches are likely to emerge. One involves cutting each piece of toast into four pieces and each child getting two of these pieces. The other involves cutting both slices into two pieces and a child getting one of these. Pupils may come up with other solutions but these two approaches would be the main ones to look out for. The teaching then builds on these informal solutions to help pupils express their solutions more clearly through the language and notation of fractions. The idea that cutting a slice into four pieces and labelling these as 1/4 or labelling the piece from cutting a slice into two pieces as 1/2 means that the language and notation of fractions emerges within the context of talking about pupils' solutions and refining the language of description. And already pupils are introduced, informally, to the big idea of equivalent fractions. They know both of these solutions mean each child gets the same amount of bread, so $1/2 = 1/4 + 1/4 = 2/4$.

The dialogue can go further. The deliberately ambiguous wording of the question – how much bread will each child get? – means that there are two ways of talking about the answer. Each child gets 1/2 of a slice of bread or 1/4 of all the bread. Treating the language and notation of fractions as something useful to refine and talk about informal solutions 'flips' the usual approach of teaching fractions first as an abstract idea and then providing problems to apply fractions to.

Four hungry children

Four hungry children come home from school and find two slices of bread.
If they toast the bread and share it out equally, how much bread will each child get?

I refer to such problems as foundational inquiries to suggest that they provide the foundations of mathematical ideas. Rather than teaching pupils a method for solving foundational problems, the teacher has to work with the solutions that learners come up with and to expect these to be messy, to be mathematically naïve, to be less than perfect. This requires a shift in mathematics classrooms away from the expectation that there is only one, correct, way to solve a problem towards accepting that, initially at least, a variety of solution methods is not only acceptable but also welcome. It is this variety of solution methods that provides the raw materials from which the mathematics can be crafted.

It also means providing pupils with similar versions of the problems over a series of lessons. For example, in the next lesson, pupils might be given the problem of six children sharing out, fairly, three bars of chocolate. The variation here is a change of context – chocolate for toast – and the fraction equivalents – 1/6 and 1/3 for 1/4. But the basic schema of equal shares is kept constant and the fraction of each bar each child gets is still 1/2. Thus, learners begin to draw on their experience of the toast problem to create more refined solutions to the chocolate problem. As the researcher Lyn English (English & Sriraman, 2010) puts it, teaching through problem solving means accepting that there will be 'iterations' to pupils' solution methods – a pupil's first solution to a problem will be relatively unsophisticated and may not draw on a great deal of mathematics but as she subsequently works on similar problems her solutions become more refined and her mathematical understandings deepen.

Practice and consolidation

Once pupils have worked on several foundational inquiries they need to practise and consolidate the mathematics that has emerged. Two types of activity are particularly helpful here – deliberate (or intelligent) practice and games.

Deliberate practice

Deliberate practice is a term coined by the psychologist Ericsson from the study of expert sportspeople (Ericsson, Krampe, & Tesch-Romer, 1993). Ericsson found that one of the things separating 'experts' from 'amateurs' was the nature of practice they engaged in. The experts kept making what they practised harder to the point of failing, while the amateurs simply kept repeating what they could already do. This has resonances with what Carole Dweck describes as the difference between a 'growth' and 'fixed' view of ability: learners with a 'growth' mindset view their abilities as amenable to change and so they will persevere with challenging tasks in the expectation that this will help them to improve. In contrast, learners with a 'fixed ability' mindset prefer to work on tasks that they can already do (Dweck, 2000). Fixed mindset learners give up on challenging tasks as they believe that struggling means they have reached the limits of their ability.

In mathematics, we often make practice harder simply by introducing bigger numbers or expecting exercises to be done more quickly. Deliberate practice means finding other ways of adding challenge to activities, so that pupils still have to think and be mindful of what they are doing as they work through the practice. For example, practise in naming fractions often provides examples that are all very similar to each other, as illustrated in Figure 1.1.

Which shows 1/2?

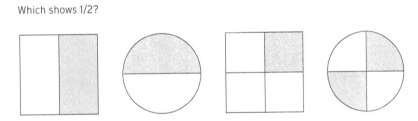

Figure 1.1

Contrast that with the examples in Figure 1.2.

Which shows 1/2?

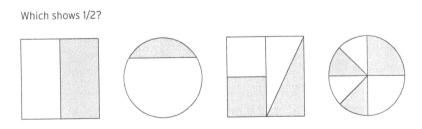

Figure 1.2

Games

There is truth to the adage 'use it or lose it' and we cannot assume that the pupil fluent in recalling, say, the four times table in Year 3 is, without continued practice, going to be just as fluent in Year 5. Games are the ideal task for keeping skills fluent. *Deal-em*, for example, is an activity for pairs to practise multiplication or division in spare moments.

Deal-em

Pairs of pupils need a pack of playing cards with the picture cards removed.

Version 1: A pupil decides which multiplication facts they want to practise, say, multiplying by seven. Their partner takes a card from the pack, reads out the number and counts, silently, to five. If their partner gives the correct answer to multiplying that number by seven within that time, the card goes in the 'correct' pile; otherwise, it goes on a discard pile. Once all the cards have been through, the discard pile is picked up, shuffled and used again, repeating this until all the cards are in the 'correct' pile.

Version 2: In this version pupils practise the related division facts. A divisor is agreed on, say, dividing by six. This time the player looking at the card multiplies the value on the card that they can see by the agreed number (say they are looking at a five, in this case they would say '30'). Their partner has to say the value of the card. As before, cards are dealt into 'correct' or 'discard' piles.

In choosing games, I'm always on the lookout for 'frame games' – games that provide a basic game structure that can be adapted to practise different mathematical skills. *Deal-em*, for example, could be changed for younger pupils to practise, say, adding or subtracting ten. In the examples in subsequent chapters I've included games that can act as frames in this way.

Extension challenges

Foundational inquiries involve problems for which learners are able to find informal solutions that can then be worked on to become more mathematical. Extension challenges also develop the learners' mathematics, the difference being that these involve problems where coming up with a solution is harder and will draw on a range of mathematics. Extension challenges are not just about applying an idea to harder problems. Learning is still occurring on the assumption that, through the struggle to find solutions, learners re-organise and deepen their mathematical understandings. Types of extension challenges include:

- modelling tasks
- practical problems
- whole class challenges.

Modelling tasks

Modelling tasks are real world problems where the challenge is to simplify the world and create a mathematical model of it. Applied mathematicians work with modelling problems all the time – they take the messiness of the real world and stress certain aspects while ignoring ones that may not be relevant to the task in hand. Pupils can engage in modelling through problems that are not 'neat', for example a problem like *Every day a shower!*

Every day a shower!

A shower uses 8 litres of water per minute.
How many litres might a person use in a year?

Given such a problem, many pupils will say that it cannot be solved, on the basis of not having been given enough information. Dialogue can bring into their awareness the fact that at least some people in the room will have had experience of showers, so data can be gathered on approximately how long a shower lasts and how many showers a typical person might take in a week. Pupils can then use this information to create a model of the situation.

There are particular types of modelling problems called Fermi problems that some learners find intriguing. Fermi problems are named after the Italian Nobel Prize winner Enrico Fermi. He enjoyed playing with problems along the lines of 'How many train carriages are there in the UK?' Or, 'How many piano tuners are there in greater Manchester?' Clearly such problems cannot be calculated precisely but Fermi showed that, by making reasonable assumptions, selecting sensible estimates and using simple calculations, surprisingly accurate answers could be reached.

Primary pupils can get deeply involved in Fermi-type problems, such as:

- How many trees are used each year to keep the school in paper?
- How many litres of water does the school use each week?

Practical problems

Practical problems are problems that require something to be built or have some solution that will be followed through.

Classic examples of practical problems include investigating how tall a tower can be built using straws and blu-tak or rolling up newspaper and finding a way to use the rolls to make a 'bridge' between two tables which is strong enough to support a pupil sitting on it.

Practical problems also include situations where the outcome matters; for example, adapting a recipe for making peppermint creams for an end of term party, or drawing up a timetable for who gets to work on the computer.

I counsel against what I call pseudo-practical tasks; for example, providing pupils with a set of travel brochures, giving them an imaginary budget and asking them to plan a holiday. Or asking the class to imagine that they are planning a week's worth of food for a camping holiday they might one day go on. Although some mathematics can emerge from such problems I think they have drawbacks. First, the pupils never get to test out if their solutions will actually work. It doesn't matter if your imaginary holiday goes over budget or you run out of food on the second day of your fantasy camping trip. I am also not keen on such problems because they inevitably carry some implicit messages about the sorts of lives that pupils should aspire to, for example that going on expensive holidays is the norm.

I do, however, think primary school learners can engage with problems that use realistic data and which might engage them in thinking about issues over and above the mathematics. Many pupils are aware of issues like the decline in the number of tigers or pandas and looking up the data on the Internet and interrogating it can lead to some valuable application of mathematics and to cross-curricular activities such as investigating what conservation programs are in place at a local zoo.

Whole class challenges

Whole class challenges are situations where smaller groups take on different parts of a large problem to solve.

Such challenges can take two forms, either one inquiry where different groups tackle it at different levels of difficulty, or alternatively, selecting a challenge that involves several different aspects and so different groups can take on different parts that collectively resolve the whole challenge.

Chocolate boxes

Chocolate boxes is an example of an inquiry where different groups can explore the same context at different levels of difficulty. (This activity is adapted from the work of Marten Dolk and Cathy Fosnot; see, for example, Fosnot & Dolk, 2001a.) The inquiry is about exploring area and volume by looking at different possible arrangements for making boxes of chocolates. So, for example, everyone might start by working on designing boxes to hold 24 chocolates. Some pupils may work on designing a box that has only a single layer of chocolates, looking at the different arrays that can be created from the factors of 24. Others may be challenged to create boxes with more than one layer and so move into exploring volume: finding three factors that multiply together to make 24 lays the foundations for meeting the formula for calculating the volume of cuboids.

This core inquiry can then be extended in a number of ways. As well as exploring different sizes of boxes, for example holding 36 or 48 chocolates, pupils could be offered the choice of different types of chocolates to make up their box, say, three types of chocolate costing 20p, 25p and 50p. How much would the box of chocolates cost? The level of difficulty can be adjusted by giving different versions of the challenge to different groups. Some groups may be asked to find the cost of a box of chocolates where the chocolates are all the same price, while others may be asked to fill their box with two prices of chocolate, still others with all three prices of chocolate. A further variation on this would be to fix the cost of the box of chocolates but to change the number of chocolates in the box, for example, exploring how a £5 box of chocolates could be made up.

The inquiry could then turn to looking at the amount of paper needed to cover the boxes, or the amount of card needed to make up the nets of the boxes. Do the different nets of different boxes all use the same amount of card or do some nets use less card than others? My colleague at Monash University, Peter Sullivan, came up with a nice extension problem. If a box is going to be tied up with ribbon (in the usual fashion as illustrated in Figure 1.3) and you know that 50 cm of ribbon is used up in tying the knot and the total length of ribbon is 2 m, then what are the possible dimensions of the box?

Figure 1.3

Pupils can work through such inquiries at different paces and according to what captures their interest. Some may get involved in looking at the costs of different boxes, others at the different amounts of card to make up the boxes, still others on which nets of boxes are most economical (if several nets are punched out of a larger sheet of card, then which net wastes the least amount of card?).

One advantage of linking together a number of inquiries in this way is that it helps build a 'collective memory'. Rather than mathematics lessons being a series of short tasks which over time become difficult in memory to distinguish one from another, it is possible to refer back to and effectively recall when the class were working on chocolate boxes and revisiting topics like volume or surface area can thus be anchored to this collective memory.

Organising the end of term party is an example of a whole class challenge where different groups can embark on different aspects of the challenge. Organising a party is too complex for any one group to do alone, so the various tasks that need to be done have to be identified and different groups assigned to work on them. One group might work on finding out what foods everyone would like and costing this. Another group might develop fundraising activities to help pay for the party. Yet another could survey the games that the pupils like and draw up a timetable of these for the afternoon of the party. Such large-scale challenges provide rich opportunities for mathematics across the curriculum. How well the party actually goes becomes the focus of reflection after the event for the pupils to evaluate how effective their problem solving was.

Finally

As I said at the beginning of this chapter, tasks are at the centre of learning mathematics: you can only learn mathematics by working on something. The choice of tasks is a non-trivial matter once we start to look beyond the surface details, beyond the obvious 'direct object of learning' of a task to the potential 'indirect object of learning'. This involves shifting from (not only) asking 'what do learners to need to do to complete this task?' (for example, multiply decimals or identify fractions) to also asking 'what is it about mathematics that they will be learning through this task?' (reasoning about when multiplying can make numbers smaller or reasoning about when 1/4 can be bigger than 1/2).

Carefully selecting tasks with aims and proficiencies in mind has to be complemented by attending to how the pupils will be encouraged to develop their reasoning, problem solving or fluency as the lesson plays out. Research shows that because problem solving or tasks involving reasoning can require more effort from pupils than that required by routine tasks, tasks chosen with these proficiencies in mind can, as a lesson unfolds, be met with resistance from learners. Lessons then become more focused on fluency, as teachers reduce the challenge in order to help pupils feel less uncomfortable. As I argue in *TPM*, it is more productive to acknowledge such struggles and help pupils work through them than to remove them.

In the examples in the chapters that follow I've included what I see as the potential indirect object of learning of the tasks. Whether these come into being in a lesson is as partly a consequence of how the learners are supported in carrying out the tasks, and what tools are available to them, which is the subject of the next chapter.

2 Tools

This chapter examines a number of key tools that support learners in developing mathematical understanding: contexts, models, actions and symbols. Taken together, these four tools provide the learning and teaching experiences from which mathematical meaning can emerge.

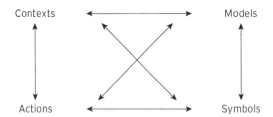

Contexts

You may be wondering in what sense context is a tool. As I argue here, and elaborate through examples in later chapters, setting tasks in contexts helps learners to understand the mathematics (and not, as commonly assumed, the other way round, that is, abstract mathematics helps you understand concrete contexts). Consider these two following problem scenarios:

> *Farmer Brown is planting cabbages. She has 168 cabbages to plant on a long strip of land where she can plant 6 cabbages in each row. How many rows of cabbages will Farmer Brown plant out?*

> *Farmer Brown is bagging up 168 apples to take to market. If she puts 6 apples in each bag, how many bags will Farmer Brown fill?*

To the mathematically experienced eye, it seems obvious that both of these problems involve the same calculation: 168 ÷ 6. If you regard such 'word problems' as simply providing opportunities for learners to practise carrying out calculations, then the choice of context, be it rows of cabbages, or bags of apples, will seem relatively immaterial. The calculation is the core, the context simply provides window dressing, which is not important in and of itself and can be discarded once the mathematics has been 'extracted' from the context and a calculation set up. The context can be swapped for anything else that might attract the learners' attention without any damage or change to the mathematics. Such a view of context can support practices like encouraging learners to look for key words that hint at which operation to apply.

Imagine now that, rather than these two problems being presented to a learner who already knows something about division, they are offered as foundational inquiries to a pupil with less experience of division but who can imagine setting objects out in rows or putting things into bags. The problems now are offered in the expectation that pupils will be able to use informal inquiry methods, particularly pictures or diagrams, to find solutions.

In this scenario the context does matter: different contexts will provoke different images and actions. In the case of cabbages in rows pupils' models (literally, with cubes or counters) or drawings are likely to be organised in an array-like fashion, perhaps rows of cabbages represented by setting out rows of six cubes or sketching rows of circles, adding additional rows and keeping a running total until reaching 168. In the case of apples in bags pupils are more likely to draw circles to represent bags with six tallies or dots in each to represent apples, adding additional circles and again keeping running total until they have used up all 168 apples.

If both problems boil down to keeping a running total of adding sixes, then do these differences matter? Yes, as the different representations provide different opportunities for the teacher to develop the mathematics. A pupil's representation of rows of cabbages lends itself to being linked to creating and describing arrays. Pupils could, for instance, be offered squared paper to help them organise their solutions, opening up the possibility for a conversation about exploring shortcuts – once ten rows of six have been shown to represent sixty cabbages then that could be used to show another ten rows representing a total of 120 cabbages, which then leaves only the remaining 48 cabbages to sort out.

Although 'apples in bags' does not preclude a similar exploration of arrays, that context makes it less likely that pupils will organise their drawings of the bags in an orderly fashion, making links to arrays and looking for short cuts less likely to emerge.

Rather than being chosen because learners might find them interesting or fun, problem contexts need to be chosen with such *pedagogic* purposes in mind, with an eye on what models and representations the context is likely to provoke learners to produce. Context then becomes a tool in the overall make-up of the mathematical experience, not simply a dressing up of the mathematics.

To take another example, problems about sharing out food are a good way to introduce pupils to fractions. A typical problem is something like:

> *Six hungry pupils shared four pizzas equally. How much pizza does each child get?*

Does it make any difference if the context of the problem is changed from pizzas to, say, 'submarine' sandwiches or bars of chocolate? Setting aside issues of which of these foodstuffs pupils might be more drawn towards, it again does make a pedagogical difference. Dividing a circular image into thirds or sixths is considerably more difficult for pupils to do than it is for them to divide a rectilinear shape into thirds or sixths. The pizza version of the problem is actually harder for learners to solve (reasonably accurately) than a submarine sandwich or chocolate bar version of the problem.

Different contexts can also give rise to different images of arithmetical operations. Here's another pair of what, at first glance, look like very similar problems. As you read them, think about the different drawings and images that learners are likely to produce if they don't immediately know how to express these contexts in symbols:

> *Fifty-four tadpoles were swimming in the shade under a lily pad. Forty-eight more tadpoles swam and joined them under the same leaf. How many tadpoles were then under the leaf?*

> *Freddie Frog took 54 jumps then took a rest. He then jumped another 48 jumps. How many jumps did Freddie make in total?*

The tadpole problem focuses attention on quantity and an obvious type of drawing is to make a representation of the quantity. The frog problem invites the learner to represent the jumps as movement along a path – setting up the link to representing addition as movement along a number line. Although it is possible to represent the tadpole problem on a number line, it is not the immediately obvious representation and it may be that a teacher explicitly chooses the tadpole problem precisely to have a conversation about different ways to represent it. It is not that one context is better or worse than the other, but that teachers need to be mindful of the likely outcomes of choosing one or the other. For me, this means 'playing through' in my head how I imagine learners are going to respond, and changing the context if it looks like it is not going to support the sort of mathematical activity I am hoping to provoke.

To take another example, a problem like comparing the length of a mother snake to the length of a baby snake will encourage learners to make two lines, side-by-side and figure out the difference, thus fulfilling the pedagogic purpose of representing difference as a pair of points on a number line and finding the size of the line segment between the two points (see Figure 2.1).

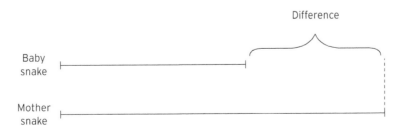

Figure 2.1

In summary, contexts need to be chosen so that when pupils 'mathematise' the situation – when they set up some mathematical model of the situation – the models they produce are likely to have some potential for being worked on and refined into more formal mathematics. I provide further suggestions for contexts in the chapters on additive and multiplicative reasoning.

Models

I have referred a lot to models and modelling, so let me clarify what I mean by those terms. A model, in the sense that I am using here, is anything that 'stands in' for something else. An architect produces models of buildings; a theatre designer produces models of stage sets; a mathematician produces models of the world. Models are created so that they can be 'played with' and explored, so that insight can be gained into the 'real' situation without having to act directly on the real world – better to have a cardboard tower block buckle than to have that happen after construction. In solving the farmer's problem, better to play with laying out rows of counters than to try and get 168 cabbages to hand. We usually think of models as three-dimensional, but they can also be two-dimensional pictures or diagrams or symbols. In learning mathematics engaging pupils in the processes of modelling is as important as getting them to work on the models.

We can think of models as lying on a continuum from being very close to the 'real thing' through to the purely abstract. Take for example:

> *Gemma had a bag of 12 sweets and she gave 4 to her brother. How many sweets did Gemma have left?*

Young pupils might be presented with a bowl of actual sweets from which they could count out 12, remove 4 and count what was left to get the answer. Working with sweets, the model is close to the 'real thing' (although this is still a model as it is standing in for any actual sweets that our fictional Gemma might have had). Older pupils are likely to know that the answer is 8 and to record $12 - 4 = 8$. The model $12 - 4$ is abstract in that it can be applied to a range of situations other than this particular problem, which is of course what gives abstract mathematics its power.

Between these two extremes is a range of models that provide stepping-stones to becoming increasingly abstract. For example, working with cubes to represent sweets; drawing sweets randomly; drawing circles, dots or tallies; organising such images in a row; finding 12 on a number track and counting back 4 spaces; marking 12 on an empty number line and making 4 jumps back; writing down $12 - 4$.

The thing to note is that right up to the point where the model becomes purely symbolic ($12 - 4$) all these models retain some sense of *quantity*. Sweets or cubes show quantity in three-dimensional terms; pictures or diagrams, being two-dimensional are marginally more abstract, but if there is one drawing for each object, the sense of quantity is still present. Number tracks embody the quantity 12 through there being, up to the square labelled 12, 12 squares on the track (and putting one counter on each square shows that quantity). The number line carries echoes of the quantity of twelve by virtue of where 12 is marked on the line. As soon as we write down $12 - 4$, however, all these representations of quantity vanish. Before using symbols, pupils need lots of experience of all these different sorts of models, so that the symbols become imbued with a host of connotations.

A literacy example illustrates what I mean here. Take the sentence:

> *As Anna was wrapping up Josh's present she remembered how last year he had such difficulty blowing out all the candles on his cake.*

Providing they have had sufficient experience, readers will conclude that Anna is wrapping a birthday present, that she was at Josh's birthday party the year before, that there were many candles on the cake and a whole host of other connotations, none of which are explicit in the printed words. The sentence makes no mention of birthdays, parties and all that goes with these. Pupils who can read the words but not tell you what the story is 'about' are said to be 'barking at print'. Pupils who can carry out arithmetical calculations, but without a sense of what the symbols might represent, could be said to be 'barking at numerals'!

The danger with much mathematics teaching is in rushing to express things in symbols, often with the (tacit) expectation that the symbols themselves 'carry meaning'. We have to remember that meaning is what is provoked in the mind of the learner; it can never be 'in' the symbols.

So although strictly speaking writing an equation like 12 − 4 = ? is setting up a model, I prefer to use model in the sense of representations - physical, pictorial or diagrammatic - that embody some sense of quantity and the relationship between quantities. Much research has shown the dangers of rushing to working purely with the symbolic as learners either cannot make sense of the symbols, or, if they start to make errors they have no means of checking or self-correcting as they cannot read meaning into the symbols. The strength of the abstract symbols is that they can be used to model an infinite number of contexts, but pedagogically that is also their weakness. For that reason I have separated out the symbolic into its own category.

Actions

Throughout the previous section, I have made reference to the actions that pupils will make as they engage with various contexts and set up models for these. These actions may be imagined and prompted through the contexts chosen - people arriving and leaving, frogs jumping, gardeners planting out seeds, bakers laying out pies - or they may be actual actions on the models that pupils create - putting out counters, jumping forwards or backwards along a number line, setting up arrays.

Actions are important not simply because of the claim that some pupils are 'kinesthetic' learners. In fact, evidence now shows that the idea of learners having a preference for 'visual', 'auditory' or 'kinesthetic' learning is not correct. While it might feel, subjectively, that one has a preference for a particular way of thinking, brain research indicates that all three modes work in conjunction with each other and we all use all three when carrying out mental activity (assuming no physical impairment).

The reason why actions are important rests on the evidence that learning is 'embodied'. We do not simply come to know mathematics through 'minds' that operate independently of our bodies. Our understandings are inextricably linked to our bodies, our positions and our movements in space.

The theory behind this view of learning comes from writers who argue that all higher levels of mathematics emerge from basic action schemas (the definitive volume on this is Lakoff and Núñez [2000]). For example, take a couple of simple questions like:

- Which is bigger: 5 or 6?
- Which is the lower number: 7 or 8?

Few primary pupils will have difficulty in answering '6' and '7' respectively, but as Lakoff and Núñez suggest, pausing for a moment we might ask, what do these questions really mean? Numerals like 5 and 6 are just symbols, abstract ideas. The symbol '5' can stand for a host of things, all perceived in different ways: five ducks, five steps, five beats of the drum and so forth - there is no single thing that *is* 'five', so how can five be smaller than six? Similarly, why is the number 7 'lower' than the number 8? Lakoff and Núñez suggest that thinking about abstract numbers as bigger or smaller arises from our embodied experiences of *collections of five objects* compared to *collections of six objects*. From the visual perception of one collection being bigger than the other collection we, subtly and not consciously, draw on such embodied experiences, to make sense of the abstract: 6 is bigger than 5. Similarly, the idea that 7 is lower than 8 has origins in considering movement from a point (upwards in this particular case) - with this action you would reach a lower point climbing seven steps than that reached by climbing eight. Lakoff and Núñez argue that metaphor is at play here: numbers are like quantities or they are like positions (along or up). We make sense of the abstract mathematics through these metaphors and there is no one metaphor that we use to make sense of numbers - the metaphor will vary according to the circumstances. Comparing, say 6 and 5, we might think of 6 as bigger than 5 through the metaphorical reasoning that a pile of six cubes will be seen to be bigger than a pile of five, but comparing 656 to 655 that metaphor lets us down - we would not be able to discern just by looking which of those piles of cubes would be bigger. We do know, however, from our sense of movement that 656 is going to be 'further' along a track than 655, if we imagine passing the numbers in order, just as we do with milestones (which itself is a popular metaphor for tracking achievements).

Metaphor, I used to think, was the stuff of poetry, but my reading around these theories convinces me that there is much to the argument that our thinking is based in metaphor. It is beyond the scope of this book to go into the details but if you are interested in reading more about this, I highly recommend *Metaphors We Live By* (Lakoff & Johnson, 1980). Reading this was, for me, that clichéd thing, 'life-changing'. I could not, cannot, think about language in the same way after reading it.

When it comes to number, Lakoff and Núñez argue that there are four core action metaphors that under-gird arithmetic (underpin, are the foundation of, at the base of, . . . choose your own metaphor. Ok, I'll stop):

1   arithmetic as object collection
2   arithmetic as object construction
3   the measuring stick metaphor
4   arithmetic as motion along a path.

1. Arithmetic as object collection

Wherever you go to school you are likely to be introduced to adding and subtracting *numbers* by adding and subtracting *quantities*. Putting collections of things together and taking them apart are core experiences providing metaphorical links to pure arithmetic.

2. Arithmetic as object construction

'How may tens are there in 36?' 'Twenty-one is made up of three lots of seven'. Here numbers are thought of as being made up of other numbers, but again, as numbers are essentially abstract this talk of 'in' or 'made up of' is metaphorical: images of wholes being made up of parts are being brought into play. The idea that numbers can be made up of other numbers is based in the everyday actions of taking discrete collections – say, red, yellow and green bricks – and combining them into a larger collection.

3. The measuring stick metaphor

Taking a unit – a stick or a knotted length of string – to measure is a well-established activity, an extension of the embodied actions of using body parts as units for measuring (echoes of which remain in the imperial units of feet, spans and cubits). The actions of measuring, in particular repeatedly using a body part of unit, provide root actions for later metaphorical abstractions. For example, longer lengths are used to make sense of the idea of greater numbers (the length of the corridor at 12 m is longer than the length of the classroom at 6 m, so 12 must be greater than 6) or comparing two lengths helps to make sense of the idea of the difference between two numbers.

4. Arithmetic as motion along a path

Moving or jumping along a number line is linked to the embodied experiences of moving along a path, of things we pass on the way, and the order in which we pass them.

While Lakoff and Núñez argue for thinking of multiplication as arising from repeated addition, I would add a fifth core metaphorical action that underpins multiplication:

5. Covering surfaces into two directions

Spreading out sheets on the bed, painting a sheet of paper, filling a tin by smoothing out the cake mix – all these form the everyday actions that lead to making sense of the idea of multiplication as finding the surface covered.

All this may simply sound like a fancy argument for providing pupils with 'concrete' experiences out of which they 'discover' the 'real' mathematics. But the point is subtly different. These actions are not a substitute for the 'real' mathematics, in that once they have served their purpose they can be discarded. These actions are the basis of the 'real' mathematics and the abstract only makes sense by them being drawn upon.

Symbols

As I have argued, although we often start mathematics through introducing symbols, I think they are best introduced as a compact way of representing contexts, models and actions, otherwise we run the risk of confusing the symbols with the mathematics; of confusing a representation with an idea. Again, to make an analogy with reading, suppose you were sitting next to me with a book and looking at the sentence 'Cats are cute'. If I pointed to the word 'cats' and said, 'These make me sneeze', many things are likely to come to mind: cat hairs, watery eyes, a YouTube video and so forth. What is highly unlikely is that you would think that what I meant was that the printed letters - c, a, t, s - make me sneeze. When reading, we do not mistake the symbols on the page for the thing they have come to represent for us. Yet that is what we often do in mathematics - we think the symbols are the mathematics, when in fact the relationship between, say, the numeral '5' and an actual pile of five stones is as arbitrary as the relationship between the letters c, a, t, s and the furry creatures to which I am allergic. When reading, we know that the symbols - words and letters - don't 'carry' any meaning in and of themselves. Meanings come into being when the reader brings to bear their host of connotations and associations, to bring 'cats' to life in the mind, to conjure up in the imagination - something a computer will never be able to do, even though it can 'read' the word 'cats' out loud.

Similarly, mathematical symbols are brought to life through the wealth of associations and ideas that the mathematician (and by this I mean anyone engaged in mathematics, not just professional mathematicians) can bring to mind in response to engaging with the symbols.

Take, for example, the numeral '64'. This might bring to mind a large pile of randomly organised bricks, or the same quantity organised in some way. Most likely this organisation would be imagined as six groups of ten and four single ones. But we can also organise such a quantity as an array of eight squares by eight squares, and that in turn may provoke an image of a chessboard, the squares alternating in colour. Or we could imagine how 64 unit cubes could be assembled to make a four-by-four-by-four cube. That might then bring to mind the question of whether there are other ways to arrange 64 unit cubes to make a cuboid. Or 64 may conjure up images of two groups of 32, and how each of those could be split into two groups of 16, and groups of eight, four, two or one (and why then stop there?). For some, 64 may have particular connotations - only one more year to retirement - or bring snatches of the Beatles song to mind about still being loved at that age.

We can express each of these actual or imagined models and actions on them in concise symbolic form:

$60 + 4$

8×8

4^3

$2 \times 2 \times 2 \times 2 \times 2 \times 2$

But all these symbols are inert if the learner cannot bring to mind such rich networks of associations. Exploring different ways of playing with and expressing 63 and 65 can illustrate just how different these numbers are from 64, making them all the more interesting than simply being three consecutive numbers in the sixties.

Symbols are important but the person interacting with them has to imbue them with meaning, has to bring to mind contexts, models, actions. Symbols are not the pinnacle of mathematics, not the goal that as we move up through primary education contexts, models and actions can be discarded. Yes, symbols at some point do become 'objects' in their own right that can be played with and manipulated without having always consciously to root them back in any model or context but contexts, models and actions still remain in the background. Hence there are dangers in only looking at learners' symbolic representations and assuming that these reveal what they know about the mathematics. Many learners are good at learning the rules of how to manipulate symbols without having a strong sense of the connotations that the symbols might provoke (I know, I was one of those pupils).

To summarise, in Bruner's (1960) terms, this linking of the concrete (contexts), iconic (models) and symbolic (to which I add actions, the enactive) is something that we need to be invoking at all points of learning mathematics, as a set of linked experiences that learners of any age or ability need to work with. The final element of the teaching tripod, talk, is what helps learners bring all these experiences together.

3 Talk

This chapter examines the importance of talk in gluing together mathematical tasks and tools. In *TPM* I wrote about thinking of talk in mathematics classrooms as happening in two 'spaces' - private talk and public conversation - that acknowledges that different types of talk serve distinct purposes.

Private talk

Private talk recognises that the mathematics classroom has to provide learners with time and space to talk about their mathematical ideas in ways that are non-judgmental and non-threatening. A space where it is okay to be wrong, where it is acceptable to try and articulate half-formed ideas and where pupils can work with someone else on refining and developing their thinking. Often we expect pupils in mathematics classrooms to be able to quickly articulate mathematical ideas, to be instantly coherent and correct, but learning needs phases of mulling, being less than coherent and being comfortable with an initial lack of certainty about answers.

When working on a task, learners will often get a sense of 'what is going on' but the move to turning that nascent sense of understanding into meaningful words is far from easy. As John Mason puts it, it is not easy to 'say what you see'. Time for private talk supports the struggle to articulate what learners are developing a sense of. Take for example, a string of calculations like these ones and the question as to whether each one is true or false:

$$6 + 6 = 6 + 7 - 1$$

$$26 + 6 = 26 + 7 - 1$$

$$345 + 259 = 345 + 260 - 1$$

Pupils can establish that each of the first two equations is true by carrying out the calculations. In the third example, however, the numbers are chosen to be awkward enough to discourage learners from immediately calculating each side of the equation. Although learners may be convinced that they know each side of the equation is equivalent articulating a coherent and convincing explanation is not easy: 'If you add 260 to 345 instead of adding 259, then you've added on one more, so you need to take one off to keep the answer the same'.

This talk of actions on quantities and what has to be done to keep everything in balance is the beginning of realising that there is a possible generalisation here. Although challenging, it is worth pursuing and encouraging pupils to articulate a general statement: 'If you add two numbers together, then take one of these numbers and add one more than the other number, this second answer is always going to be one more than the first answer'. Why go to that bother? First, the struggle to articulate such 'noticings' is an important part of establishing a 'conjecturing classroom' - articulating what you have a sense of and getting it into a form where it can be checked out. Second, it provides the justification for algebra - learners can begin to appreciate that expressing this as $a + b = a + (b + 1) - 1$ is just a shorthand way of saying the same thing.

In lessons there are at least two opportunities for private talk. One is through the frequent use of 'turn and talk' within whole class sessions. One of my 'relentless practices' is to ask pupils to turn and talk to a partner before taking answers from the class. Just a minute or so gives everyone the opportunity to share their thoughts or answers with a partner, to see if they agree and perhaps adjust their thinking if they do not.

The other opportunity for private talk is when the pupils go off to work independently on tasks – the vast majority of such times I expect them to work in pairs. The research evidence is clear: working individually is best for independent practice, paired work is best for developing understanding and small group work is best for extension activities (for a synthesis of the research leading to these claims, see Kutnick et al., 2005). As I argue in TPM the evidence also shows that, provided pairs work well together, paired talk raises the achievement of each partner, even if at the start of a task there is a difference of attainment between the pair.

Public conversation

Public conversation is the complement to private talk. It is during public conversation that learners' different ideas, methods and solutions are shared, collectively examined, refined and agreements worked towards. During public conversation the teacher collects together and makes public different mathematical senses and solutions that individuals and pairs have arrived at, and crafts these, through dialogue, into generally accepted mathematical meanings. Of all the aspects of teaching advocated here, this is, I think, the hardest to implement. This type of public conversation differs from what research shows is the dominant form of whole class interaction in mathematics classrooms – initiation, response and evaluation (IRE) – where the teacher asks a question, elicits learners' answers and immediately evaluates these, most often in terms of whether they are right or wrong and a common response to an evaluation that an answer is wrong is to seek other answers until the correct one is elicited. 'What is seven times eight? Jimmy?' 'Fifty-four?' 'Selma?' 'Forty-eight?' 'George?' 'Fifty-six?' 'Yes, thank you George'.

Although IRE appears to move a lesson forward, it does not help those pupils giving incorrect answers. A more productive response is to note down the various answers on the board without 'giving away' which is the correct one (easier said than done – pupils are very good at reading a teacher's face). Pupils can then turn and talk about which they think is the correct answer. That provides time for the teacher to listen in to what pairs are saying or to have a conversation with pupils providing an incorrect answer and try to understand why they gave that answer. Sometimes wrong answers are the result of slip-ups (and in private talk pupils may self-correct), but they are more often the result of some misunderstanding or alternative interpretation. If that is the case then it is likely that more than one pupil holds such ideas and so it is worth talking about these in the public space. That is no guarantee that learners' understanding will be 'corrected' there and then, but having a clear idea of what and how the learners are thinking is the first, formative, step in deciding what might need to be done to work on changing their ideas.

At the heart of this is the idea that lessons need to play out in ways that not only provide plenty of opportunities for talk but also for listening, listening that goes beyond evaluating the 'correctness' of answers to listening that helps everyone gain access to each other's thinking. Listening is central both to generating collective mathematical meaning and to helping the individual learner.

Relational and attentive listening

Rinaldi (2001, p. 3) describes listening as a relational process based around being 'orientative, curious and responsive as opposed to pre-determined, disinterested and pre-scriptive'. At the heart of relational listening is the attitude that there is such a thing as 'pupils' mathematics' – that is, pupils engage with their worlds in ways that are mathematical, and in doing so come up with mathematical ideas and that their ways of reasoning, whilst possibly not fitting with the canon of mathematical ideas considered to be correct, do, nevertheless, construct a mathematics that has a certain logic to it. Listening in a relational way means listening for the pupils' logic and it makes a big difference to how the mathematics unfolds. Let us look at a small case study.

A 7-year-old boy I worked with was confident in correctly answering questions like $7 + 2 = [\ ]$ or $9 + [\ ] = 14$. However, when presented with $11 + 9 = [\ ]$ he equally confidently claimed that the answer was 11. Asked why, he explained that that, 'Nine plus 1 is 10, plus the other one is 11'.

This is, I think, an example of what Eleanor Duckworth calls a 'wonderful idea' in her claim that intellectual growth comes from everyone having their own, unique, wonderful ideas, irrespective of their level of development. 'The having of wonderful ideas, which I consider the essence of intellectual development, would depend [. . .] to an overwhelming extent on the occasions for having them' (Duckworth, 2006, p. 181).

Of course, thinking of 11 + 9 = 11 as a 'wonderful idea' does not deny that it is mathematically incorrect, but getting the idea articulated gave me, as teacher, material to work with in ways that may be more productive than simply correcting or explaining. Sharing this example recently with a class of pre-service teachers, there was a gasp of delight at the boy's explanation, and comments about how skillful I had been to elicit this. When I asked the students why they thought this, there was general consensus that in the classrooms they had been visiting, the majority of such interactions, from the point of the boy getting it wrong, involved teachers showing the correct solution (the IRE cycle). For me, it is not that my questioning was particularly skillful (I simply kept asking, 'How did you get that answer?'). I think it is more to do with the attitude behind the questioning. Asking a pupil how they got the answer works best when underpinned by an attitude of curiosity; by a belief that behind every pupil's answer - correct or incorrect - there is some sense making, some wonderful idea.

The writers Empson and Jacobs (2008, pp. 262-264) identify four reasons why they think listening is important in mathematics lessons:

1   It improves learner's understandings - having to explain to someone who is really listening to your explanation improves the quality of that explanation.
2   It is a powerful means of formative assessment - listening to understand what the learner is saying and thinking provides different insights than those gained when listening simply to judge whether or not their answer is correct.
3   It supports 'generative learning', that is learning that goes beyond simply succeeding at the task in hand.
4   It increases a teacher's mathematical knowledge - listening to and actively making sense of learners' explanations is mathematical work, as you have to think about whether what they are saying makes mathematical sense.

Given that pupils' mathematics is going to be (one hopes) less sophisticated than the teacher's, then in what sense is listening to pupils' explanations mathematical work and so likely to increase a teacher's mathematical knowledge? In *TPM* I wrote about a learner I met who was confident that 2, 4, 6 and 8 were even but was equally confident that 9 was also even. When I asked him how he decided if a number was even, he explained that it meant it could be 'split it into even amounts' demonstrating this by taking six interlocking cubes, making two equal towers that were 'even' (putting his hand flat across the top of them). Asked about nine, he showed how nine cubes could be arranged to make three equal 'even' towers. Listening evaluatively, the response that 'nine is even' is going to be heard as wrong. Listening relationally - in being curious about whether there was a logic to his answer - not only revealed something about the pupil's thinking but also made me, as the teacher, think about the mathematics of even numbers, composite numbers and factors. Composite numbers are those numbers that are not prime - they have factors other than one and themselves. Nine is a composite number as $3 \times 3 = 9$. Thinking about the boy's response, I realised that I had never really thought of the even numbers as a particular subset of the composite numbers (even numbers have a factor of two). My own mathematical understanding was changed.

The demands that relational and attentive listening place on teacher subject matter knowledge of mathematics may be one reason why such listening is difficult to do in lessons, as teachers have to make mathematical sense, in the moment, of learners' ideas. But this cognitive demand can be eased. Techniques such as 'revoicing' (see TPM) - getting other learners to explain in their own words what they think a peer said - provides time and space for everyone in the class - teacher included - to process and make sense of what is being said.

Breaking set with the idea of the lesson as the primary 'unit of learning' can also help as pupils' work can then be considered between lessons. Technology is opening up new opportunities for this. For example, pupils working on tablets can record short 'movies' that capture the construction of images and solutions along with a 'voice-over', allowing for viewing and listening outside actual lesson time. A lesson I saw in Singapore had learners working on laptops and not only were their stages of activity being recorded but the teacher was also able to monitor everyone's progress in real time, as all the work was being streamed to her computer.

Relational and attentive listening means not only expecting learners to have some mathematics to communicate but also treating learners as already competent communicators of mathematics. Judit Moschkovich argues that growth in mathematical talk occurs through learners taking part in mathematical conversations in whatever ways they can. This means setting aside expectations of correct mathematical talk and working with the communicative resources that pupils do bring to school, including gestures and social resources (Moschkovich, 2007).

Relational and attentive listening also poses challenges to learners. They need to listen to each other's solutions, not just out of politeness, but to think about the connections to their solutions and to help each other refine methods and explanations. The sharing of methods can then be followed up with asking learners to try out a particular approach and see if other problems could be done in that way. The evidence from psychology is that this leads to better learning. Being, in the psychologist Ellen Langer's term, mindful of the fact that there are choices – that, say, a calculation could be done in several ways – results in deeper and more flexible learning than that arising from insisting that something must be done in a particular way (Langer, 1997).

Creating conjecturing classrooms

I mentioned the importance of creating a culture of conjecturing, so what can help promote this? One aspect of preparation for conjecturing classrooms where talking and listening are two aspects of mathematical dialogue involves careful choice of examples. In the examples discussed earlier ($6 + 6 = 6 + 7 - 1$; $26 + 6 = 26 + 7 - 1$; $345 + 259 = 345 + 260 - 1$) the first example can be readily checked in the head, and the second example could be checked mentally but it could also be justified by referring back to the first example. The third example, as noted previously, was chosen so that the calculation is too cumbersome to work out and to encourage the learners to reason rather than calculate. There is a logic and progression to the examples to prompt a move from the specific to the general, from a closed answer to a general reason, to conjecturing about how equations function.

Let us look at another example: adding using a compensation strategy – rounding one of the numbers to a multiple of ten, adding that multiple of ten and then adjusting the answer appropriately. Consider these examples as choices to work on:

$47 + 39$

$35 + 38$

The first, $47 + 39$, may be likely to provoke a compensation strategy: rounding 39 to 40, adding 40 to 47 and then taking 1 off 87. The second, $35 + 38$, although amenable to compensation (add 40 to 35, take 2 off 75 to get 73), might also provoke a near-doubles strategy (double 35 is 70, add 3 on to that). So, although each example *can* be answered using a compensation strategy, in choosing which examples to present to pupils we have to think about whether the desired strategy is the one they *are* likely to choose. It is not that one example is better than the other but that examples have to be thought through in terms of the strategies that pupils might use. Examples are not all equal.

This choice of examples is easier said than done. If I decide that the direct object of learning of the lesson is going to be compensation, if that is foremost in my mind when preparing for a lesson and selecting examples, then $35 + 38$ probably seems as good an example as any other. But it is one thing to have (as teacher) a strategy in mind and then choose some examples; it is quite another to be presented (as learner) with an example and be expected to choose exactly the same strategy that the teacher had in mind. Trying to imagine yourself in the position of the learner is an important part of preparation.

Dialogue

In *TPM* I discuss the distinction that the physicist David Bohm makes between discussion and dialogue – the former is associated with having a position that one is trying to convince the other of adopting, whereas dialogue is characterised by exchange of ideas, which means holding lightly to one's position.

In my experience, working with dialogue sets up a virtuous circle in classrooms. As pupils learn that the culture is one in which is it safe to make mathematical offerings – conjectures – and that it is alright to sometimes be wrong, so they begin to make more offerings. Recently, a teacher and I addressed ways of working with a class where a couple of boys had established themselves as the mathematical experts and a number of the girls had 'switched off'. We worked on two things to explicitly change the pupils' expectations. First, we introduced 'thinking thumbs' to replace 'hands up', so there was no 'rush' to be the first to volunteer. Second, we selected pupils to explain their thinking rather than asking for volunteers. Initially we were met with much resistance from the pupils: the boys were not happy at no longer being recognised as the quick experts and the girls were reluctant to offer anything in case they were wrong. But in under a month the class was transformed, with these same girls willingly explaining their solutions to problems and the same boys providing helpful feedback. A shift towards dialogue means the advantages extend beyond simply improving standards in mathematics. As Robin Alexander (2006) points out, dialogue is at the heart of developing caring learners:

> Dialogue requires willingness and skill to engage with minds, ideas and ways of thinking other than our own; it involves the ability to question, listen, reflect, reason, explain, speculate and explore ideas; to analyse problems, frame hypotheses, and develop solutions; [. . .] Dialogue within the classroom lays the foundations not just of successful learning, but also of social cohesion, active citizenship and the good society. (p. 5)

4   The number system

This chapter looks at how to help pupils develop a sound understanding of the number system. Three aspects are examined:

- the development of counting and ordering;
- teaching place value, not only for whole numbers, but also so that it leads to an understanding of decimal fractions;
- learning about fractions.

Big ideas

- Numbers have a unique position on the number line.
- Placing numbers on a number line connects discrete and continuous quantities.
- We can think about place value in two ways: additively (counting out and exchanging groups of ten) or multiplicatively (scaling up and down by a factor of ten).
- There are two roots/routes to fractions: measurement and sharing.

Making connections

- Being fluent in flexible counting strategies lays the foundations for effective calculation strategies.
- Thinking about place value in multiplicative terms leads to decimal fractions.
- Fractions, decimals, measuring and division are all connected ideas.

Progression in counting and ordering

Young pupils are often proud of the fact that they can count – that is, recite the number words in the correct order – but it takes time for them to connect this oral counting to finding the number of objects in a collection. Even more challenging is learning to count collections and not count every object singly. For example, a pupil may learn to orally count in twos – 'Two, four, six, eight . . .' – but given a collection of buttons, and asked to count them in twos, will point to a single button in time with saying each of, 'Two, four, six . . .' rather than marking off the buttons in pairs. There are two processes in play here that learners have to master. One is 'unitising' – handling two objects (a pair of buttons) as though they a single object (one group of two). The other is becoming fluent in counting flexibly and switching between, say, counting in twos then into ones (this is much harder than simply counting only in twos). Mastering each of these processes is itself a challenge and learning to coordinate the two will take time and is best practised little and often. *Twos, fives, tens* sets out a number of direct instruction tasks that help learners connect their ability to skip count orally with productive ways of enumerating a total quantity.

In addition to being fluent in flexible counting, there is strong research evidence that working with number tracks or lines helps pupils develop good number sense (the researcher Robert Siegler has examined this extensively – see, for example, Siegler, 2010). As I noted in Chapter 2, tracks are easier to start with as objects can be matched to spaces on the track. Most tasks start by providing pupils with pre-prepared tracks or lines, but it is important also to provide pupils with experience of creating number tracks and number lines for themselves. This not only helps deepen their understanding of putting numbers in order, but also the actions of placing numbers on a track or line helps develop understanding of the relative size of the numbers. Intuitively it can seem that numbers get closer together as they get larger – the difference between a pile of three and four bricks can be easily discerned, but given a pile of 1,003 and 1,004 bricks it is impossible to tell which is the larger pile. So when pupils place numbers on an empty line they often 'bunch up' the numbers as they get larger, rather than space them out equally. Helping pupils develop the skill of equally spacing consecutive numbers has been shown to support their understanding. This in turn connects with then using an empty number line to develop calculation skills and understanding. *Order on the line* provides suggestions for a foundational inquiry that helps learners develop the skill of creating reasonably accurate number lines.

As pupils move into Key Stage 2 it is tempting to think that they will have learned all they need to know about oral counting forward and backwards, but this is not always the case. Pupils need to continue to practise counting in ones forward or back from any number, and they also need to be confident in fluently counting on or back in, say, multiples of 10, 50 or 100 from any number. Without such fluencies they will be hampered when coming to work with larger numbers and in calculating mentally. *Choral counting* provides suggestions for engaging ways to practise flexible counting. I would not recommend trying to create an entire lesson out of the activities suggested there, but practising and playing with counting little and often will help pupils' confidence to grow. *Closest to* connects ordering numbers to place value. It is a frame game – the basic form of the game can easily be adapted to be easier or more challenging.

In relation to the history of mathematics, negative numbers are relative newcomers to the family of numbers and it took mathematicians many decades to accept that they could be considered legitimate numbers, so it is hardly surprising that primary pupils find them difficult. The number line continues to provide a good model for numbers as pupils move into thinking about negative numbers. Temperature is the context within which we most often meet negative numbers (until, perhaps, we get bank accounts and overdrafts!) and *Exploring temperatures* provides some direct instruction suggestions for introducing negative numbers (integers) onto the number line.

Rounding is an important skill in helping learners estimate answers to calculations. It is also helpful in developing mental strategies: rounding a number up or down to a multiple of 10, 100 or 1000 helps with addition and subtraction strategies involving compensation. For example, $356 + 278$ can be calculated by rounding 278 up to 300 by adding 22: then $356 + 278 = 356 + 300 - 22 = 656 - 22 = 634$. *Rounding up or down?* illustrates how to take another frame game idea – connect four – and use it to create a practice activity. In setting up the board for the game, pupils get practice in rounding, to different levels of accuracy, four-digit numbers and they then gain further practice in this as they play the game. Over and above this, the game involves strategic thinking, so it is richer than, say, simply a worksheet of numbers to round up or down. Don't be put off by the instructions: it is easier to set up than describe!

TWOS, FIVES, TENS

Foundational inquiry.

Stages

Key Stage 1.

Direct object of learning

Count collections in twos, fives and tens.

Indirect object of learning

Fluency: develop flexible counting strategies.

Tools

Interlocking cubes, the number line.

Preparation

Put around 25 loose cubes into a clear, lidded container (or a shallow tray that the pupils can look down into). Set up a similar container with around the same number of cubes but with around 2/3 of the cubes joined together in pairs. Have a 1-30 number track on the board (or number line, depending on which the pupils are confident with).

Prepare similar collections of cubes (each a mix of twos and ones) for groups to work on and number tracks or lines to record on.

Task

Public talk

Show the class the jar of single cubes. Ask the pupils to turn to the person next to them and to share how many cubes they think are in the jar.

Take suggestions from the class as to the total and mark their suggestions on the number track or line.

Empty the cubes out onto the mat and invite someone to come and count them. As she reaches ten, get her to set aside that group of ten, so that the final total can be checked by counting, 10, 20, 21, 22 . . .

Did anyone estimate correctly the number of cubes? Which estimate was closest to the actual total? Which was furthest away? How do they know?

Repeat this with the jar containing single and cubes joined in pairs.

When a learner comes to count these cubes, he may want to break the pairs up to make the counting easier – discourage him from doing this. He may also make errors like counting each pair as one, or counting the single cubes as twos. Help him count correctly, with the class joining in, starting with the twos and then switching to counting in ones.

Check the total number of cubes by reversing this: counting the singles and then switching to counting in twos.

Which do the pupils think is easier – starting with the twos, or starting with the ones?

Private conversation

Give groups a collection of cubes (a mix of pairs and singles) and a number track or line. Each person in the group records on the track or line their estimate for the number of cubes. The group then count the cubes. Encourage learners to try and figure out how far away from the actual number of cubes their estimates were – counting forward or back along the track or line can help here. Given a different collection of cubes, do pupils get better at estimating and at counting in twos and ones to find the total number of cubes?

Assessment

- Are the pupils using strategies that help them to keep track of the objects they have counted from those they have yet to count?
- Are they fluent in switching from counting in twos to counting in ones?

Public talk

Split the class in two: one half is going to count in ones, the other in twos. 'Conduct' rhythmic counting by switching from one half of the class to the other: 1, 2, 3, 5, 7, 8, 10, 12, 13, 14, 15, 17 . . .

Variations

Have a collection of cubes, some of which are joined together in fives.

Have a collection of cubes, some of which are joined together in twos and some in fives.

Have a collection of 2p and 1p coins (total value up to around 30p). Work with the class on finding the total by counting up the 2ps in twos and then switching to counting in ones.

Work with a collection of 5p and 1p coins, then 5p, 2p and 1p.

ORDER ON THE LINE

Practice and consolidation.

Stages

Key Stage 1, but adaptable for other ages.

Direct object of learning

Position numbers appropriately along an empty number line.

Indirect object of learning

Reasoning: Understand the relative size of numbers.

Tools

The empty number line.

Task

Public talk

Take suggestions from the class for ten numbers up to 100 and note these on the board.

Draw an empty number line on the board and mark it 0 at one end and 100 at the other.

Model thinking aloud your strategy for placing one of the numbers, say 72, in an appropriate position on the line.

> *Seventy-two? Hmm, I know that 75 is 3/4 of the way along the line. Now 50 would go about here (indicating half way along the line), so 75 will go around here (at the 3/4 position). Seventy-two is a bit less so will be around here.*

See Figure 4.1 for further illustration of this point.

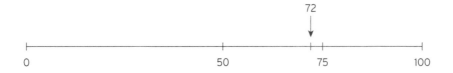

Figure 4.1

Invite individuals to give you instructions to place the other numbers appropriately. Does everyone agree with the positions suggested?

Private conversation

Put up ten more numerals. Working in pairs, pupils draw up an empty number line to share and take it in turns to give each other instructions on where to place a numeral on the line.

Learners who find this difficult could start by marking the multiples of ten on the line.

When finished they make up their own set of numbers to work with.

Assessment

- Can the pupils explain their reasoning for why they placed numbers in particular positions on the line?

- Point to a position on the line. Can pupils make a reasonable approximation for the number they would place in that position?

Public talk

Reverse the process: put up an empty number line and mark a position on it. Have a dialogue with the class about what value that point could be indicating.

Variations

Work with placing multiples of 2, 50 or 100 or decimal numbers, or negative numbers.

Change the start and end numbers: explore where to place multiples of 10 up to 100 on a line beginning at 0 and ending at 150. Or one beginning at 180 and ending at 240.

CHORAL COUNTING

Practice and consolidation.

Stages

Lower Key Stage 2, but adaptable to other ages.

Direct object of learning

Count in multiples of 10, 50 and 100.

Indirect object of learning

Fluency: be able to say 10, 50 or 100 more or less than a given number.

Tools

None.

Task

Public talk

There are many ways that counting on and back can be done with the whole class. Variety is important, both to develop flexibility and to break set with always starting from small numbers.

Here are three ways to practise counting on or back to encourage flexible fluencies.

I'LL SAY THREE, YOU SAY THE NEXT

Set up a count of three in a pattern – pupils chorus back the next number in the sequence.

Teacher: Fifty-six, sixty-six, seventy-six . . .
Class: Eighty-six.
Teacher: Fifty-six, one hundred and six, one hundred and fifty-six . . .
Class: Two hundred and six.

ME, YOU, ME, YOU

Tell the class what the counting on pattern is going to be. Teacher and class take it in turns to say the next number in the count.

Teacher: We're going to count in tens, starting at eighty-seven. Eighty-seven . . .
Class: Ninety-seven.
Teacher: One hundred and seven.
Class: One hundred and seventeen.

A variation on this is to split the class in two and each half takes it in turn to advance the count.

SWITCH THE COUNT

The count switches between two or more different patterns. For example, write 10 and 50 on the board. Start the count off with skips in one of these values – when you tap on the other the class has to switch to counting on by that amount.

Teacher: We'll start by counting in tens from thirty-four.
Class: Thirty-four, forty-four, fifty-four.
Teacher: (Point to fifty.)
Class: One hundred and four, one hundred and fifty-four, two hundred and four, two hundred and fifty-four.
Teacher: (Point to ten.)
Class: Two hundred and sixty-four, two hundred and seventy-four . . .

This can be adapted further with three different counting on values.

Private conversation

CLAP AND COUNT

In pairs, get the pupils to practise a 'patty-cake' style clapping pattern: facing each other, they clap their own hands together and then clap both of their partner's hands, repeating this until they can perform it smoothly. They then add in a counting pattern that they say when they are clapping each other's hands. For example, starting at 35 and counting on in fifties. Clap, 35, clap, 85, clap, 135 . . .

Assessment

- Can the pupils describe any patterns they can hear in the counting?
- Are they confident counting backwards as well as forwards?

Variation

These activities for counting can all be easily adapted – working with counting in twos, threes, fives and so forth. Count back from various multiples. Count in fractional increases or decimals. The variations are limitless and 5 minutes' daily practice will keep fluency in flexible counting sharp.

Source

Adapted from the work of Bob Wright (see for example Wright, Stanger, Stafford, & Martland, 2006).

CLOSEST TO

Practice and consolidation.

Stages

Lower Key Stage 2.

Direct object of learning

Round any number to the nearest 10, 100 or 1000.

Indirect object of learning

Reasoning: Consider the effect of the value of digits in different places.

Tools

A 0-6 or 0-9 die for each pair of pupils.

Note - the version of the game described here is for rounding numbers to the nearest 100. This is a 'frame game' that is easily adapted to other multiples (or other targets, for example, the nearest multiple of six).

Task

Public talk

Demonstrate how to play the game by playing against the class.

Put two sets of three empty boxes on the board, as illustrated in Figure 4.2.

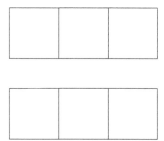

Figure 4.2

Roll the die - the score gives the multiple of 100 that is the target, for example, a roll of 4 means the target is 400.

The class goes first - someone rolls the die. They choose which of their three squares to put the score in. Then it is the teacher's turn. After all six boxes are filled in, the winner of that round is the player with the number closest to the target score. For example, the class scores 368 and the teacher scores 489 - the class wins that round.

For each round players draw a joint blank number line and record the position of the three numbers - the target number and the two scores. If they can, they figure out the difference between the number scored and the target number.

Private conversation

Pupils play in pairs, determining how many rounds they will play.

Assessment

- Can pupils explain how they know for certain which number is closer to the target number?
- Can they use the number line to figure out how far away from the target number each number is?

Public talk

Talk about strategies the pupils developed. Could they predict if someone had won before the end of the game? Use a number line to model how they could calculate the exact difference between each of their scores and the target number (see Figure 4.3).

Target: 400

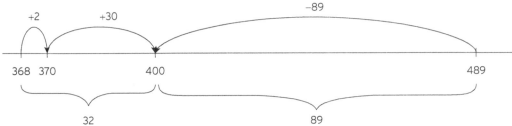

Figure 4.3

Variation

A popular adaptation of this game is the 'nasty' version – the score on the die can either be recorded on a pupil's own board or on her partner's.

Another adaptation is for pairs to work collaboratively: they can put the digit rolled on either board and when both boards are filled they find the difference between each number and the target. These two differences are added together for the score for that round. After, say, five rounds, the pairs total up their five overall scores. Which pair got the *smallest* overall score?

The type of target number can be adapted: the largest even number, the smallest multiple of three, a number between 200 and 500 and so forth. Players may decide to allow a limited number of 'lets' with these variations – if they do not like the number rolled on the die they can roll again.

Source

I have come across this game in so many places it is difficult to know its origins. A version of it is described in Kirkby (1992).

 ## EXPLORING TEMPERATURES

Practice and consolidation.

Stages

Upper Key Stage 2.

Direct object of learning

Interpret negative numbers in context.

Indirect object of learning

Reasoning: understand negative numbers and the effect of changes of temperature.

Tools

Whiteboard images of thermometers with the scale in degrees Celsius and copies printed out for pupils to work with.

A die and a coin.

A set of temperature cards as follows:

–9°C, –5°C, –2°C, 0°C, 3°C, 6°C, 8°C

(The task described here is in terms of temperatures in London; obviously you could adapt this for a local city.)

Put the names of the seven days of the week on the board. Shuffle the temperature cards and put one under each day, in a random order.

Task

Public talk

Talk about this chart showing an imaginary set of temperatures over the course of a winter's week in London. Ask questions like:

- *Which was the warmest day?*
- *Which was the coldest?*
- *How do you know?*

Who can come and show the temperatures on the image of the thermometer?

Between which two days did the temperature go up the most?

Between which two days did the temperature go down the most?

Who can explain how they know? Can anyone use the image of the thermometer to show how to figure out the difference in the temperatures?

Pose the following question:

One day the temperature was 4°C. Overnight the temperature changed by 6 degrees. What was the temperature showing on the thermometer after that change?

Is 10°C the only possible answer? How might –2°C be the answer? Point out to the pupils that you did not say whether the temperature went up or down. How could that be made clear? Can the pupils come up with a solution for distinguishing between a change of 6 degrees being an increase in temperature and being a decrease? If no one suggests it, show how using the positive and negative signs can indicate an increase or decrease respectively.

Give out copies of the thermometer image to pairs of pupils.

Roll the die - this gives a starting temperature - and toss the coin to determine positive or negative (heads being positive, tails negative), say –4°C.

Pupils to work in pairs and mark this temperature on the thermometer. Roll and toss again noting the result on the board, say, +5°. This is now the change in temperature. The pairs agree on what the temperature will be after this change. Do several more examples (each change being applied to the temperature just arrived at).

Private conversation

Roll the die and toss the coin to establish a new starting temperature.

By rolling and tossing, put up seven changes of temperature.

Working in pairs, the pupils record the starting temperature and the subsequent temperatures after each change.

Early finishers can challenge each other by giving a starting temperature and a change - their partner has to figure out what the changed temperature is.

Assessment

- Given two temperatures, can pupils say what the difference in temperature is between them?
- Can they distinguish the difference between the temperature going up from, say, –2°C to 5°C and it going down from 5°C to –2°C?

Public talk

Go over the answers, checking that everyone is counting forward or backward appropriately.

Variation

Instead of specifying a starting temperature and change, put up a series of temperatures. Working in pairs, pupils have to figure out what the changes in temperature were and record these appropriately.

Pupils could use the Internet to investigate the temperatures of cities around the world. Taking the temperature of their hometown as a base-line temperature, how many degrees hotter or colder are places like Beijing, Stockholm, Sydney and Santiago?

Play a number line game with negative numbers on the line – now + or – indicates the direction of travel along the line.

ROUNDING FOUR IN A ROW

Practice and consolidation.

Stages

Upper Key Stage 2.

Direct object of learning

Round any whole number to a required degree of accuracy.

Indirect object of learning

Fluency: round up and round down numbers in the context of a strategy game.

Tools

A 10 000s place value chart – one for each pair of pupils – as in Figure 4.4.

1000	2000	3000	4000	5000	6000	7000	8000	9000
100	200	300	400	500	600	700	800	900
10	20	30	40	50	60	70	80	90
1	2	3	4	5	6	7	8	9

Figure 4.4

Each pair also needs a blank 6 × 6 grid and a collection of counters in two colours.

Task

Public talk

Remind the class of the rules for rounding a number to the nearest ten. (If it ends in five then it rounds up to the next multiple of ten.) So, for example, 72 458 rounds, to the nearest 10, to 72 460. Go over rounding to the nearest 100 (72 500), nearest 1,000 (72 000) and nearest 10,000 (70 000).

The task is set up in two parts – first pupils work together in pairs to create a playing board, then the game.

Explain setting up the playing board as follows:

Players take it in turns to put five counters on the place value chart – one on each row. They writ the five-digit number that they have created. Model this on the board.

Their partner moves the five counters somewhere else on the place value chart and writes down the new number created. When they have written down nine five-digit numbers, they round each one to the nearest 10. The rounded numbers are written onto the blank 6 × 6 grid – players are free to choose where they write these.

Once these nine multiples of ten have been written on the grid, pupils again take it in turns to place the five counters on the place value board, record another nine five-digit numbers, each of which they then round to the nearest 100. These nine multiples of 100 are added to the playing the board.

In a similar fashion they create on the board nine multiples of 1000. The remaining nine spaces on the board are filled with nine multiples of 10 000.

Private conversation

Send the pupils off to make their playing boards.

Public talk

Model how the game is played.

Player 1 places five counters on the place value chart to make a five-digit number. They announce that they are going to round this number either to the nearest 10, 100, 1000 or 10 000. Both players agree on what the rounded number is and if that number is free on the playing board player 1 can cover it with a counter.

Player 2 now makes a different five-digit number. This time they can only move one or two of the counters on the place value chart – the remaining counters have to stay where they are. As for player 1, they announce the degree of accuracy that they are rounding the number to, and claim that space on the board, if the number is available.

Play continues in this way (players miss a turn if their rounded number is not on the board or already covered). The winner is the first player to get four counters in a row, vertically, horizontally or diagonally.

Variation

This is a frame game version of four in a row and can be adapted in many ways. For example, the board could be filled with products of numbers from 1 × 1 to 9 × 9. The digits 1–9 are set out in a row. Player 1 covers two of the digits with counters (or one digit with both counters). If the product of the two digits covered is free on the board, they claim that space. Player 2 can only move one of the counters to create a new product.

Place value and decimals

Understanding place value is central to learners' understanding of the number system and this in turn is the basis of sound mental and written calculating. It is tempting to think that once learners have grasped the structure of hundreds, tens and units, then it is simply a case of applying this knowledge to larger numbers. However, I suggest that as pupils move up through primary school we need to extend and deepen their understanding of place value and in particular encourage them to think about it not only in additive terms (collecting ten ones to exchange for one ten and ten tens to exchange for one hundred and so on) but also in multiplicative terms (imagining a single one being scaled up by a factor of ten to create a ten and a ten in turn being scaled up by a factor of ten to create a hundred). It is this latter multiplicative reasoning that leads to understanding decimals.

Progression in place value

A key understanding in Key Stage 1 is knowing how the position of a digit in a number gives its value. To adults this can seem almost 'natural' – it is just the way that numbers are. Given this apparent simplicity, it can seem that explaining this and then giving pupils plenty of practice in saying or writing what various digits 'stand for' will develop understanding. Many pupils can, however, learn the 'trick' of saying there are, for example, six tens in 60 but without really understanding what that means. This can also lead to a misunderstanding: How many tens are there in 261? There are 26 tens, not six. A foundational inquiry like *Stocktaking* helps pupils understand that place value provides a way of organising large quantities so that they are easier to count and compare. *Stocktaking* also provides a practical problem-solving situation that helps learners connect together organised actions (grouping quantities in tens) with mathematical records (the place value system). This approach to introducing place value is based in the Dutch research on mathematics arising from 'mathematising' the world, which sees place value as invented by mathematicians to help counting be more easily organised and recorded. So rather than starting with a numeral like 42 and talking about the number of tens and ones, the approach recommended here is to start with a large quantity of things and count these by organising them into groups of ten and bringing to the pupils' attention how the notational system reflects the physical grouping. (The idea of 'mathematising' can be read about in Gravemeijer [1997].) *Market stalls* exemplifies this 'flipping' of the traditional teaching approach on its head and like *Stocktaking* is another example of mathematising the world. Again the idea here is that the context (plates of ten), the action of putting out fruit and the representations together provide an embodiment of the abstract idea that 52 represents five tens and two ones.

As pupils move into Key Stage 2 it is important to make sure that their understanding of place value is still strongly grounded in images of quantity and does not simply become focused on reading or manipulating symbols. *Greater or smaller* is a game that helps strengthen understanding of the connection between a quantity (a number) and how that quantity is represented in numerals. It encourages pupils to reason about place value not simply in terms of the position of numerals but how that relates to quantities.

Order, order builds on this understanding to work with four-digit numbers. Over and above this, it puts the skill of comparing and ordering numbers into a strategic context: rather than simply deciding which of two numbers is the larger, the challenge is to put a sequence of numbers in order through only exchanging two adjacent numbers at a time. Thus pupils are not only given the opportunity to practise comparing the sizes of numbers, they are also challenged to think strategically. Pupils who are already confident in comparing numbers can be challenged to think about the most effective strategy for putting the numbers in order, while pupils who still need to practise ordering numbers are given ample opportunity to do so.

As learners start to work with larger numbers, it can become more difficult for them to relate to the quantities involved. I might be able to read that 1000000 is 'one million' but what exactly does that 'feel' like as a quantity? Large numbers can be quite meaningless unless linked to some context. By comparing very large numbers that the pupils have no experience of with more local, smaller numbers that they do have a sense of, the scale of big numbers can be better appreciated. *Sleep tight* uses an everyday context for developing a sense of 'one million'. Is it likely that someone will sleep for a million hours over the course of a lifetime? Hooking pupils' interest into something they might one day experience can provide a way into solving a problem that not only involves large numbers but also requires a mathematical model to be set up by estimating and thinking about the operations needed to solve the problem.

Cities of the world uses real data to explore large numbers. Beyond the recording and reading of numbers in the millions, this challenge encourages learners to think about what is really being conveyed when larger numbers are reported. For example, is the population of Singapore really exactly 5312000? Such questioning can prompt further inquiry into the nature of rounding numbers. What could be the maximum population of Singapore? And the minimum?

Place value and multiplicative reasoning

As pupils move into the upper primary years we can help them come to understand that place value is not only a big idea that relates to whole numbers but is also the big idea underpinning decimals. This means developing the idea behind whole numbers getting larger by focusing attention on the idea of scaling up – as digits move a place to the left in the place value system they represent quantities that become ten times larger. Reversing this, quantities become ten times smaller. Base ten blocks can be used to model the relationships in multiplying or dividing by 10, 100 or 1000. Instead of using a counting out strategy – exchanging ten ones for one ten, then ten tens for one hundred and so forth – work with the pupils on handling the bricks in a multiplicative way (accompanied with appropriate language). One unit multiplied by ten gets scaled up to become a ten stick that in turn gets scaled up by a factor of ten to become a hundred square.

Once pupils are confident in the imagery and language of scaling up this can be reversed to look at scaling down. By the time pupils reach Year 5 or 6 they can find it difficult to think of, say, the 100 'flat' as representing anything other than 100, so a little preparation helps them break set with this. Take a collection of base ten materials – small ones, ten sticks, hundred 'flats' and thousand 'blocks' – and wrap them up. Newspaper is fine. Covering the blocks in paper makes them look sufficiently different for the pupils to be able to talk and think about them differently and yet be familiar enough to still draw on their previous knowledge. This helps pupils to attend to the ten-times-bigger or ten-times-smaller relationships between the blocks (as opposed to thinking of the blocks as absolute quantities).

Now it is possible to hold up, say, a wrapped ten stick and a wrapped hundred square and ask, 'If this is one (the ten stick) then what is the value of this (the hundred square)?'

Pupils usually know that the larger shape must then have a value of ten, but it is worth time discussing, 'What must happen to this one (the stick) to become one ten (the flat)?'

Initial answers may focus on needing ten of the smaller one to make one of the larger one. You need to make it clear that this is fine, but it is the answer to a different question: how many of the smaller 'one' are needed to make the larger 'ten'. Pupils need help focusing on what would have to happen to the smaller 'one' to become the larger 'ten' without anything being added. The imagination has to come into play here – part of the reason the additive image of the relationship between base ten blocks comes to pre-dominate is because it is easier to demonstrate how ten units can be placed alongside the 'ten' stick to show the equivalence. But a single wooden brick cannot be, literally, pulled and stretched to be ten times larger. Gesture and lots of talk is needed to help bring this scaling up image into the learners' minds.

The conversation thus shifts from talking about the relationship between the two pieces as additive – you need ten of those to make one of these – to a multiplicative relationship – the smaller piece needs to become ten times as large. Once that is established you can talk about the reverse relationship. What would have to happen to the 'ten' to become the 'one'? It would need to become ten times as small.

Play around with other relationships. What has to happen to the 'one' (that is the stick) to become the biggest piece (the cube)? It has to become a hundred times as large. For the largest (the cube) to become the 'one' (the stick)? It needs to become a hundred times as small.

I recommend any recording of this only after lots of handling and talking and imagining the blocks and these relationships between them. Once pupils are comfortable with all this talk of growing and shrinking, they are ready to look at how to position the same digits in different places to record these changes. Note that multiplying or dividing by 10, 100, or 1000 is not, in itself, about moving digits. An imagined quantity has to be scaled up or down and as a result of that multiplicative change, the digits then have to move to record the final quantity.

The scene is then set for moving into decimals. If the 'stick' is 'one' what has to happen to this to become the smallest piece? Ten times as small. We cannot simply write the digits for this to the right of the digits for the 'ones', hence the need for the decimal point. And then all this can be played with the 'flat' as a 'one', leading to hundredths.

STOCKTAKING

Foundational inquiry.

Stages

Key Stage 1.

Direct object of learning

Use place value to read, write and compare numbers up to 100.

Indirect object of learning

Problem solving: count large collections of objects by grouping in tens.

Tools

Nothing aside from the materials and equipment around the class.

Task

Public talk

Explain that you want to make a note of how many there are of various things in the classroom, such as rulers, brushes, scissors (choose items where there are at least 30 but probably no more than 100).

Assign pairs of pupils to go off and count how many there are of one type of object in the classroom. At this stage do not give any guidance on how they should record the total number of items – let them decide to record them in whatever way they like.

Private conversation

As the pairs are working on counting the numbers of items, wander round and watch how they are going about this. If anyone is having difficulty keeping track of what they have counted, work with them on putting the objects into groups of ten to keep track of the things that have been counted.

Assessment

- Can the pupils use grouping and counting in tens to quickly show you how many objects they have?
- Do they know how to record the number of objects?

Public talk

Bring everyone together and draw up on the board a record of the items and the number there is of each. For example:

Item	Total
Brushes	36
Scissors	42

Invite one or two pairs of pupils to show how to keep track of and check the total by putting the objects into groups of ten. Add to the information on the board the numbers of groups of ten and the number of single items left over.

Item	Total	Groups of ten	Total tens	Ones over
Brushes	36	3	30	6
Scissors	42	4	40	2

Send the pairs back off to find out how many groups of ten and single ones there were in their collection.

Back as a whole class, add to the table the groups of ten, total tens and ones for all the items counted. Do the pupils notice any patterns in the table? Why do they think those patterns are there?

Variations

Provide pairs with collections of small items, such as dried pasta, beads, buttons or shells. Also provide each pair with something to organise their collections into groups of ten; for example, egg cartons or dry paint palettes. The pairs find the total number of items by counting out groups of ten, putting one group of ten into each division of the egg carton or palette. They record the total number of items. Work with the pairs on checking the total by counting in tens and then the single ones.

Source

This activity is adapted from the work of Cathy Fosnot and colleagues at Math in the City, City College, New Year. An extended account of the inquiry is given in Cameron, Hersch, and Fosnot (2004).

MARKET STALLS

Foundational inquiry.

Stages

Key Stage 1.

Direct object of learning

Recognise the place value of each digit in a two-digit number (tens, ones).

Indirect object of learning

Reasoning: explore patterns in the number system through grouping in tens.

Tools

A 0–99 number square (with 0 in the top left hand corner so that the first column contains 0, 10, 20, 30, . . .).

Task

Public talk

Set up the problem context of knowing someone who works in a market selling fruit. Explain how she does not sell the fruit by weight but that she has plates that she puts ten pieces of one type of fruit on: ten apples, ten oranges and so on. Talk about going and buying crates of fruit that the market stallholder then opens to put out in plates of ten.

The challenge for each pair is that they will be assigned a fruit and told the number of pieces of that fruit in a crate. Their job is to figure out how many plates of ten could be made from the numbers in the crates, and how many single pieces of fruit would be left over.

Assign pairs a fruit and the number of that fruit in a carton; for example, a carton of 52 apples. They can record as they choose how they are going to find out how many plates of ten could be made from the number in their carton.

Private conversation

As the pupils are working, watch and listen to their approaches. If any of them are recording the numbers of pieces of fruit by drawing or representing them in a haphazard manner, talk about how to organise their recording so that it is easy to keep track of the numbers of groups of ten.

Any pair who are confident that they know the number of groups of ten, because, say, they know that 52 will have five groups of ten can be challenged to find the number of tens for two crates, the total of which exceeds 100; for example, a crate of 67 kiwi fruit and a second crate of 75.

Assessment

- Are the pupils recording their results in a systematic fashion?
- Do they notice any patterns in their results?

Public talk

On the board draw up a table of everyone's results:

Fruit	Number in crate	Plates of ten	Total tens	Ones over
Apples	52	5	50	2
Oranges	76	7	70	6

What patterns do the pupils notice? Why do they think those patterns have emerged?

Locate the numbers in the crates on the hundred square and talk about the multiples of ten in the left hand column and the single digits in the top row. How does the position of, say, 52, on the number square relate to the plates of ten and ones over? How is that linked to the numbers at the head of the row and column that 52 sits in? Why is that?

Variations

Prepare a page with multiple images of, say, stars on it – they could be arranged in an orderly fashion with, for example, 15 in each row, or they could be scattered randomly across the page. Ask the pupils to work on their own to find the total number of stars on the page. Do not tell them to draw around groups of ten to make the counting easier but watch out for pupils who do realise that this is helpful and get them to explain to the class why they chose to do that.

Source

This is based on a lesson I taught and is described in more detail in the companion volume, *Transforming Primary Mathematics* (Askew, forthcoming).

GREATER OR SMALLER?

Practice and consolidation.

Stages

Lower Key Stage 2 (but adaptable to other stages).

Direct object of learning

Compare and order numbers up to 1,000.

Indirect object of learning

Reasoning: order numbers using place value and concrete representations.

Tools

Base ten blocks, a coin or die per pair of pupils.

Task

Public talk

Set up how to play the game by you playing against the class.

Whoever goes first writes down a three-digit number, say, 246.

Their partner writes down another three-digit number by changing exactly one digit, say 286.

Roll the dice or toss the coin to decide if the target is to have the greater or smaller number (rolling an even number – greater; odd number – smaller. Tossing a head – greater; tail – smaller).

Whoever thinks they have won (suppose in this case a head was tossed, so the player writing down the greater number wins, 286) has to convince their partner that they have won the point by modelling both numbers using base ten blocks and showing why this proves that theirs was the winning number.

Private conversation

Pupils play the game in pairs. As they play, watch and listen and encourage them to use place value language appropriately. For example, '246 and 286 each have the same number of hundreds, so we have to look at the tens to decide which is larger. 286 had eight tens compared to only four tens in 246, so 286 is the larger number'.

Players agree either to play a certain number of rounds or to play until one player has scored a certain number of points.

Assessment

- Can the pupils read out the numbers correctly?
- Who can explain which of a pair of numbers is the larger without using place value blocks?

Public talk

Play the game again against the class – can they convince you which is the winning number without using the base ten blocks to prove it.

Variations

The game can be adapted to numbers with more or fewer digits. The goal could also be changed. For example a ten-sided die could be rolled to set a target of a particular number of hundreds, for example, 600. The winner is the player who wrote down the number closest to that target.

Confident pupils could score the difference between the two numbers, so if 286 beats 246 then that player scores 40 points. After a set number of rounds, the die or coin decides whether the winner is the person with the greatest score or the least score.

ORDER, ORDER

Extension challenge.

Stages

Lower Key Stage 2.

Direct object of learning

Understand the value of each digit in a four-digit number.

Indirect object of learning

Reasoning: order numbers using place value in the context of a strategic game.

Tools

0–9 digit cards or a 0–9 die. Slips of paper or card and blu-tak.

Task

Public talk

Use the digit cards or die to generate four four-digit numbers. If using the cards, turn over a card to represent the ones, replace it in the pack and select another card (which could be the same one again) to set up the tens and so on for the hundreds and thousands. If using a die, roll it four times for each number. Record each number on a separate slip of paper and attach them to the board one under the other in the order in which they were generated:

2 678

3 459

1 882

7 627

Work with the class on putting the numbers in order from the largest at the top to the smallest at the bottom. This has to be done in the following fashion: any two adjacent numbers can be swapped over – that counts as one move. For example, the first move might yield:

2 678

3 459

7 627

1 882

A question then to ask is – is it better to swap the 3 459 and the 7 627 next or the 3 459 and the 2 678? Keep a tally of the number of moves it takes to put the numbers in order.

Private conversation

Generate five new four-digit numbers on the board. Pupils work in pairs to put the numbers in order, greatest to least, using the system of only switching pairs of adjacent numbers each time. Some pupils may benefit from writing the numbers on slips of paper.

As pairs complete the task, write up on the board the number of moves that they took. Encourage the pupils to look at these scores and if someone seems to have done it in fewer moves than they have then to put the numbers back in the original order and see if they can do it in fewer moves.

Early finishers could generate another set of numbers, and perhaps explore six numbers.

Assessment

- Can pupils explain how they know for certain which of a pair of numbers is the larger?
- What strategies do they develop to sort the numbers in the fewest number of moves? Can they explain the basis of their strategies – why they think they will work?

Public talk

Invite pupils to come and share their solutions to the ordering problem. What strategies did they use to decide which was the best pair of numbers to swap? While one system is to keep moving one number until it is at the top or bottom and then work on the next number in order, looking ahead to see whether another number can be brought closer to where it will finally end up can reduce the number of moves.

Variations

Numbers with more or fewer digits could be used, and the number of numbers to order increased or decreased.

 SLEEP TIGHT

Extension challenge.

Stages

Upper Key Stage 2.

Direct object of learning

Work with numbers up to 1 000 000.

Indirect object of learning

Problem solving: model a situation mathematically.

Tools

Calculators.

Task

Public talk

'Ah,' the old man said, 'I must have slept for a million hours.'

Discuss this quote with the pupils. Do they think it is possible for someone to have slept for a million hours? How could they investigate this? There is not enough information provided to be able to just do a calculation, so they will have to decide things like, how old might the old man be and how many hours, on average, might a person sleep each night.

Private conversation

Set pupils off in pairs to investigate whether or not they think the old man's claim is reasonable. As they work, encourage them to make clear any assumptions they are making and how they are carrying out the calculations.

Assessment

- Are the pupils comfortable with having to make assumptions in setting up the problem, for example how old the man might be, how many hours per night an adult sleeps?
- Can they break the inquiry down into manageable steps?

Public talk

Rather than bring the whole class together, a problem like this provides a good opportunity to have some sharing of approaches and solutions in smaller groups. Divide the class up into three groups. Each group arranges themselves so that they can see and hear everyone else in their group. Appoint, or have the group appoint, a chairperson and a timekeeper. Each pair has, say, five minutes to present their work in progress to the rest of the group – the timekeeper makes sure that they do not take up more than their allocated five minutes. The chairperson encourages other people in the group to ask questions that help everyone become clear about what was done.

Private conversation

Back in their pairs, pupils review what they did and decide whether they need to make any changes in the light of the feedback they got from their peers and what they heard that other people had done. They prepare a poster showing whether or not they agree that a person could have slept for a million hours and their reasoning (a reasonable estimate is that an 80-year-old might have slept for around a quarter of a million hours).

Public talk

Select two or three posters – the creators of these come and share their thinking with the class.

Variations

Pupils could explore other 'millions' – how long would a million seconds be? How long would it take to breathe a million breaths? How long would a million heartbeats be? How far could you walk in a million steps?

Source

I first came across this in a BEAM publication from years ago (although I cannot track down which), but the source of the problem probably is earlier.

CITIES OF THE WORLD

Extension challenge.

Stages

Upper Key Stage 2.

Direct object of learning

Read, write, order and compare numbers up to 10 000 000.

Indirect object of learning

Problem solving: examine how large numbers are presented in data.

Tools

Calculators.

Task

Preparation

Gather together data on the population of a dozen or so capital cities of the world. You could do this yourself, or ask the pupils to find the information on the Internet. The data used here is for illustrative purposes – it may well be out of date by the time you read this.

Also prepare local data of interest – the number of pupils in the school, the population of the nearest town and so on.

Public talk

Present the city data on the board.

Mexico City	8 851 080
Washington, DC	601 723
Bangkok	8 249 117
Brussels	1 080 790
London	8 174 100
Singapore	5 312 000
Berlin	3 520 000
Warsaw	1 771 324
Copenhagen	562 253
Tokyo	13 189 000
Hong Kong	7 136 300
Hanoi	3 398 889

Invite pupils to read out each capital city and its population.

Discuss why the digits are presented in groups of three and how that helps when reading the numbers.

Discuss what they notice about the numbers. Draw attention to, say, the recorded population of Singapore – 5 312 000 – and Warsaw – 1 771 324. Is it likely that Warsaw has exactly 1 771 324 people living there? How would you know? And Singapore – does 5 312 000 look as precise as 1 771 324? Discuss what some of the population figures would be if they were rounded. Why might that be done? What do some numbers look to have been rounded to (the nearest thousand)? Can a city's population ever be counted exactly?

Private conversation

Working in pairs the pupils round all the figures to the nearest thousand and then list the cities in order of population.

Assessment

- Can the learners respond to questions about rounding to other powers, say the nearest ten thousand or hundred thousand?
- Can they explain how to decide whether to round a number up or down?

Public talk

Introduce some local data about populations. For example, there are 750 pupils at the school, Wembley arena can hold 12 500 people, the estimated population of Coventry is 321 700. Challenge the pupils to work together to pose and answer questions that compare the relative sizes of the capital cities with this local data. For example:

- How many times could the population of Singapore fill Wembley arena?
- How many times bigger is Tokyo than Coventry?
- Encourage the pupils to be creative and to find further data on the Internet. For example: If 1/10 of the population of Hong Kong goes to school, how many schools the size of ours does Hong Kong need?

Private conversation

As the pupils work on their problems, discuss what to do with the numerical answers they get – do these need rounding to be sensible? Is it better to round up or down?

Public talk

Invite pupils to come and share some of their findings.

Variations

Populations of countries could be explored, alongside the areas that they cover. For example, Coventry covers about 100 square kilometres (98.64 according to the web at the time of writing). Tokyo covers approximately 13 500. Which city is more densely populated?

Fractions

For many pupils, learning about fractions marks the beginning of the end of any affection towards or confidence in mathematics. Talking to some teenagers about likes and dislikes in mathematics, one summed up a popular feeling: 'I don't like fractions, 'cos they're not real numbers'.

Actually, fractions are real numbers (indeed, to the mathematician, they are Real Numbers) but she was partially correct. Fractions are not real in the sense of you will never 'find' 1/2, or 5/6 in the real (physical) world any more than you would find a singing penguin or flying horse. Such creatures, like fractions, are products of the imagination, not descriptions of pre-existing 'things' and the fact that fractions are not tied to any particular real world situation is what gives them their power. Take the idea of a 1/3. I can use this to think about:

- the 1/3 of the pizza leftover for tomorrow;
- how I'm 1/3 of the way through the book I'm reading;
- liking my latte to be 1/3 espresso and 2/3 hot milk;
- how a tree is about 1/3 of the height it will grow to.

In such examples '1/3' does not stand for a 'thing'; it expresses a relationship. You don't need to know how many pages long my book is, how large I like my latte, or what type of tree is growing – the idea of 1/3 as a relationship is clear without the specific details. Even the pizza example, which looks like it is describing a quantity, is, at heart, about a relationship – the relationship between the amount of pizza there was to start with and the amount remaining.

Teaching fractions as relationships

Most learners initially meet fractions as 'things' – 1/2 an apple, 1/8 of a pizza. That's where the problems start, because what gets (unintentionally) learned is that fractions have to 'look' right. So the first image in Figure 4.5 shows a 'correct' 3/4, but the pupils think the second is wrong because it doesn't look like 3/4 'should'.

Figure 4.5

The key to helping pupils develop sound understanding is to start with the relationships, not the fractions: to work on problems about relationships with answers best expressed through the language and notation of fractions. At heart, there are essentially two such types of problems:

- measurement problems
- division problems.

Fractions from measurement problems

It is common practice for learners to engage in measuring problems like using crayons to measure a book – say the book is three crayons long. It is less common to turn this situation on its head and measure a crayon in terms of 'books', but doing that provides an opportunity to introduce the language of fractions. The book is three crayons long; the crayon is 1/3 of a book long.

This may seem contrived but it is the reasoning behind the classic introduction of, for example, 1/2 an apple. Produce two apples from a bag and these can be described as – obviously – two apples. But that is only because – so subtly that we do not notice it – we are 'measuring' the quantity of apples, with the unit being one apple. There are two (of) one-apples. We can change the unit – take pairs of apples. Now we have one (of) a pair-of-apples and a single apple could be described as half of a pair of apples. When we cut an apple in half the unit of measure is one-apple and the amount measured is half (of) one apple.

The language, and subsequently the notation, of fractions can arise from a foundational inquiry like *Eating toast*: an imaginary friend cuts her piece of toast into two pieces but only eats one of them. Such contexts introduce learners to the language of 'halves'. But fractions were developed for a purpose – not simply to describe things but to compare them. Hence the problem has a second part – if the toast is cut into four pieces and two of them eaten, is that more or less than was eaten the day before? Pupils are thus encouraged to reason about when two seemingly different fractions might be used to represent the same amount. This approach to teaching fractions is based on taking a realistic context to which we can then apply the language of fractions, which is different from the more common approach of producing a relatively abstract image of a fraction and giving it a name. Research shows that pupils' understanding fractions is more secure by starting with realistic contexts out of which the language of fractions emerges rather than starting with the abstract idea and applying it to the world (see, for example, Van Galen et al., 2008).

In a similar way, *How many at the party?* is a foundational inquiry that introduces learners to thinking about a big idea in fractions: that a half can represent a whole range of quantities and in talking about halves (or any other fraction) it is important to be clear about it being a half of what? Given a situation like the number of people at a party, the challenge can be turned around: talk about going to a party and looking around the room and noticing that there were exactly the same number of boys and girls at the party. Pupils investigate how many pupils might have been at the party. How many boys were there? How many girls were there? How many children altogether? Rather than the idea of 'a half' being limited to one particular image, young learners can reason about a half being one of two equal parts, and it does not matter how big or small each part is.

Fractions from division problems

Give three pupils six bars of chocolate to share out 'fairly' and they can do it, no problem.

Give three pupils two bars of chocolate to share out 'fairly' and, messier though it may become, they can still find a way to do it.

Whereas at the end of sharing out six bars they will know that they have two bars each, at the end of sharing two bars between three, learners may only be able to say that they have 'some' chocolate, and less than a bar each. Over time, talking about such amounts learners can come to refine their description – 2/3 of a bar each. Such sharing problems are the second root of fractions: division situations with answers that are less than one. *The twins' party* is another foundational inquiry for introducing learners to such division situations. Once again an element of comparison is built into the problem to provide the reason for describing amounts in fractional terms.

I want to stress that a problem like *The twins' party* is not intended to be treated like a 'classic' word problem – printed out on a worksheet, handed out and pupils left to muddle through. For pupils to engage with a problem like this, time needs to be spent setting up the context, perhaps getting pupils up to act out being at the different tables and making clear that when they go off to work on the problem, whatever way they solve it – pictures, diagrams, cutting up circles – is fine. The purpose is to reach a point where everyone is happy that the boys and girls got the same amount of pizza – only at that point can the ideas and notation of fractions be most effectively introduced in the discussion as it then has a purpose – to clearly communicate the reasoning behind everyone getting an equivalent amount.

When a problem like this is set up in this open way, pupils will solve it in different ways and through discussing and comparing their different solutions the idea (and possibly the language) of equivalence can emerge. For example, one solution to the problem of sharing two pizzas between four people is to cut each pizza into four pieces, each person then getting a piece from each pizza. Another is to cut each pizza in two, so everyone gets only one piece (see Figure 4.6).

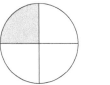

Solution 1: each person gets 1/4 + 1/4 of a pizza   Solution 2: each person gets 1/2 of a pizza

Figure 4.6a   *Figure 4.6b*

The teaching comes in from introducing and using the language and notation of fractions to label and describe these different parts.

Deepening understanding of fractions

All that I know is an example of a practice and consolidation task that helps pupils consolidate what they know, learn from each other and provide the teacher with formative assessment information. This is also a frame task: the context of fractions could easily be changed to many topics: shapes, measure and so forth.

As pupils move into Upper Key Stage 2, so their understanding of equivalent fractions develops into working with mixed numbers. Although pupils might be comfortable with the idea that a fraction less than one can be expressed in a variety of equivalent ways, the idea that a fraction might contain within it a whole number – that, say, 5/2 is equivalent to 2 1/2 – is an extension of the idea of equivalent that many pupils do not find immediately obvious. *Fill the wall* is a game providing the basis for practice and consolidation of mixed numbers, improper fractions and different, equivalent, ways of expressing these. It is likely that in the early stages of playing the game pupils will think that they have rolled scores on the dice that mean they are stuck and cannot shade in any part of the fractions wall. This is the moment to talk about improper fractions, about equivalences and ways of splitting up fractions.

Percentages are often introduced as though they are a distinct topic, whereas they are just a particular set of equivalent fractions – fractions with 100 as the denominator. Over time we come to think that getting, say, 75% in a test is a piece of meaningful information in its own right, but it really only has meaning if put into the context of what other people scored on the test. If the overall average score was 50% then getting 75% might be good news, but if the overall average was 85% then 75% no longer looks like such a good score: percentages are most often used for making comparisons. *Best at* sets up such a comparison situation. It also introduces the idea of finding percentages by setting up a double number line as a tool – the bottom of the number line is fixed as going from 0% to 100% with the top from 0 to whatever the total quantity being converted to a percentage is. For instance, if the total possible score on a test was 60 marks, the initial double number line will have 0-60 on the top and 0-100% on the bottom. Key, benchmark, percentages that are easily calculated such as 50%, 10%, 25% and so forth can then be placed on the line and the equivalent test scores marked in (see Figure 4.7). The double number line thus serves two purposes. First, it acts as a ready reckoner for converting to and from percentages. Second, it provides a strong visual reminder that the big idea of percentages is to compare amounts by converting them to a 'standard' of 100.

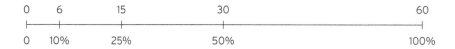

Figure 4.7

HOW MANY AT THE PARTY?

Foundational inquiry.

Stages

Key Stage 1.

Direct object of learning

Recognise, find and name a half as one of two equal parts of a quantity.

Indirect object of learning

Reasoning: understand the relationship between halving and doubling.

Tools

Counters.

Task

Public talk

Set the context for this enquiry by talking about parties. What parties have the pupils been to? Who has had a birthday party recently?

Talk about going to a party and looking around the room and noticing that there were exactly the same number of boys and girls at the party. Ask the pupils to turn to the person next to them and talk about how many boys and how many girls there might have been at the party. As the pupils are chatting, listen in and choose one or two pairs to share with their thoughts with the class.

Set the pupils off to work in pairs to investigate how many pupils might have been at the party. Ask them to record how many boys there were, how many girls there were and how many children were at the party altogether. Tell the pupils they can record their work in whatever way they want.

Private conversation

As the pupils are working, look out for who needs support – they could use counters in two different colours to represent the boys and girls and to find the total number of children. Pupils are likely initially to represent the situation using pictures: support these pupils to start to use numbers as well. Engage the pupils in conversations around questions like:

> *If there were ten pupils at the party, how many were boys and how many were girls?*
> *If there were six boys at the party, how many children were there altogether?*

In this way, introduce the language into the conversation of there being double the number of boys or girls at the party, and of half the total number of children being boys or girls.

Select two or three pairs who will come to the front to share their working.

Assessment

- Given the number of boys or girls at the party, can pupils say how many pupils would be at the party altogether?
- Told that there were, say, 12 pupils at the party and 6 were boys, can the pupils talk about this using the language of halves?

Public talk

As the pupils are explaining what they found out about the different numbers of boys, girls and total number of children, record their solutions on the board as ordered pairs with the number of boys or girls written above the total number of children. At this stage you won't talk about equivalent fractions but this way of presenting the answers gives a hint of what's to come later. For example:

Girls	5	10	12
Children	10	20	24

Use the pupils' examples to talk about the total number of children being double the number of boys or girls, and how if you know the total number of children at the party you could halve this number to find the number of boys or girls.

Variations

The task can be varied either by changing the context or changing the fractional relationship. For example, the context could be changed to a sport such as football or hockey where each team scores the same number of goals. What might be the number of goals scored by each team and the total goals scored? Or the context might be something like blueberry and chocolate muffins on a plate, where there is the same number of each flavour. This could then be adapted to change the fraction: a quarter of the muffins of chocolate, the rest are blueberry, how many muffins might there be on the plate?

Source

Adapted from *Fractions and Decimals; Online Interview Classroom Activities*. Department of Education and Early Childhood, Victoria. Downloadable from http://goo.gl/COwC9O.

EATING TOAST

Foundational inquiry.

Stages

Key Stage 1.

Direct object of learning

Understand simple equivalent fractions.

Indirect object of learning

Reasoning: explore equivalence through problems with fractional answers.

Tools

Paper and pencil.

Task

Public talk

Set the context by talking about eating toast. Explain that you have a friend who likes to have some toast for breakfast in the morning but that she is usually not very hungry and so cuts a slice of toast up and only eats some of it.

Set the problem:

> On Monday your friend toasted one slice of bread. She cut it into two equal pieces and ate one of the pieces. On Tuesday she cut the same size slice of toast into four equal pieces and ate two of them.

Explain to the pupils that you were wondering if your friend ate more toast on Monday or on Tuesday. What's puzzling you is that she had a bigger piece of toast on Monday but she had two pieces to eat on Tuesday. So, did she eat more on Monday or on Tuesday?

It is likely that some pupils will start to argue that this is the same amount of toast on each day. Rather than immediately getting into a conversation about that, tell the class you want them to go off and put something on paper that will convince you that it is the same amount of toast on each day (or not). Ask the pupils to work in pairs on the problem and to record their solutions in any way they wish.

Private conversation

As the pupils are working on their solutions, talk to them about what they are finding out and introduce the language of fractions into the conversation. 'So on Monday she cut her toast into two equal pieces. That means each piece is 1/2. Do you know what we might call the pieces she cut her toast into on Tuesday?'

For those pupils that you think are ready, introduce the fractional notation.

Assessment

- Shown a picture of a piece of toast cut into two unequal pieces, can pupils explain why this does not show halves?
- Asked to cut two slices of toast into four equal pieces, can pupils describe these pieces using appropriate fraction language?

Public talk

Back as a whole class, invite some pairs to come and share their solutions with the class. Does everyone agree that your friend ate the same amount of toast on each day? How can you be sure? Use the fractional notation to label the images of pieces of toast that the pupils produce. Introduce the idea that the 2/4 could be written either as 1/4 + 1/4 or as 2/4 and that this is the same as 1/2.

Variations

The fractions could be varied: it's difficult for pupils to produce images of thirds or sixths so best to have the toast cut into eight pieces. The context can also be changed both to other continuous images such as bars of chocolate or cutting up lengths of ribbon. But it can also be changed to discrete quantities: a bag of grapes could be shared into two equal parts or four equal parts.

THE TWINS' PARTY

Foundational inquiry.

Stages

Lower Key Stage 2.

Direct object of learning

Recognise and show, through diagrams, equivalent fractions with small denominators.

Indirect object of learning

Problem solving: solve division problems that have fractional answers.

Tools

Paper and pencil.

Task

Public talk

Set the context of twins – Anna and Josh – having a birthday party. Frame the story around the twins going to a pizza parlour for their party and the boys and the girls sitting on separate tables. There were 12 girls at one table (Anna and 11 of her friends) and 8 boys at the other table (Josh and seven of his friends). Their father knew that the pizzas were too big for the children to eat a whole one each, so he ordered nine pizzas for the girls' table and six pizzas for the boys' table. Being good friends, the children on each table shared the pizzas fairly.

    After the party, on the way home, the twins were chatting about how much they got to eat. Anna said the girls got more to eat because they had more pizzas on their table. Josh said he thought the boys got more to eat because there were not as many people sitting on his table.

    Ask the pupils to turn to their neighbour and to discuss who they agree with, Anna or Josh?

    After taking some 'soundings' from the class, send the pupils off in pairs to produce something on paper to show whether the boys had more to eat or the girls, or whether they think each had the same amount.

Private conversation

As the pupils are working on the problem encourage them to use appropriate fractional notation to record the amount of pizza everyone gets to eat. Pupils who find the problem too challenging can be encouraged to draw the pizzas or even cut out circles to represent them and cut into pieces.

Join up pairs of pupils into groups of four to share their approaches and solutions.

Look out for different solution methods to share with the class. For example, some pupils may share the 9 pizzas between the 12 girls by cutting 6 pizzas into 12 halves and the remaining 3 into quarters, giving everyone 1/2 + 1/4. Others may cut all 9 pizzas into quarters, producing 36 1/4s so that everyone gets 3/4.

Choose which pairs will share their working with the class and alert them to this.

Assessment

- Can pupils use the language of fractions in explaining their solutions?
- Can they make up another situation where the children would also have the same amount of pizza to eat?

Public talk

Bring the class together to discuss their results. Is everyone convinced that the boys and girls got the same amount to eat?

Who can convince the class that 1/2 + 1/4 is the same amount as 3/4?

Variations

The obvious variation is to change the numbers of children and pizzas so that different equivalences are explored; for example, two pizzas and three boys compared to four pizzas and six girls. Discrete quantities could also be used: sharing bags of grapes or nuts – the pupils do not have to know how many items there are in each bag, only that each bag has the same number of items.

ALL THAT I KNOW

Extension challenge.

Stages

Lower Key Stage 2.

Direct object of learning

Recognise and write decimal equivalents for simple fractions.

Indirect object of learning

Reasoning: understand how different symbols can represent the same underlying mathematical idea.

Tools

Number line.

Preparation

Make up a set of 11 cards with the decimal fractions 0.1 through to 0.9, and 0.25 and 0.75. Also make a set of about 24 cards with the same amounts expressed as fractions and simple equivalents: 1/10, 1/2, 3/4, 5/10, 4/5, 8/10, 16/20 and so forth. You need enough sets of these cards to have one set for each group of four pupils.

Task

Public talk

Give every pupil one of the cards from a set. Ask them to turn to their neighbour and to take it in turns to tell them everything they know about the number on their card. There are two rules they must follow in doing this:

1 They cannot show what is on their card to their neighbour.
2 They cannot directly say what is on the card.

Model this for the class. For example, if you have the card with 0.3 on it, tell them things like:

> 'This is a decimal fraction.'
> 'It is bigger than 0.2 but smaller than 0.4.'
> 'It is equivalent to 3/10.'

After each person has had a chance to talk about the number on their card ask the pupils to find someone who has an equivalent number on their card. How are they certain that the numbers are equivalent?

Now ask them to find other people in the room so that when the numbers on all their cards are added together the total is exactly one.

Finally, get everyone to line up in order, from the smallest number to the largest.

Private conversation

Get the pupils into groups of four and give each group a set of the fraction cards. They mix the cards up and share them out across the group. (It does not matter if some players have more cards than others.) Taking it in turns, the pupils say all they know about one of their numbers - as before, they cannot show the group their card nor can they say the number directly. Other people in the group check other things about the number by posing questions. For example, if one person has said that his or her number is equivalent to 3/4, someone might ask, 'Is it also equivalent to 6/8?'

When they have exhausted everything they can say about that number, the card is placed face up on the table. Whoever has a card that is equivalent to that number places it above or below this card.

The next person then talks about a number in her hand. When that card is placed on the table, it is positioned relative to the cards already there, as if the cards were being placed along a number line.

The pupils continue in this way until all the cards have been placed on the table. They then individually make a 0-1 number line, placing all the fractions on the line that they have on the table. Groups that finish early can be given blank cards to make more equivalent fractions.

Assessment

• Listen in to the conversation and note down the ideas and language being used.
• Are the pupils paying attention to making the spaces between the fractions appropriate when placing them on a number line? If so, what strategies are they using to do this?

Public talk

Put a large 0-1 number line marked in tenths on the board.

Point to different divisions on the line and invite pupils to offer fraction or decimal fraction labels for these points.

Variations

The range and variety of fractions can easily be adapted to make the task easier or harder.

Source

Adapted from *Fractions and Decimals; Online Interview Classroom Activities*. Department of Education and Early Childhood, Victoria. Downloadable from http://goo.gl/COwC90.

FILL THE WALL

Practice and consolidation.

Stages

Upper Key Stage 2.

Direct object of learning

Recognise mixed numbers and improper fractions and convert from one to the other.

Indirect object of learning

Reasoning: understand equivalences.

Tools

Fraction wall as in Figure 4.8.

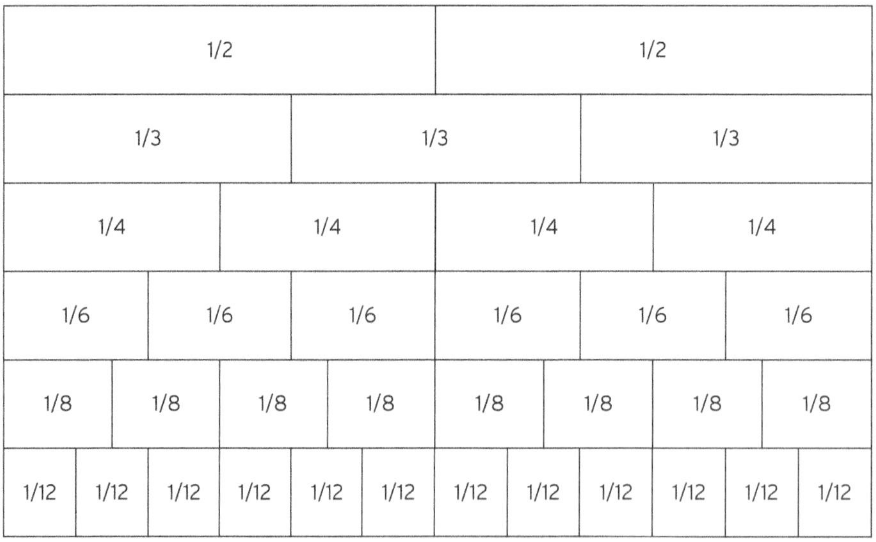

1/2						1/2					
1/3				1/3				1/3			
1/4			1/4			1/4			1/4		
1/6		1/6		1/6		1/6		1/6		1/6	
1/8	1/8		1/8		1/8		1/8	1/8		1/8	1/8
1/12	1/12	1/12	1/12	1/12	1/12	1/12	1/12	1/12	1/12	1/12	1/12

Figure 4.8

Preparation

Each pair needs a copy of the fraction wall each and two dice: one regular 1-6 die and one marked: */2, */3, */4, */6, */8 and */12.

Task

Public talk

Explain how to play the game.

Each horizontal slice on the wall is one whole, making the total on the board six wholes.

In pairs, players take it in turns to roll both dice. They combine the two scores to make a fraction, for example rolling 3 and */6 creates 3/6.

They shade in on their wall the equivalent of this fraction they have just rolled. So in the case of rolling 3 and */6 they can shade in the 3/6 in row four, or half of any other row, or 1/4 of a row and 3/12 of the bottom row or any other combination making 1/2.

None of the pieces in the wall can be cut smaller – whole pieces have to be shaded.

If a player cannot shade in the fraction they rolled they miss that turn.

The winner is the first player to shade in their entire wall.

Private conversation

The nature of the dice means that leaners will create some improper fractions. Watch out for anyone treating, say, 6/4 as '4/6'. Also look out for pupils who think they cannot go when they can. For instance rolling 3/3 and already having one of the thirds shaded in, some learners may think that they cannot go. Work with them on the idea that 3/3 is equivalent to one-whole, so any complete strip can be shaded in.

Playing also involves thinking about addition of fractions, as towards the end of the game a fraction rolled may have to be split up. You might want to ask learners to keep a list of the fractions they rolled and what they shaded in – this could later be used to look at recording addition of fractions: Rolled 5/8. Shaded 1/8 and 1/2. So 1/8 + 1/2 = 5/8.

Assessment

- Can pupils identify at least two different parts of the fraction wall that they could shade in for a particular roll of the dice?
- Can they suggest ways that a fraction could be split into two or more smaller ones?

Public talk

Talk about the game. What were good fractions to roll? Were any not so advantageous?

Variations

Learners could shade in on each other's walls – the goal of the tasks is then to complete both walls with as few rolls of the dice as possible.

Source

Adapted from *Fractions and Decimals; Online Interview Classroom Activities*. Department of Education and Early Childhood, Victoria. Downloadable from http://goo.gl/COwC9O.

BEST AT?

Foundational inquiry.

Stages

Upper Key Stage 2.

Direct object of learning

Understand percentages.

Indirect object of learning

Reasoning: use percentages to make comparisons.

Tools

Double number line.

Task

Public talk

Set up the context for the problem. Introduce this problem verbally, putting sufficient information on the board to act as a memory jogger when the pupils go off to solve the problem. A pupil – call him Mike – got some test results at another school.

> *Mike got 18/20 on a mathematics test and 23/25 on an English test.*
> *Mike said he was better at English, because he got more questions right than he did on the mathematics test.*
> *His friend Ash said Mike was equally good at mathematics and at English, because he got two questions wrong in each test.*

Who do the class agree with?

Private conversation

As the pupils are working in pairs on this problem most should realise they need to get each test to be out of the same mark – and 100 is the obvious one.

A double number line both helps the conversion of the scores into percentages and also acts as a visual reminder that whatever is being compared is set up against a benchmark of 100. Help the pupils draw up an appropriate double number line. For the mathematics test they have a scale from 0 to 20 on the top and from 0% to 100% on the bottom.

Pupils can write in 'benchmark' percentages along the bottom and then the equivalent value above the line. For example, 50% is halfway along the bottom, and so must be matched with 10 above the line for the mathematics test. Marking 50% makes it easy to fill in 25% and 75%. Similarly, 10% is 1/10 of the way along the line and so 2 must be 10% of 20 (see Figure 4.9). The other percentage multiples of ten can then be marked along the bottom and matched to values on the top. Some pupils may need to fill all of these in to see that 18 marks on the mathematics test are the same as 90%. Others may notice that 18 is two back from 20, so if 20 is 100% and two marks are 10% then 18 must be 90%. Look out for such different reasoning and note which pupils you will invite to share their thinking with the class so that a range of approaches can be discussed.

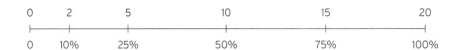

Figure 4.9

The double number line for marks out of 25 is set up in a similar way. This time it is easier to mark the 20% benchmarks first – each 20% will be 25/5 or 5. The multiples of 10% can then be filled in and 23 marks established as 92%.

Assessment

- Do the pupils realise that they need to make the number lines for each test the same size so that 100% is equivalent in length in each case?
- Do they use the line to make reasonable estimates of where 50%, 10% and 25% are and use these to mark off other percentages in appropriate places?

Public talk

Invite your selected pairs of pupils to come and share how they decided which subject Mike was better at. Does everyone agree? Which method of finding percentages do the class think is the most sensible?

Variations

Changing the context provides other opportunities for comparing. For example, breakfast bars - given the total weight and weight of fat or sugar - which of two bars (of different weights) is the healthier? Or syrup in a drink: if two drinks have different sugar content (e.g., 15 ml in 50 ml versus 6 ml in 20 ml) - which is sweeter?

Give the pupils a percentage amount of something, for example 50% is £40. Given this information what else do they know?

5 Additive reasoning

This chapter looks at how to help pupils develop a sound understanding of calculating involving addition and subtraction (multiplication and division are addressed in the next chapter). There are two aspects of arithmetical understanding that we need to foster:

1   when to do a particular type of calculation, be it addition, subtraction, multiplication or division;
2   how to carry out the calculation.

Lessons often focus more on the latter than on the former partly because teaching pupils how to carry out a calculation appears to be easy, and partly because of the assumption that if learners do know *how* to carry out a calculation then they will know *when* to carry it out, although the link between knowing how and knowing when is not that simple. So rather than talk about teaching addition and subtraction, I prefer to talk about additive reasoning which encompasses both how and when to calculate.

Big ideas

- It is helpful to think about two types of arithmetical reasoning: additive and multiplicative.
- Addition can be done in any order, but subtraction cannot.
- Additive reasoning has roots in situations that typically involve questions that ask about how much more or how much less.

Making connections

- Modelling addition and subtraction on the number line helps pupils not only to appreciate the connection between these two operations but also to work flexibly between them.
- There are core types of problems that are the roots of addition and subtraction: change, part-part-whole and compare.
- Any addition or subtraction problem can be represented symbolically in many different ways.
- Any addition or subtraction number sentence can represent a multitude of different real world situations.

Calculating effectively and efficiently

I have £3001 pounds in a savings account. How much will be left after I have paid £2999 for a motorcycle?

The current kilometre reading on the motorcycle is 5472 km. When I bought it the meter reading was 3778 km. How many kilometres have I ridden?

How would you figure out the answers to these two problems? Most people are happy to mentally figure out the answer to the first problem, but the second problem is not quite so straightforward.

Each problem is essentially a subtraction – on a calculator you would enter the first number, hit the subtraction button and enter the second number. However finding the answer without a calculator does not necessarily mean carrying out subtraction: knowing that adding 2 to 2999 makes 3001 works well for the first calculation, whereas writing down

```
  3001
 −2999
```

and 'doing a take away' might eventually lead to the right answer but is more time consuming and is more likely to involve a slip-up than working mentally.

While asking, 'What do I need to add to 2999 to get 3001?' is, for most people, the most effective and efficient method, in finding the difference between 5472 and 3778 the decision over which method to use is less clear-cut. Some people are confident in working out mentally what to add to 3778 to make it up to 5472; others feel more confident finding the answer using a standard paper and pencil method (if not using a calculator).

Deciding whether or not to calculate mentally (perhaps with some jottings) or using a standard algorithm thus rests on two questions:

- Is the chosen method effective – am I confident that the method will give me a correct answer?
- Is the chosen method efficient – am I confident that the method will get me the correct answer with minimum effort?

Dealing with calculations flexibly means encouraging pupils to explore and share different methods of calculating and helping them appreciate that there may not be one best method. And whichever method you choose carrying it out rests on being fluent in knowing the number bonds to 20.

Developing fluency in number bonds to ten

Building up a repertoire of calculation methods relies on a sound base of known or quickly derived number bonds. There are 100 number bonds from 1 + 1 to 10 + 10 that form the bedrock not only of mental calculation but also of addition and subtraction of larger numbers. Unlike committing the corresponding multiplication bonds (100 from 1 × 1 up to 10 × 10, or the 144 when going up to 12 × 12) these 100 addition bonds are not worked on as the addition tables (one plus one is two, one plus two is three and so on) but there are ways that we can help pupils move from having these bonds, literally, at their fingertips to rapidly recalling them, and ways to work on these number bonds that helps pupils come to know them not simply as 100 disparate pieces of knowledge.

Informally solving addition and subtraction problems with numbers up to ten may involve the use of concrete materials such as counters or cubes. This informal modelling, which stays 'true' to the original context of the problem can only go so far as the unstructured nature of the materials can mean that learners do not develop more sophisticated approaches based on the structure that mathematics can bring to a context.

Helping pupils become fluent in the number bonds to ten means helping them to move away from treating collections of objects as made up of several individual items to working with collections as units in their own right. When pupils first learn to count collections of objects, each object is treated separately and moving objects one at a time to distinguish what has been counted from what is yet to be counted is a key skill in learning to count accurately. But for pupils' understanding of addition and subtraction to grow, they have to progress from the use of 'unit' to refer to a single object to the use of 'unit' to refer to a group of objects. The mathematical structure most often focused on here is place value – the mathematical structuring of groups of tens can result in more effective and efficient strategies than counting in ones. There is research evidence, however, that working with the structure of five plus five making ten helps young learners not only to learn number bonds but also to develop a sense of how calculations can be carried out without relying on counting.

One model to use is our built-in structure of five fingers: getting pupils to 'show' seven by putting out fingers and not counting them singly – being able to rapidly hold up five and two, or three and four – establishes the idea that there are 'numbers within numbers', that, in this instance, seven is not simply made up of seven single units, but can be decomposed into various subgroups and thus the foundations are laid for knowing the number bonds within seven (or six, eight or nine).

A class demonstration ten-bead string – five large white and five large red beads threaded on a cord with enough slack to be able to separate them easily – provides a structured way to explore this idea (see Figure 5.1).

Figure 5.1

Working with this bead string starts by holding it up to show one of the sets of five beads and making sure everyone knows, without repeatedly counting, that there are five beads of each colour. From there you progress to hiding, say, three of the ten beads in your hand.

Holding up the bead string only long enough for pupils to see that there are five beads and two more and not long enough for them to count all seven encourages the mental activity of subitising – being able to enumerate small quantities without counting the individual objects. As five is around the number of objects young learners can subitise without counting, the five-five structure of the bead string builds on this. Asking how many beads the learners think they saw and how they knew, leads to explanations like, 'I can see the five and the two and that makes seven together'.

You can then progress to asking how many beads are hidden: the structure of five again helps pupils come to know without counting in ones that there must be three beads hidden. Thus pupils begin to make several connections:

- That seven is five and two.
- That five is two and three.
- That ten is seven and three.

Repeating this activity little and often means pupils come to easily remember the number bonds to ten.

From the bead string, it is a relatively short step to the number track model. Matching the beads and other objects to the spaces on the track helps learners come to understand that the last number covered on the track tells how many objects or spaces on the track there are up to and including that number (see Figure 5.2).

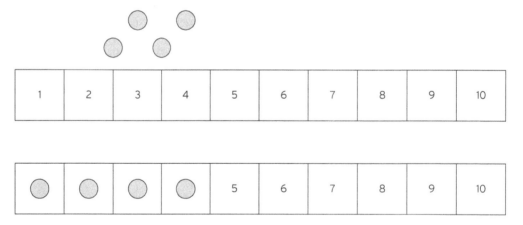

Figure 5.2

The move from the number track to the number line is a non-trivial one. Counters can be put out along a track, making it clear that it is the squares on the track that are counted. On a number line, however, it is the *jumps* that are counted. The best way for pupils to get to grips with this is through track and dice games like snakes and ladders. As I pointed out earlier, the power of such games is such that research findings show that children entering school with limited experience of mathematical activity can close the gap between them and their peers in only a few weeks by playing simple games on straight number track games (circular tracks are less effective than ones with straight-line tracks [see Siegler & Ramani, 2009]).

Developing fluency in number bonds to 20

A 20-bead string takes this further in developing the number facts to 20. Again, the beads are strung in groups of five rather than two groups of ten, so that quantities can be recognised without having to count in ones. Now the structure helps pupils see (and use) two things to calculate: the structure of teen numbers being made up of ten and something, and the knowledge of complements to ten (what needs to be added to a single number to make it up to ten). Showing, say, 8 + 7 on the bead string provides a visual cue that two more onto the 8 makes it up to 10, and the remaining five beads makes 15 (see Figure 5.3) – thus the structure encourages learners to move away from, say, counting on in ones from 8 to 15. (The 20-bead string in the following task examples elaborates the teaching moves here.)

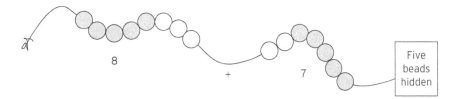

Figure 5.3

Once pupils are confident with this, the number line can be used introduced, co-constructing the line, the jumps and the numbers being landed on (see Figure 5.4).

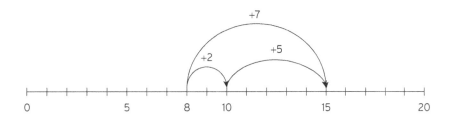

Figure 5.4

This can then be recorded as:

$8 + 7 = 8 + 2 + 5 = 10 + 5 = 15$

The empty number line then provides a visual, action and verbal bridge into larger numbers, for example 28 + 7 or 78 + 7, as shown in Figure 5.5.

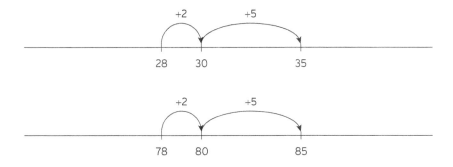

Figure 5.5

Subtraction, as take away, can be modelled in a similar fashion. So, for example, 14 – 7 is modelled by sliding 14 beads to the far left – without counting them singly but by noting that this is one bead less than the three groups of five that make up 15. From these 14 beads, 7 can be separated off again, making use of the five structure to first slightly separate four and then the remaining three (all by using the structure of five to identify where to do the splitting without counting single beads). That there are seven left is again 'obvious' from the five red and two white (see Figure 5.6).

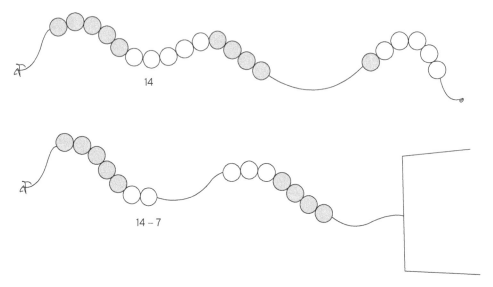

14

14 − 7

Figure 5.6

I have described this at length to make it clear that there are two learning objects in play in such activity. The first, the direct object, is to find the answer to particular calculations, but a second, indirect object, is to draw attention to the underlying structure provided by the arrangement of the beads in groups of five. In doing so, more than one number bond is being worked on – in adding 7 to 8, not only the bond to 15 is explored but also the reinforcing of 7 as 2 + 5 and 8 as 3 + 5. A further indirect object of learning is the idea that additions and subtractions can be carried out by decomposing numbers into constituent parts. While some pupils, when working individually, may still count on seven single ones in adding 7 to 8, through frequent, brief, exposure to the bead string model, they will come to appreciate that there are more efficient ways to add small numbers.

Bead strings continue to provide a model that can help bridge into the more abstract number line. A 100-bead string, with the beads now arranged in groups of ten, tautly strung across the board, means pupils can be invited up to show where, say, the 24th bead ends. Drawing a number line below the string prompts a conversation about where to make the mark to represent 24 on this line. Should the mark sit below the middle of the 24th bead or at the end of the position of that bead? Helping pupils to appreciate that it makes most sense to mark the position of the end of the bead connects to the idea that on a number line the mark for 24 is actually marking the first 24 jumps along the line. This is why the number line includes zero – no jumps yet made – whereas a number track needs to start at one (see Fosnot and Dolk [2001b] for a fuller discussion of this).

Developing understanding of addition and subtraction

Variation theory (see Askew, forthcoming and Marton et al., 2004) provides a way of thinking about how to select and order the examples chosen to maximise the indirect object of learning, so that understanding of addition and subtraction is developed alongside calculation skills. For example, in working on number bonds to 20, a typical sequence of examples might be:

8 + 7
8 + 9
9 + 7

The variation in these examples is that they all have answers in the range of 15–19. With the indirect object in mind of working with decomposition and the structure of five to bridge through ten, then the choice of examples might be:

8 + 7
38 + 7
78 + 7

The variation in these examples is designed to encourage learners to realise that decomposition is a strategy that applies to adding a single digit to *any* whole number. This means setting aside common, but unsubstantiated, expectations that because learners are, say, 6-year-olds they can only cope with working with numbers up to 30. In selecting a sequence of examples to work on, think of them as 'reasoning chains' – chains of linked calculations encouraging reasoning about how one calculation relates to the one that follows. Often all that needs to be done is a re-ordering of the examples. Taking the earlier first three, they might be presented in the order:

8 + 7
9 + 7
8 + 9

Now a conversation could be had about the relationship between the answer to the first calculation (15) and the second (16). Did anyone spot that the answer was going to be one more? How did they know? And can they use that second answer to figure out the sum 8 + 9 without having to start from scratch? The reasoning here relies on the big idea that addition can be done in any order. Pupils can explore this through simple games involving rolling a dice and collecting the number of counters corresponding to the dice scores recorded as an addition. So a roll of 5 followed by a roll of 3 could be modelled by counting out five cubes and then another three, recorded as 5 + 3 = 8

This can be extended to rolling two dice and talking about which order to add them in and whether it makes any difference to the total.

'I've rolled a five and a two. Let's start with two and add on five. Three, four, five, six, seven. Now you try starting with the five and adding on two. Which is easier? Why?'

Modelling such calculations with counters or cubes can help pupils come to understand that it does not matter which order numbers are added in and that it is usually easier to start with the larger number.

It is a short step from situations where an initial quantity is made larger to one where a collection of objects is made smaller by removing some. Again a simple game might involve starting with a collection of, say, ten items and rolling the dice to decide how many to put back in the pot.

While pupils experience few problems with the introduction of the addition sign, I recommend not rushing to introduce the subtraction sign because too much emphasis too soon on 'reading' 7 – 3 as 'seven take away three' can mean that pupils come to think that this is the only meaning to attach to the minus symbol. Indeed, this is a default reading for most adults: ask someone to read out 2 001 – 1 997 and they are likely to say 'take away' when reading the subtraction symbol. Why is that a problem? If pupils 'over-learn' that the minus sign stands for 'take away' they can find it difficult to associate the same symbol with finding a difference. That then can lead to them using taking away as their preferred strategy for carrying out a calculation but as we saw earlier, a calculation like 2 001 – 1 997 is better off treated as finding the difference than trying to, literally or metaphorically, remove 1 997 from 2 001.

At the heart of such simple games and experiences is the setting up of situations involving combining and separating: combining five cubes with two cubes, separating (taking away) two cubes from five cubes. But there are two other sorts of situations that can be mathematically modelled using addition and subtraction – part-part-whole problems and compare problems, as discussed later in this chapter. It is important that pupils get plenty of experience with each of these as well, so that their understanding is broadened.

To summarise, learners building up a repertoire of known facts and simple strategies for deriving facts acquire the tools for finding answers that they do not instantly recall. At a minimum, pupils need to be confident in:

- using the commutative law to start with the larger number, for example 2 + 8 = 8 + 2;
- knowing the complements to 10: the pairs of numbers that add to 10, 2 + 8, 3 + 7 etc;
- being able to add 10 instantly to a single digit;
- being able to rapidly add 9 by adding 10 and taking off 1;
- knowing the doubles to 10 + 10;
- being able to 'bridge through ten'; that is, use knowledge of complements to decompose a number to make bond to 10, for example, 8 + 5 = 8 + 2 + 3.

Strategic approaches to addition and subtraction of two-digit numbers.

Once learners are confident with the addition and subtraction bonds to 20, there are further strategies that they might use to help them mentally add any two-digit numbers. To build such strategies four key fluencies are needed:

- Continuing to put the larger number first: given any addition, encourage learners to ask themselves whether it is sensible to start with the larger number: 15 + 37 is more easily done as 37 + 15.
- Adding a multiple of ten to any two-digit number: being able to rapidly answer calculations like 35 + 20, 48 + 30 and so on. If learners need to break the calculation down, encourage them to count on in tens – 35, 45, 55 – rather than adding tens and ones separately – 35 is 30 + 5, 30 + 20 = 50, + 5 is 55.
- Knowing complements to the next multiple of ten: given any two-digit number, pupils can say what needs to be added to make the number up to the next multiple of ten: 36 – add 4 to reach 40, 72 – add 8 to reach 80.
- Bridging through multiples of ten: 36 + 8, 36 + 4 gets me to 40, four more, 44 (note that this skill rests on fluently knowing complements to multiples of ten).

Those are four core fluencies that pupils need to keep practising. Once these are established then there are two key strategies that pupils can work with that are worth exploring in detail.

The first strategy I'm calling, in line with other writers, 'splitting' and it is the one that is most familiar. Adding say, 56 + 37, is done by splitting the numbers into their tens and units, adding each of these separately and then recombining them – 50 plus 30 is 80, 6 plus 7 is 13, 80 plus 13 is 93. It works and it is the method that pupils will often come up with if you ask them to figure out the answer.

The second method is jumping. The difference between jumping and splitting is that jumping means keeping the first number whole and only splitting the second number. In the case of 56 + 37, this time you would calculate 56 + 30 to get to 86 and then add the 7 on to that to get to 93. That second step some pupils might do by bridging through a multiple of ten: adding on 4 to bring the 86 to 90 and then adding on 3 to get the 93. All this is made clearer to learners by modeling it on the empty number line, as shown in Figure 5.7.

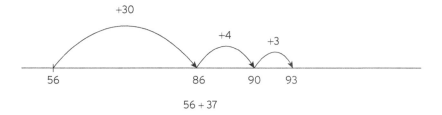

Figure 5.7

I recommend encouraging jumping over splitting. Why? Both strategies work fine for any addition, but jumping is more straightforward for subtraction and less prone to error. For example, calculating 56 – 37 using the jumping method goes along the lines of 56 – 30 = 26, and then 26 – 7 = 19. Just as bridging through ten can simplify adding a single digit, it can also support some pupils in subtracting a single digit: 26 – 6 = 20, one more off is 19. Figure 5.8 shows the number line model for this.

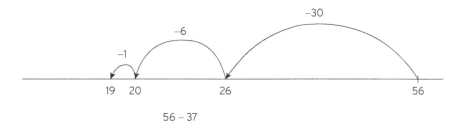

$$56 - 37$$

Figure 5.8

The same calculation done using the splitting method gets trickier. Splitting the numbers gives two calculations: 50 – 30 and 6 – 7. If you are confident that 6 – 7 can be done and the answer is –1, then 20 + –1 = 19. Most younger pupils do not, however, have that depth of understanding and the 6 – 7 step confuses them, resulting in them arguing along the lines of, 'Okay I know the difference between six and seven is one. So what do I do with that one? Do I add it or take it away?' It all goes a bit pear-shaped! Using the jumping method means pupils are more likely to get a right answer.

The jumping method also means that you can start to play with bigger numbers with young pupils. Something like 456 + 125 goes: 456 + 100 = 556, 556 + 20 = 576, and 576 + 5 = 581 (doing this in real time, some of the intermediate answers might need to be jotted down to keep track of them). With the jumping method, because you are building each time on a partial answer, it helps you to keep hold of, mentally, information as the answer builds up from 456 to 556 and then 556 to 576, 576 to 581. Again, we can help pupils get to grips with this by showing them how it works on a number line, as shown in Figure 5.9.

$$456 + 125$$

Figure 5.9

In contrast, the splitting method makes it harder to keep track of all the intermediate steps: '400 + 100 = 500, 50 + 20 = 70, so that's 570, and then 6 + 5 = 11, so that's . . . '. There is too much information to keep track of to do this in your head.

The purpose of modeling on the number line is not so much to clarify what an individual pupil is saying, but to make that pupil's method accessible to the rest of the class. The intent is not that the number line model is an accurate representation of what is in a learner's head (which we could never know anyway) but to translate the learner's words into a model that is helpful to as many pupils as possible. If you are interested in reading more about this, I highly recommend Cathy Fosnot and Maarten Dolk's book (Fosnot & Dolk, 2001b). The use of the empty number line in this way can be thought about through a theoretical lens developed at the Freudenthal Institute in Holland (see for example, Gravemeijer, 1999). These Dutch researchers distinguish between:

- models of
- models for
- tools for understanding.

Over time, if pupils are given plenty of experience in explaining their solutions to calculation and the teacher consistently creates *models of* these on the number line, then pupils will start to use the number line themselves. They will start to draw number lines to help them figure out answers. There is a shift from the teacher providing a *model of* the solution method to learners taking this on as *model for* them to use themselves.

The Dutch research shows that eventually, if the model is a good one (and the empty number line is proven to be one) then learners come to be able to work with the model, but without needing to make actual marks on paper: the model is imagined and has become a *tool for* thinking with. Thus one point of working on an empty number line is not about ways of doing paper and pencil calculations that are non-traditional, but that such models are stepping-stones to becoming mentally proficient.

To summarise, teaching that is focused on strategic approaches to addition and subtraction is important for several reasons:

- It helps pupils to make links between what they know (known number facts) and what they do not know (derived number facts).
- It helps emphasise that learning mathematics involves thinking about and choosing methods as much as it is about getting right answers.
- Pupils explaining how they worked something out is a powerful way of learning.
- It helps pupils realise that there is more than one way to work things out.
- It builds pupils' confidence and helps them realise that mathematics is something to be worked on, not something that some people can just do and others cannot.

Deepening calculation strategies

Playing around with one or two calculations and modelling these on an empty number line can help pupils deepen their understanding of the relationship between addition and subtraction and develop their mental mathematics.

Take a calculation like 637 – 389 and the different ways that this can be modelled on an empty number line.

Starting with 637 marked towards the right hand end of a line and interpreting the calculation as 'taking away', it can be modelled by jumping back 389 on the line. Pupils doing this will usually start by jumping back by the largest amount, 300, then the 80 and then the 9 (Figure 5.10).

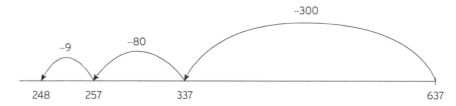

Figure 5.10

The beauty of the empty number line is the potential it has for other, possibly more efficient, strategies to be explored. For example, noticing that 389 is close to 400, we could subtract 400 and then 'compensate' for the fact that we took away more than we needed to (Figure 5.11).

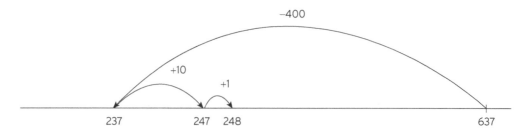

Figure 5.11

We can also model interpreting 637 – 389 as finding the difference. Now, rather than marking 637 and jumping back, we mark both numbers on the line and work out the size of the distance between them. We can do this by counting up from the smaller number to the larger (Figure 5.12).

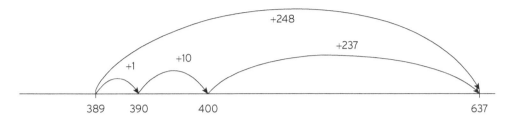

Figure 5.12

Here again the number line lends itself to playing with the numbers. Attending to the fact that 389 is close to 390, we might add 1 to each number, thus keeping the difference between the two numbers constant and creating a difference that is easy to calculate – this difference between 390 and 638 (see Figure 5.13 – the method is known as, not surprisingly, constant difference).

Figure 5.13

We can make things even easier. Add 11 to each number (Figure 5.14).

Figure 5.14

Now all we have to do is find the difference between 300 and 648 – that's easy, 248.

These models for carrying out subtraction on the number line then lend themselves to becoming mental methods.

'Six hundred and forty-eight subtract 289. Well I can take away 300, that's 348 but that's 11 more than I need to take away, so 11 onto 348 is 359.'

Or

'Six hundred and forty-eight subtract 289. What's the difference between these two? Making 289 up to 300 means adding 11 to it. Adding 11 to 648 will preserve the difference. So that's 659. The difference between 659 and 300 is 369.'

And if the learner gets lost in the mental reasoning then a quick sketch of a number line can extend the mental screen.

Understanding additive reasoning

At heart, additive reasoning comes into being through experiencing, representing and thinking about three core situations:

1   change situations
2   part-part-whole situations
3   compare situations.

(See Carpenter, Fennema, Franke, Levi, and Empson [1999] for a detailed description and analysis of each of these.)

Change situations

Pupils' early experiences of addition and subtraction are closely linked to the everyday actions of adding items to or removing items from another set. Typical change problems follow the structure embedded in problems like:

> *Russell had five t-shirts and was given two more for his birthday. How many t-shirts did he then have?* (Change, increase, leading to addition.)
>
> *Hamsa had five eggs. She ate two eggs for breakfast. How many eggs did Hamsa then have?* (Change, decrease, leading to subtraction.)

Because change problems – adding to or taking away from a set – have 'action' built into them they are the easiest problems for young learners to solve. Possibly for that reason they tend to be the most commonly used, but change problems need to be balanced with two other types: part-part-whole and compare.

Part-part-whole

To complement change – increasing or decreasing – situations we need to provide pupils with experiences of 'part-part-whole' situations: contexts where everything is present the whole time, nothing changes over time, as in for example:

> *Sami is carrying home a basket of eight eggs. Five of the eggs are white, the other eggs are brown. How many brown eggs are there in the basket?*

This is a typical part-part-whole situation. There is a whole – a basket of eight eggs – made up of two distinct parts – white and brown. Unlike change situations, nothing is added or taken away – the number of eggs in the basket is the same at the beginning of the 'story' as it is at the end – but the context can still be mathematically modelled in terms of addition or subtraction.

Talking about the relationships between the parts and the whole in a part-part-whole situation leads to linking addition and subtraction. As presented earlier, the egg problem is in the form where the problem is that given the whole number of eggs (eight) and the number of one part (five white eggs), the other part needs to found.

Pupils can solve this problem informally and we can use and build on their informal approaches to help them progressively 'mathematise' the situation. What might this look like? Initially the pupils may use counters or drawings to solve the problem. For example, a pupil may put out five white counters and add brown ones until there is a total of eight. This sets up modelling the situation as a missing addend calculation (what needs to be added to five to make eight?) and can be recorded on a number track by putting the five counters in the first five squares and then adding on the three more (see Figure 5.15).

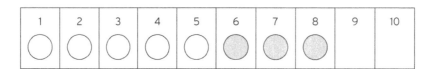

Figure 5.15

As pupils become confident with using the number track in this way, they can be introduced to using a bar diagram to represent the situation. This is set up to represent having a total of eight eggs, five of which are white and the question being how many other eggs are needed to make up the eight (see Figure 5.16).

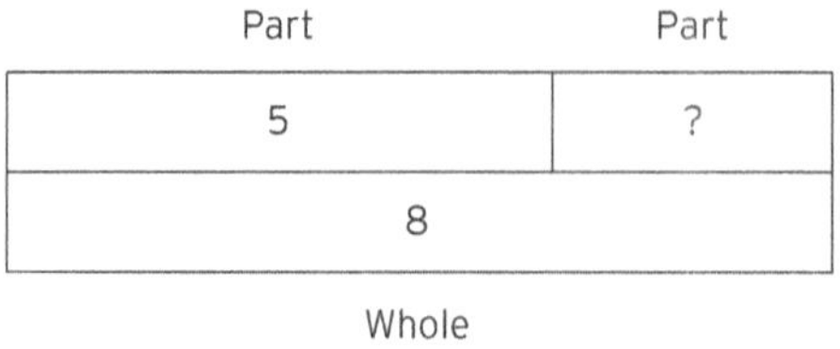

Part	Part
5	?
8	

Whole

Figure 5.16

This leads to introducing the formal notation of a missing addend calculation:

5 + [ ] = 8

Another pupil might initially draw eight eggs, cross out five and count up the remaining three. This can be linked to representing this on the number track by putting out all eight eggs and then removing five.

Again, the bar diagram can be introduced and learners encouraged to make the connection that the model is essentially the same in both approaches: there are a total of eight eggs, part of which we know comprises five, the remaining part needing to be found.

Now the alternative number sentence can be introduced:

8 – 5 = [ ]

This may seem like taking a sledgehammer to those eggs! Why bother with counters, number tracks and bar diagrams, why not just go immediately to recording the number sentence?

The first thing to note is that in that in both cases, nothing has been added or taken away. The number of eggs is constant. Although that seems obvious to the experienced learner, it is not to the novice. If a pupil has come to read the subtraction sign as 'take away' the question in their mind (not necessarily consciously, but implicitly) is, 'How come you can use the subtraction sign for a calculation where nothing is taken away?' Similarly, setting up the situation as a missing addend calculation raises the issue of, 'How come you use the add symbol when nothing has been added?'

At heart here is the big idea that the same mathematical symbols can be used to represent many different real world situations. If we over-emphasise the use of the addition and subtraction symbols as only representing change situations – increase or decrease – then pupils have difficulty associating them with other situations like part-part-whole ones (or, as follows, compare situations).

The other reason for this elaborated movement through counters, tracks and diagrams is so that an abstract representation like 8 – 5 = [ ] becomes imbued with meaning – when the learner meets these abstract symbols echoes of the contexts, actions, and diagrammatic images are brought to mind, as discussed in Chapter 2. The mathematically savvy learner comes to 'see' lots of different interpretations in the symbols. The more naïve learner who can only 'see' this number sentence as 'take away' limits the possibilities. If I can only 'see' 600 – 289 as 'take away' then working out the answer is rather more complicated than 'seeing' this as, say, part-part-whole (a whole of 600, part of which is 289) and being confident in then knowing that the other part of the whole must be 311 by counting up.

We do all of this so quickly as adults it can seems almost instinctive, but it is not instinctive in the sense of having been born with that understanding. As teachers we need to recognise that what now seems obvious to us was not always so, and we need to work to help learners reach the same insights.

Typical contexts that can be used to model part-part-whole include people on a bus – standing and sitting on a single decker or upstairs and downstairs on a double decker. Or fruit in a bowl – apples and pears. Encourage pupils to come up with their own stories that they can ask such questions about.

Compare

The third type of situation giving rise to addition and subtraction are compare problems, such as, 'Mike has £8, Sheila has £5, how much more money does Mike have?' Compare problems are harder for pupils to learn than either change problems or part-part-whole problems. Contrast the first compare problem, with, 'Mike has £8 and he gives £5 to Sheila, how much money does Mike have left?'

Both of these problems can be modelled mathematically with the number sentence 8 – 5 = [ ] and in each case the answer is 3. In the second case, when Mike has given some money to Sheila then the £3 he is left with can be seen – it is, literally, in Mike's hand. The answer 3 in 8 – 5 = 3 represents three specific objects, pounds in this case. But in comparing Mike's £8 to Sheila's £5 there is no particular £3, no specific three £1 coins that is the actual money that makes the difference. The 3 in 8 – 5 = 3 represents a *relationship* between two numbers rather than a specific quantity, and that makes difference harder for pupils to understand.

There are two other things in the story of the development of addition and subtraction that complicate things still further: where the unknown comes and choosing an appropriate operation.

The position of the unknown

Louise had 74 stickers and she gave her friend 39. How many stickers did Louise have left?

This is a relatively straightforward change problem that most pupils have little difficulty modelling as 74 − 39 = [ ] based on the understanding of the problem as 'result unknown'. There are two other related problems that can be created from this same situation:

Louise had 74 stickers and she gave her friend some. Louise then had 39 stickers left. How many stickers did Louise give her friend?

The structure of this problem is one of 'change unknown'. In contrast to the previous problem, the start and result are given in the situation, making it harder for pupils to take the structure of this problem and represent it symbolically. The mathematical sentence most close to the situation is:

74 − [ ] = 39

As we will look at shortly, it is, mathematically, quite sophisticated for the pupil to know that the answer to this can also be obtained by solving 74 − 39 = [ ].

The third possible situation is where the start is the unknown:

Louise had some stickers and she gave her friend 39. Louise then had 35 stickers left. How many stickers did Louise have to start with?

The most obvious number sentence here is:

[ ] − 39 = 35

This is difficult for pupils to solve and many will use trial and error, guessing what the initial quantity might be and adjusting that guess until they get an answer. Again, the move to realising that the answer can be found by adding 39 and 35 is not a simple one – after all, as far as the learner is concerned this is a 'take away' problem, so how can the answer be found through addition?

The same shifting of the unknown can be applied to part-part-whole problems and to compare problems, although it is now more based in where the unknown is in the setting out of the problem rather than the action of the story.

Part-part-whole

There were 48 girls and 37 boys at the park. How many children were there altogether at the park? (Whole unknown.)
There were 48 girls at the park and 85 children altogether. How many boys were at the park? (Second part unknown.)
There were some girls at the park and 37 boys there. There were 85 children altogether at the park. How many were girls? (First part unknown.)

Note that each of these problems has the word 'altogether' in them, but only one of them is an addition situation – being told that 'altogether' means you need to add does not work with the other two problems.

Compare problems

There were 58 white sheep and 74 black sheep in a field. How many more black sheep were there than white sheep? (Difference unknown.)
There were 58 white sheep and 16 more black sheep in a field. How many black sheep were there? (Second amount unknown.)
There were some white sheep in a field and 74 black sheep. If there were 16 more black sheep than white sheep, how many white sheep were in the field? (First amount unknown.)

Again, treating 'more' as a key word – telling pupils it means add – will not lead to correct interpretations of which operations to use in all of these cases.

Choosing the calculation

A further complication in moving from a realistic situation to a mathematical model of that situation, arises from the fact that the 'action' of a problem may not suggest the most appropriate way to carry out the calculation. For example, consider this change problem:

Sally was a keen collector of postcards and had a collection 304. When she decided to take up collecting stamps instead, Sally gave away 297 of her postcards. How many postcards did she have left?

This is a relatively easy problem for learners to understand – a change, result unknown problem. The 'action' of the problem is one of 'giving away', close to taking away and implicitly suggesting that, literally, taking away 297 from 304 is the mathematics to do. However, mathematically, the solution is much easier to find through finding the difference between 304 and 297. In other words, it is easier to figure out what to add to 297 to make 304, than it is to take 297 from 304.

The Realistic Mathematics Education research from the Freudenthal Institute in the Netherlands makes the distinction between 'horizontal' and 'vertical' mathematising (Gravemeijer, 1997, p. 21). The horizontal move is to go from a realistic situation to a mathematical model of the situation – thinking about what this horizontal 'move' might produce in the way of representations is behind what I was arguing earlier for careful consideration of choice of context. In the case of Sally and her postcards the horizontal move is to set up the model of 304 – 297.

Having set up a mathematical model, there may also be an element of 'vertical' mathematising that involves thinking about how best to work with the mathematical model set up. Making this vertical mathematising move means setting aside, for the moment, the context that gave rise to the model and thinking about the relationship between the numbers, the operation and how best to coordinate the two. So 304 – 297, solved as 'taking away' is close to the context 'action' of giving away postcards; no vertical mathematising is needed. Tackling 304 – 297 by counting forward from 297 involves a vertical mathematising – realising that the numbers involved make counting up a more effective strategy than 'taking away' even though this does not mirror the action of the context.

A teaching strategy that I find helps here is to get pupils to record the mathematical sentence that they think best represents a problem, but *not* to actually go on and figure out the solution. In this instance they might record

304 – 297 = [ ]
or
297 + [ ] = 304

Talking these through with the class or group helps the pupils to understand that what we do mathematically may not always be the same as what is suggested by the 'story' of the problem.

The danger of emphasising key words

As indicated previously, another understanding that needs to be worked on here is not being lulled into thinking that particular words in a problem provide the 'clue' to which operation to use. Look at this pair of problems:

Russell had saved £27 towards buying a jacket. His gran gave him £35 more on this birthday. How much does Russell now have towards his jacket?

Jennie had saved £27 towards a ticket for the theatre. The ticket costs £35. How much more does Jennie have to save towards her ticket?

The wording of each problem is somewhat similar but the underlying mathematics is very different: a change, result unknown addition in the first case and a compare, difference unknown, in the second. Often this subtle difference passes pupils by and they focus simply on the fact that both problems contain the word 'more', remember being told that 'more' means 'add' and so they add in each case. Once pupils start out on this route, it is difficult to break them out of it: the fact that sometimes 'more' actually does mean 'add' results in the being correct sometimes and a partial reward system is set up. Research shows that partial reward systems – sometimes, rather than always getting a reward – are actually more reinforcing of the behaviour than a total reward systems.

Getting the pupils to create simple diagrams of the elements of the problem can help them sort out their thinking. They sketch out the information in the problem and then use this to create an image of what they are trying to find, and bar diagrams help as we saw earlier.

Progression in addition and subtraction

The approach to developing addition and subtraction that I advocate rests on three things:

1   Starting with contexts that pupils can relate to and make sense of, however informally, and using these as foundational inquiries.
2   Making sense of the context through actions – either acting out the situation, or acting on physical objects – and drawing pictures or diagrams.
3   Moving to representing the situation, actions and images with mathematical symbols.

Just as I argued for the teaching of fractions, this is a reversal of how arithmetic is often taught by starting with the symbolic and setting up a situation to represent the symbols. I advocate this 'flipping' of the order because I want learners to appreciate that mathematical symbols can 'stand in' for a whole host of situations – there is no simple one-to-one mapping between the real world and the mathematical world. *Birthday presents* provides a description of how a foundational inquiry can be used to build up this learning.

Complementing the understanding of the roots of addition and subtraction is the development of fluency in number bonds, particularly those for addition and subtraction of numbers within the 1–20 range. As discussed earlier, the 20-bead string provides a powerful structured introduction to this and *20-bead string* sets out a typical type of practice and consolidation task to develop such fluency.

As pupils move into Key Stage 2, another fluency that will serve them well is to know the complements of two-digit numbers to 100 – quickly being able to establish what you need to add to any two-digit number to make it up to 100. *Pairs to 100* provides a model of practice and consolidation of this fluency.

As pupils work on word problems they need to develop the awareness that they have to read and engage with what is written in a flexible fashion. Unlike reading a simple story in a book, word problems might not be best read from beginning to end: you might want to look to see what the question is before reading the rest of the problem, and you often need to go back and re-read what is in the problem to check the correctness of a solution. Breaking up the information in a problem and presenting it to learners as a collaborative task encourages this flexibility – *Buying lunch* provides an example of how to do this and provides a framework for practice that can be applied to other types of problems.

When it comes to dealing with addition and subtraction of three-digit numbers, pupils will be taught to use column arithmetic, but there is still a place for exploring such calculations on the number line to ensure that when working with larger numbers, pupils continue to develop a sense of the changes in quantity that are happening and do not end up simply manipulating digits. *Adding and subtracting large numbers* provides a model of practice and consolidation for paired work that both provides individuals with some practice in working with larger numbers and also, through having to share their work with a partner, engages them in reasoning about what is happening.

Work on problems in Upper Key Stage 2 moves into dealing with word problems that involve more than one step and may include information that is redundant: *Multi-step problems* looks at the sort of extension challenges that can help pupils understand these ideas.

BIRTHDAY PRESENTS

Foundational inquiry.

Stages

Key Stage 1.

Direct object of learning

Solve addition and subtraction problems, using concrete objects and pictorial representations.

Indirect object of learning

Reasoning: use bar diagrams as a model for representing additive, part-part-whole, relationships.

Tools

Interlocking cubes.

Task

Public talk

Set up the following two problems. Do this orally, putting only the essential information on the board – this is not about reading and decoding 'word-problems' but about making mathematical sense of a situation.

> *Jo has five white t-shirts and was given three blue t-shirts for her birthday. How many t-shirts does Jo have now?*

> *Sam has five books. His uncle gave him some more books for his birthday. Sam now has eight books. How many books did Sam's uncle give him?*

Provide the pupils with paper, pencil and interlocking cubes. Encourage them to work together and to record their solutions to the problems in any way they like.

Private conversation

As the pupils work on the problems, help them model the first problem with cubes by putting out five for the white t-shirts and another three for the blue ones. In a third colour, help the pupils set up a 'train' of cubes that matches the total length of eight. (Strictly speaking, they don't actually need this third length of eight as they could just count the five and three that were put together, but the image of the five and three alongside the eight helps to talk about the structure of the problems.)

Help them set up a similar model for the second problem.

Assessment

- Can pupils describe what the cubes are representing?
- Can anyone record the problem using numbers and symbols?

Look out for anyone who can then use the cubes in a similar fashion to model the second problem. Alert these pupils to the fact that you will be inviting them up to share what they have done with the class.

Public talk

Invite the pupils you identified to share their solutions of the problems with the class.

Set up the model for problem one with the cubes and show the pupils how this can be recorded: at this stage you'll need to draw a 'closed' bar diagram' – one with all the units clearly marked. Over time this can be turned into an 'open' bar diagram, where the bars are approximately the appropriate lengths and the numbers written in rather than all the units being shown (see Figure 5.17).

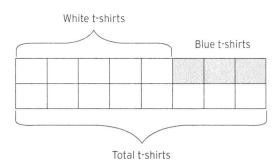

Figure 5.17

Use the cube model and diagrams to introduce the language of part-part-whole. The white t-shirts are the first part, the blue ones are the second part and the final total is the whole. Work with the pupils on how the number sentence for this problem can be written as 5 + 3 = [ ].

Keep the images for this first problem up on the board as you work through the second one. In the case of the second problem, model this with the cubes and talk about how you know one part – the number of books Sam had to start with and the final whole: it is the second part that is missing (see Figure 5.18).

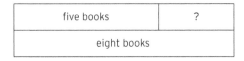

Figure 5.18

Can anyone suggest what might be a suitable number sentence for this problem? Work on setting up 5 + [ ] = 8.

What do the pupils notice was similar about the two problems?

What was different?

Variations

The pupils will need lots of experience of problems like this. The first here is a change problem where the result is unknown. The second is a change problem with the result unknown and the change needing to be found. Making the start unknown can increase the difficulty: Mike had some postcards. He bought three post-cards and now he has eight postcards. How many postcards did Mike start off with?

20-BEAD STRING

Practice and consolidation.

Stages

Key Stage 1.

Direct object of learning

Fluent recall of addition and subtraction facts to 20.

Indirect object of learning

Fluency: develop effective calculation strategies including bridging through ten.

Tools

A class demonstration 20-bead string: 20 large beads in two colours, strung in groups of five. Smaller, similar bead strings for pairs of pupils to work with. The empty number line.

Preparation

Fix the demonstration bead string to the board.

Task

Public talk

Start by getting everyone familiar with the structure of the bead string. Slide all the beads to the right hand end of the string and then count them by sliding them back to the far left one at a time.

Now slide them all back to the right and count them in fives.

Ask the pupils how you knew where to split the beads when counting in fives.

With all the beads to the left of the string, count all 20 beads without moving them, thus establishing ordinal value of each bead.

Point to various beads - what number along the string is each bead at? Look out for pupils using the structure of five to be able, for example, to say that the 7th bead is in that position without having to count all the way from one but because it is two more than the five. Get these pupils to explain how they are using the structure of five to say the numbers quickly.

Work on using the structure of five to identify the position of various beads – for example, noting that the 12th bead is two after ten, or the 9th bead is one before ten.

When the pupils are confident in using the structure of the beads, model additions of numbers between 6 and 10 with addends between 5 and 10 by adapting the following example.

Put 8 + 6 on the board. Move all of the beads to the far right of the string.

Invite a pupil to come and move eight beads to the left - can they do this without counting the beads singly (by using the structure of five to identify where the 8th bead is and sliding them back in one go)?

With the eight beads as the far left, slide six beads towards these, but leave a reasonably sized gap between the two groups of beads. Establish that this is showing the 8 + 6 and the total is when they are all put together (also establish that the remaining beads can for the moment be ignored - you may want to cover these up).

Who can say how many beads there are altogether? Can anyone say how he or she knows that there are 14 without counting them all? Work on the noticing that the two white beads from the 6 make up the numbers 8 to 10 and then there are four more beads to add on. Model this on an empty number line (see Figure 5.19).

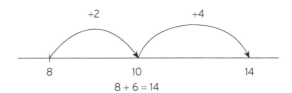

Figure 5.19

Do several examples like this.

Private conversation

Working in pairs, the pupils make up similar calculations to do and use the bead strings to model the situation. As they are doing this, watch out for pupils who are counting the beads in ones - encourage them to use the structure of five and work with sliding groups of beads rather than single one.

Assessment

- Can pupils say how many beads are hidden as well as how many they can see?
- Can pupils show the same structuring of five and a bit on their fingers?

Those pupils working confidently with the bead string can be encouraged to record what they are doing on an empty number line.

Public talk

Go over some of the pupils' examples. Over time, move towards pupils visualising this and talking through the strategy:

'Eight add six, well eight add two is 10, and four more is fourteen.'

Variation

This task will need to be revisited on several occasions – it is better to work on such examples little and often than to expect the learners to 'get it' in one or two lessons.

PAIRS TO 100

Practice and consolidation.

Stages

Lower Key Stage 2.

Direct object of learning

Add and subtract numbers mentally.

Indirect object of learning

Reasoning: use known number facts to support mental calculation.

Tools

The empty number line.

Task

Public talk

Write on the board a multiple of ten above 50, say 70, and ask the pupils to figure out what to add to this to make 100.

Take answers from the class and check that everyone is happy that 30 is the answer.

Write the calculation as a missing addend and record the complement as a jump on the empty number line. Leave these records on the board.

70 + [ ] = 100

Write up a number slightly smaller than the first multiple, say 68, record the calculation and get the pupils to figure out what to add to that to make 100.

68 + [ ] = 100

Write up suggested answers: if not everyone got 32 invite pupils to explain their thinking until the class is agreed on the answer.

Talk about whether anyone used the answer to 70 + [ ] = 100 to help them figure out this second calculation. Provide a model of how the two calculations are related on the empty number line (see Figure 5.20).

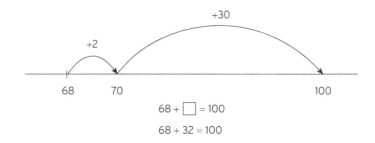

Figure 5.20

Repeat this for other pairs of numbers, for example, 60 and 56, or 80 and 77.

Put up a number just below a multiple of ten, say 48, and ask the pupils to use this strategy of making it up to a multiple of ten to find the complement to 100. Share answers and draw number line models of the strategy.

Repeat for other examples.

Write up a collection of two-digit numbers on the board, all with unit digits equal to or greater than five, for example, 46, 57, 66, 78, 89 and so forth.

Private conversation

In pairs pupils act as solver and recorder: one pupil has paper and pencil. Their partner selects one of the numbers from the board and gives their partner the instructions for drawing the number line model for finding the complement to 100.

Assessment

- Can pupils find complements to 100 by 'bridging through ten' – making the number up to a multiple of ten and then adding on the required tens?
- Can they clearly show their working using a number line?

Public talk

Go over one or two examples.

On a sheet of flipchart paper, work with the class to agree on a couple of examples to record to create a poster that will help them to remember this strategy. Agree on a name for the poster.

Variations

Finding complements of multiples of 100 to 1000.

Finding complements of decimals with two places of decimals to the next whole number.

BUYING LUNCH

Practice and consolidation.

Stages

Lower Key Stage 2.

Direct object of learning

Solve addition and subtraction two-step problems in contexts, deciding which operations and methods to use and why.

Indirect object of learning

Reasoning: choose appropriate models for representing problems.

Tools

Empty number lines.

Preparation

The main preparation here is to turn two-step problems into cooperative problems. Finding, or creating problems is relatively easy (use old test papers!) and setting up a template in a word processor makes creating such problems relatively easy.

Sample problem:

> *Russell bought a bottle of juice for £1.25 and a sandwich for £2.30. He paid with two £2 coins. How much change did Russell get?*

The problem has to be presented on a set of three 'clue' cards – each card contains the question and one (or more) item(s) of information:

How much change did Russell get?	How much change did Russell get?	How much change did Russell get?
Russell bought a bottle of juice for £1.25	Russell bought a sandwich for £2.30	Russell paid with two £2 coins

Task

Public talk

Model how the pupils are going to work together by inviting two pupils up to work with you.

Explain how everyone is going to get a card with a question on it – everyone's question is the same. Each card also has a piece of information that will help in answering the question. Emphasise that there is a 'ground-rule' that everyone in the group must obey:

> *You can read out what is on your card, but you must not show your card to anyone in the group.*

Publicly work through the problem with two volunteers.

Check if the pupils have any questions about how they are to work. Send them off in groups of three with a selection of problems to work on.

Private conversation

As the pupils are working, check that everyone is involved with their group.

Assessment

- Can pupils decide what they think is the best order in which to deal with the information?
- Can pupils record their solution steps appropriately?

Public talk

As well as going over some of the solutions to the problems, discuss what is it was like to work in groups in this way. What helped the group to work well together? Did any group experience difficulties? Were they able to overcome them?

Variation

The variations here are limitless – the complexity of the problems can be altered, the number of clues changed – although I suggest keeping to a maximum group size of four. With more clues than that pupils can have more than one clue each.

Source

I first came across this way of structuring problems in Erickson, T. (1989) *Get It Together*. Peter Gould has written about it too: Gould, P. (1993) *Co-operative Problem Solving in Mathematics*.

ADDING AND SUBTRACTING LARGE NUMBERS

Practice and consolidation.

Stages

Upper Key Stage 2.

Direct object of learning

Add and subtract numbers mentally with increasingly large numbers.

Indirect object of learning

Reasoning: choose strategies on the basis of the numbers in a calculation.

Tools

Empty number line.

Task

Public talk

Put two calculations on the board:

> 326 + 152
> 326 + 198

(The calculations used here are illustrative – they can be changed to be easier or harder.)

Ask the pupils to turn to their neighbour and talk about whether they are confident that they could work out the answer to each calculation mentally and, if so, how they would do it. As the pupils are talking, listen in and identify different strategies being used. In particular, listen out for pupils using a compensation strategy for adding in the second case, for example 198 by adding 200 and then adjusting the answer.

Invite pupils to share their solution methods. For 326 + 152 it is likely that some pupils will have worked this out by adding 300 + 100, then 20 + 50, then 6 + 2, finally totalling up the three sums. Accept this method but also show, if no one offers it, how this can be done by keeping the 326 whole and adding the 100, then the 50, then the 2.

Model this on the empty number line and record the sequence of calculations. Leave these and subsequent images on the board for the pupils to refer to later (see Figure 5.21).

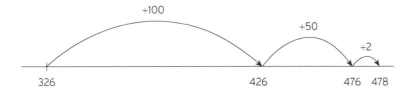

Figure 5.21

> 326 + 100 = 426
> 426 + 50 = 476
> 476 + 2 = 478
> 326 + 152 = 478

Set up a similar sequence of subtraction calculations: encourage the learners to find solution methods that keep the first number in the calculation intact:

326 – 152
326 – 198

Draw models for the subtraction, both on the empty number line and as a series of calculations (see Figure 5.22).

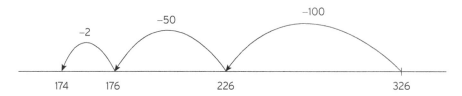

Figure 5.22

326 – 100 = 226
126 – 50 = 176
76 – 2 = 174
326 – 152 = 174

Model using a compensation method for subtracting 198 on the empty number line and as a series of linked calculations, as illustrated in Figure 5.23.

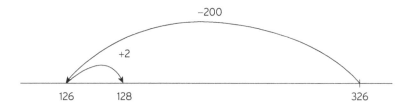

Figure 5.23

326 – 200 = 126
126 + 2 = 128
326 – 198 = 128

Now put up two sets of calculation labelled A and B:

A	B
428 + 264	537 + 144
428 + 297	537 + 399
428 – 264	537 – 144
428 – 297	537 – 399

Private conversation

Working in pairs, one learner works through the A calculations and the other through the B calculations. They have to show how the answer can be established on the empty number line and record it as a series of linked calculations - even if they are confident that they just could do the calculation in their heads. When they finish they will swap and check each other's work.

Assessment

- Do the pupils use the number line effectively and efficiently?
- Can they follow their partner's method and explain it even if it was different from their method?

Public talk

Go over the solutions by inviting learners to come and share their solutions and the models they used.

Variation

The basic structure of the paired work can be adapted for other strings of calculations.

MULTI-STEP PROBLEMS

Extension challenge.

Stages

Upper Key Stage 2.

Direct object of learning

Solve addition and subtraction multi-step problems in contexts, deciding which operations and methods to use and why.

Indirect object of learning

Reasoning: decide on the order in which to deal with the information in problems.

Tools

Paper and pencil.

Preparation

Have the problems in a form that everyone can see – for example, to project on the IWB (interactive white board).

Task

Public talk

Display this problem and get a learner to read it through.

> *On a four-day cycling and camping trip, Pierre and Polly had planned to cover 240 km. On day one they cycled 65 km. On day two they cycled 78 km, Day three they rested and only cycled 35 km. How far did they have to cycle on day four to get home?*

Get the learners to discuss in pairs what they think is the most sensible way of carrying out the calculations for this problem.

Invite suggestions for order of calculation and draw everyone's attention to how it might be more efficient to add the 65 km and the 35 km and then add on 78 km, rather than adding the distances travelled in the order given in the problem.

Put up the following two problems and set learners off to work on them in pairs and in particular to think about what might be the most efficient order in which to carry out the calculations.

Jo was selling apples at the market. She bought a crate of 240 apples and by lunchtime had sold 224, so she sent her friend to buy another crate of 240 apples. By the end of the day Jo had sold another 168 apples. Jo put 12 apples in her bag to take home and packed away the remaining apples. How many apples did Jo pack away?

At Edinburgh station, 389 people got on a train bound for London. The train stopped at Newcastle, where 156 people got off and 124 people got on. The next stop was York, where 75 people got off and 11 got on. At Peterborough, 64 people got off and 76 people got on. London, King's Cross was the last stop where everyone got off. How many people got off at London?

Private conversation

As the learners are working on the problems, talk to them about the decisions they are making over the order in which to carry out the calculations. Make a note of the learners you want to invite to share their solution methods with the class.

Assessment

- Can pupils explain their choice of order in which to do the calculations?
- Can they record their solutions methods in ways that others could follow?

Early finishers can be asked to create some similar problems for their peers to work on.

Public talk

Invite your selected pairs to share their solutions. Did anyone have what they thought was a more efficient method of carrying out the calculations?

Variation

Use the examples that the learners produce to provide further examples.

6 Multiplicative reasoning

This chapter continues to examine how to help pupils develop a sound understanding of calculating, complementing the previous chapter by turning attention to multiplicative reasoning. As with the discussion of additive reasoning, the idea here is to go beyond simply looking at the techniques for carrying out multiplication and division calculations and to consider what it means to understand the ideas behind thinking about quantities and the relationships between them in multiplicative terms.

Big ideas

- Multiplication can be done in any order, but division cannot.
- Multiplicative reasoning involves thinking about comparisons in terms of how many times more or how many times less.
- Multiplicative reasoning lies at the heart of understanding ratio and proportion.
- Given appropriate contexts, even very young pupils can engage with problems involving multiplicative reasoning.

Making connections

- Modelling multiplication through arrays, double number lines and t-tables helps pupils understand multiplication as more then repeated addition and connects to ideas of area, which involves two variables – length and breadth.
- Understanding division rests on pupils being fluent in multiplication facts and understanding multiplication.
- A good sense of multiplicative reasoning helps understanding of fractions.

Returning momentarily to additive reasoning, the examples explored in the previous chapter show how such reasoning essentially involves transforming one amount or variable. To remind you, three root situations giving rise to addition or subtraction are:

- Change situations involving an initial quantity or variable being changed either through combining another, like, quantity (adding: I have some apples and pick some more) or separating off a like quantity (taking away: I give away some apples).
- Part-part-whole situations involving a collection of one type of variable (apples) being made up of two distinct parts (red and green). Or
- Comparison situations involving two quantities of the same variable to compare (how many more green apples are there than red ones?).

Thought about in this way, addition or subtraction problems essentially involve three numbers; for example, the number of red apples, the number of green apples and the number of apples altogether. As we will see next, this is a feature that distinguishes additive reasoning from multiplicative.

The researcher Gerard Vergnaud (1983) classifies multiplicative reasoning problems into three types: simple proportions, Cartesian product of two measures and multiple proportions.

Simple proportions

These are problems where there is an implicit 'per' involved even if the proportion is not explicit. So a problem like, '*If a chew costs 20p, how much will I pay for five chews?*' has an implicit 'per item' built into it: 20p per chew, and so is a simple proportion problem: 1 (chew) is to 20 (pence) as 5 (chews) is to 100 (pence). Similarly, we readily accept that calculating the number of wheels on 5 cars is found by carrying out 5 × 4, while over-looking the hidden simple ratio here of four wheels per car. In essence, the proportional calculation involved is 1 is to 4 as 5 is to what?

Cartesian product of two measures

This fancy term applies to problems like, '*If Tom has four t-shirts and three pairs of jeans how many days can he go out and not wear the same combination of t-shirt and jeans?*' All the possible combinations can be laid out in a grid, which has the same origins as the Cartesian coordinate system (named after René Descartes who invented it), hence the name (see Figure 6.1).

Figure 6.1

Multiple proportions

A typical problem here would be:

> *Working in a cattery, a jug provides enough milk to fill five saucers of milk for cats. A pail of milk will fill four jugs. How many saucers of milk can be filled from a pail of milk?*

Again the answer here is arrived at by calculating 4 × 5 but behind this are two simple proportions: one (jug) is to five (saucers) and one (pail) is to four (jugs), leading to one jug is to how many saucers?

So although traditionally ideas of ratio and proportion are thought to be ones that are only introduced at the upper end of primary school, this analysis shows that pupils are implicitly working with these in most mul-tiplication situations that they meet. And whereas addition and subtraction problems involve three numbers, most multiplication problems that are based on simple ratios involve four numbers, the hidden number being one: one car is to four wheels, as five cars are to how many wheels?

Models for multiplication and division

The array

Just as the number line provides the ground for moving from a *model of* to a *model for* to a *tool for thinking*, in a similar way arrays support understanding multiplication. For example, given a calculation like 5×29 pupils might explain calculation methods such as:

5 times 20 is 100, 5 times 9 is 45, so 5 times 29 is 100 plus 45, 145.

A teacher's model of this explanation could look like that shown in Figure 6.2, which not only represents the solution but provides an embodiment of a particular instance of the distributive law: $a \times (b + c) = (a \times b) + (a \times c)$.

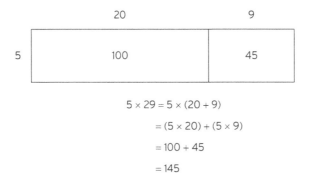

$$5 \times 29 = 5 \times (20 + 9)$$
$$= (5 \times 20) + (5 \times 9)$$
$$= 100 + 45$$
$$= 145$$

Figure 6.2

Another pupil might offer:

5 times 30 is 150. I don't want 30 lots of 5, only 29, so I took 5 off. That's 145.

A model to go with this could look like that in Figure 6.3.

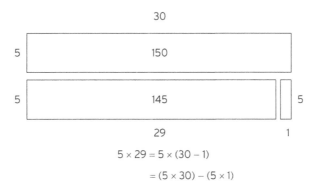

$$5 \times 29 = 5 \times (30 - 1)$$
$$= (5 \times 30) - (5 \times 1)$$

Figure 6.3

As with the use of the number line, over time, pupils will take up using the array model for working with and, with sufficient experience, can imagine it and use it as a tool for thinking with.

Progression in working with arrays

Just as the development from bead strings to number tracks, to closed and then open number lines means each image provokes, for the learner, echoes of the previous images, so arrays can similarly be introduced from concrete representations that become increasingly abstract.

Pupils' early introduction to multiplication is often through starting with a calculation like 4×5 and being taught that this 'means' 'four times five'. Pupils may then be encouraged to put out four groups of five counters to find the answer. As with additive reasoning, I suggest a reversal of this practice of starting with an abstract calculation and then setting up a physical model or diagram to represent it: that learning is deeper through starting with simple contexts that can be informally described and talked about. Take, for example, a foundational inquiry like:

> *A gardener is planting seeds in a tray of little pots. A tray holds four rows of five pots. How many seeds can the gardener plant if she puts one seed into each little pot on a tray?*

The context lends itself to pupils modelling it as a 4 × 5 array either with physical objects or drawings, as shown in Figure 6.4.

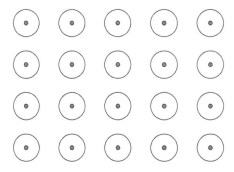

Figure 6.4

The discussion would then be around how many pots there were altogether and whether or not anyone had a quick way to find the total that did not involve counting each pot singly. Taking the learner's explanations then leads to introducing the notation of multiplication to communicate what they saw and did. For example, a pupil might say that they added five and five and five and five. The array can be annotated accordingly (see Figure 6.5) and recorded as:

5 + 5 + 5 + 5

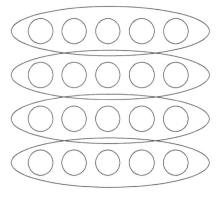

Figure 6.5

Another 'seeing' might be counting in fours, again highlighted on the array, as in Figure 6.6, and expressed as:

4 + 4 + 4 + 4 + 4

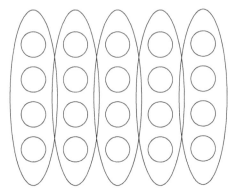

Figure 6.6

From here it is a short step to introducing 4 × 5 or 5 × 4 as a quick way of recording these totals.

The context of pots on a tray is not arbitrary as it embodies setting up the representation of pots in an array, and that image introduces, from the beginnings of learning about multiplication, that multiplication is commutative: 4 × 5 = 5 × 4. Pupils can literally 'see' this in the array.

Returning to pupils' describing how they find the total number of pots, another may say that they saw two groups of ten, arising from pairing up fives. Marking this up on an array (see Figure 6.7) pupils can see this recorded as 2 × 5 + 2 × 5.

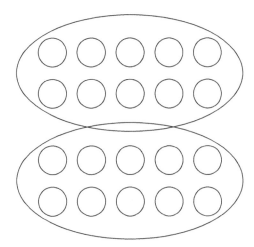

Figure 6.7

Even young children will then accept the introduction of brackets to help 'keep things tidy', for example (2 × 5) + (2 × 5).

Using arrays to model mathematical structure

The array can help deepen understanding of multiplication through working on pairs of calculations like:

   6 × 8
   12 × 4

Some pupils may think that each of these calculations having 48 as the answer is just a coincidence. Others may have an idea about this having something to do with doubling and halving, but 'double one, halve the other' does not explain why these two calculations have the same answer. Modelling with the array helps pupils begin to understand the underlying mathematical structure that allows the 'double one number, halve the other' rule to work, as Figure 6.8 shows.

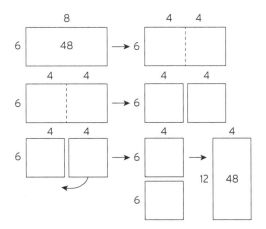

Figure 6.8

The power of such models and images is that they help learners develop a sense of how playing with the relationships between the numbers is not limited to the specific operations of doubling and halving. Take the pair of calculations:

9×4

3×12

Again, they both have 36 as the answer, but the move this time is not doubling and halving but multiplying and dividing by three with the array providing a visual 'proof' of why this holds true (see Figure 6.9).

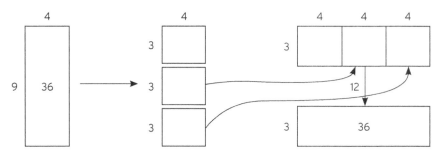

Figure 6.9

Why not just give the rule, plenty of practice and move on? There is more going on here than simply finding answers and embodied in these models and images is the big mathematical idea of the associative rule. Taking the last pair of products, in expanded form, the steps from 9×4 to 3×12 are:

$9 \times 4 = (3 \times 3) \times 4$

$(3 \times 3) \times 4 = 3 \times (3 \times 4)$

$3 \times (3 \times 4) = 3 \times 12$

It is the middle step of 'shifting of the brackets' that is the associative rule, which expressed algebraically, is:

$(a \times b) \times c = a \times (b \times c)$

This is a big idea underpinning much of the work in algebra that pupils will meet in secondary school. Working with the model of the array in such a fashion means having an eye on the 'mathematical horizon' to use Deborah Ball's term (Ball, 1993). The mathematics that pupils work on is not simply being taught in ways that get them through that day's lesson, it is taught in ways that underpin later learning.

The associative rule is one of three rules that, together, provide the structuring of arithmetic that serves learners not only into secondary school but also beyond. The other two rules are the commutative rule and the distributive rule.

The commutative rule is the one that children develop an intuitive sense of and may be able to articulate even if they don't know the name of it and it's the rule that multiplication can be done in any order:

$a \times b = b \times a$

As we saw earlier, the array provides a strong model of why this should be so.

The commutative rule also holds for addition – $a + b = b + a$ – and reversing the order of jumps along the empty number lines helps establish this.

The distributive rule underpins standard long multiplication. A calculation like 4×37 can be answered by keeping the 37 whole and finding four times it by, say, adding $37 + 37$ and then adding $74 + 74$, but that starts to become cumbersome for larger or more awkward numbers. As we know, it is permissible to partition the 37 into $30 + 7$, to multiply each of these by 4 and to add the answers. As we saw earlier the array can model this specific example and, more generally, in algebraic terms this can be represented as in Figure 6.10 and expressed:

$a + (b \times c) = (a \times b) + (a \times c)$

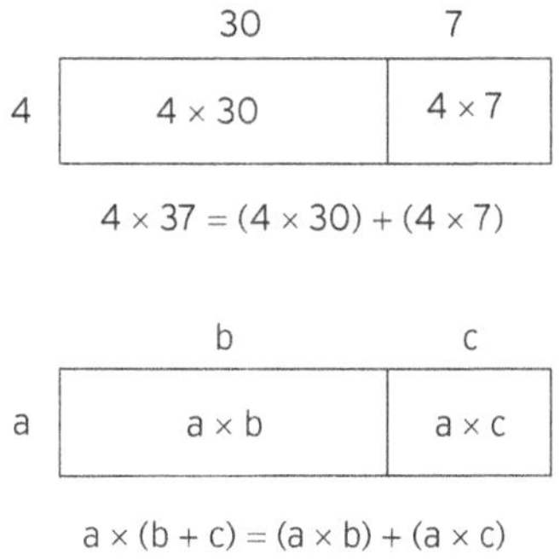

$$\begin{array}{c|c|c}
 & 30 & 7 \\
\hline
4 & 4 \times 30 & 4 \times 7
\end{array}$$

$$4 \times 37 = (4 \times 30) + (4 \times 7)$$

$$\begin{array}{c|c|c}
 & b & c \\
\hline
a & a \times b & a \times c
\end{array}$$

$$a \times (b + c) = (a \times b) + (a \times c)$$

Figure 6.10

Arrays and column arithmetic

The array supports getting to grips with column methods for multiplication. As we saw above we can represent 4×37 as an array that can be 'sliced' vertically into two parts, two 'partial products' that can be calculated separately: (4×30) and (4×7).

When learners meet the standard column algorithm for long multiplication the array helps them read into this the connotations that when multiplying, say, a two-digit number by a two-digit number there are four 'partial products'. Take, for example, 62×34. Calculating this using the standard algorithm looks like:

```
      62
    × 34
    1860
     248
    2108
```

Note that because there are two intermediate answers – 1860 and 248 – this looks like it is also made up of two partial products. But it is not; each of these intermediate steps is composed of two partial products – 1860 is the sum of 30×2 and 30×60, and 248 is the sum of 4×2 and 4×60. The array, as shown in Figure 6.11, makes explicit these four partial products.

$$\begin{array}{c|c|c}
 & 60 & 2 \\
\hline
30 & 30 \times 60 = 1800 & 30 \times 2 = 60 \\
\hline
4 & 4 \times 60 = 240 & 4 \times 2 = 8
\end{array}$$

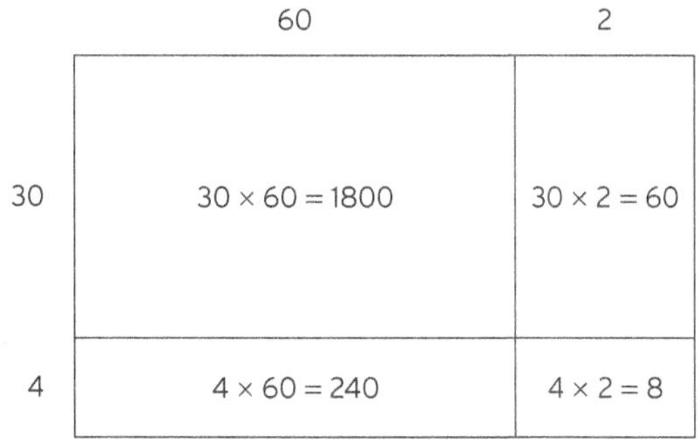

Figure 6.11

A common error that learners make when introduced to the column algorithm is to inappropriately carry over what they have learned from the algorithm for addition where you 'add the ones' and 'add the tens'.

```
     67
   + 24
     11        (from adding the ones)
     80        (from adding the tens)
     91
```

It would seem reasonable to think the same thing holds in multiplication, (especially if you have been encouraged to think of multiplication as 'just' a shorthand way of doing repeated addition) leading to the incorrect:

```
     62
  × 34
  1800   (from multiplying the tens)
     8   (from multiplying the ones)
  1808
```

Returning to the array makes clear that there are not two partial products but four.

Again the direct object of learning – learning to multiply using arrays – is not the only thing going on here: the indirect object of learning is to help learners develop insight into how long multiplication works, an object of learning equally, if not more, important than simply being able to carry out the calculation. This also has advantages for later understanding of algebra: when the expression (a + b) × (c + d) is multiplied out, it has exactly the same underlying structure as thinking of 34 × 62 as (30 + 4) × (60 + 2). Arrays help learners appreciate the algebraic expansion is not something new but just a way of expressing more generally what they have been doing for years (see Figure 6.12).

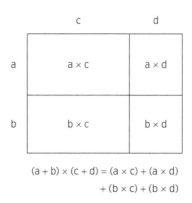

$$(a + b) \times (c + d) = (a \times c) + (a \times d)$$
$$+ (b \times c) + (b \times d)$$

Figure 6.12

Taking arrays further

Arrays are great for introducing multiplication and as a bridge into introducing the algorithm for multi-digit multiplication, but their potential does not end there. The array can also be used to help make clear the link between multiplication and division. Suppose you want to figure out 176 ÷ 8. We can set this up as an array with the value of one side missing, as in Figure 6.13.

Figure 6.13

The value of the missing side can be built up using known multiplication facts (see Figure 6.14).

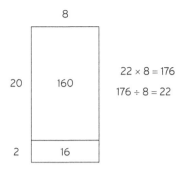

Figure 6.14

Arrays can also be used with fractions. Consider, for example, the calculation 2/3 × 2/5. Learners brought up on 'multiplication as repeated addition' can come unstuck when faced with such a calculation – how can you add 2/3 2/5 times? A quick sketch of an array moves things forward. Start with a one by one array and divide it into thirds horizontally and fifths vertically, as in Figure 6.15.

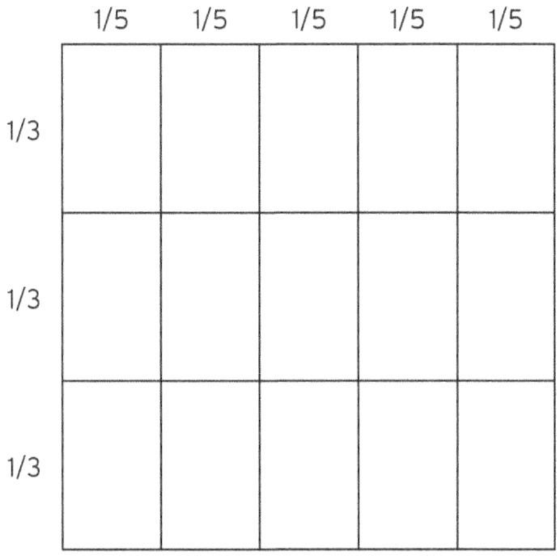

	1/5	1/5	1/5	1/5	1/5
1/3					
1/3					
1/3					

Figure 6.15

Learners who develop arrays as tools for thinking with are comfortable in thinking of the required piece as being the part of the array marked out by the intersection of the 2/3 and 2/5 (Figure 6.16). The initial unit square has been divided up into 15 parts, so each of these is 1/15 of the whole. There are four of these shaded, so the product 2/3 × 2/5 is 4/15.

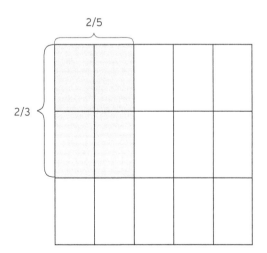

Figure 6.16

Double number lines and t-tables

A powerful pair of models that complement the use of arrays is the double line and t-table.

Double number line

The double number line is, as its name suggests a number line with two different scales on it, scales that are in proportion to each other. So for our cars and wheels context we would have the number of cars – 1, 2, 3, . . . – on one side of the line and the number of corresponding wheels – 4, 8, 12, . . . – on the other. Some writers suggest that this would first be introduced to pupils as two separate lines, matched up, others as a double line in one with one scale above the line and the other below it. I have not found that learners have difficulty working with the single line with two scales above and below and have introduced this with children as young as 6 years old (see Figure 6.17).

Figure 6.17

The progressive variation in using the double number line involves moving from a simple unitary 1:x ratio (1:4 in the case of cars) to more challenging non-unitary ratios, such as 3:5. A context that works well here in getting pupils to set up a double number line is to explore jumps of, say, frogs of different sizes.

> *If a baby frog takes three jumps for every one jump that her mother takes, how many jumps will the baby frog make if the mother takes 7 jumps? And if the baby frog takes 15 jumps, how many jumps will the mother frog have taken?*

The double number line creates a 'ready reckoner' for such problems, where the two scales can be set up and given the position on one or other of the scales, the number of jumps that matches this can be read off the other scale (see Figure 6. 18).

Figure 6.18

Varying the relationship between the number of jumps each frog makes helps learners see the power of this model (Figure 6.19).

> *If a baby frog takes 5 jumps for every 3 jumps that her mother takes, how many jumps will the baby frog make if the mother takes 18 jumps? And if the baby frog takes 15 jumps, how many jumps will the mother frog have taken?*

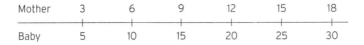

Figure 6.19

T-table

As pupils move through primary school we can deepen their understanding of the connection between multiplication, division and ratios by introducing them to ratio- or t-tables (as in looking like a T), although traditional these are usually not met until secondary school. In a t-table our car problem would be represented thus:

Cars	Wheels
1	4
3	?

When pupils first meet the t-table they treat it more or less like a vertical version of the double number line. Taking, for example, the earlier second frog problem, learners would transfer it into the t-table something like this:

Mother	Baby
3	5
6	10
9	15
12	20
15	25
18	30

Given the value in one column, the corresponding value can be read off in the other column – a vertical version of the double number line. But an advantage that the t-table has over the double number line is that the patterns and relationships in the table can be used to find ways of answering problems without filling in every pair of values. For example, if the mother takes 48 jumps, how many jumps does the baby frog make? As before the table could start with 3 and 6 jumps for the mother, and the corresponding 5 and 10 jumps for the baby, but a learner may notice that from that point it is quicker to double the entry in each column, rather than fill every entry in:

Mother	Baby
3	5
6	10
12	20
24	40
48	80

If the majority of multiplicative problems that primary school pupils meet are simple, proportional problems that involve two variables in a fixed ratio to each other, the t-table makes these ratios explicit and helps pupils deepen their understanding of multiplication.

Division problems

A further strength of the t-table is that it can be used to model division problems as well as multiplication problems. Depending on the position of the 'unknown' in the t-table we have a multiplication problem or one of either of two possible division situations. Take this t-table:

Boxes	Pencils
1	15
6	?

A problem this models is, *'If one box contains 15 pencils, how many pencils would there be in six boxes?'*
   Now consider this t-table:

Boxes	Pencils
1	15
?	90

One 'problem' that fits with this t-table could be:
   If there are 15 pencils in each box, how many boxes can be filled if there are 90 pencils?

This is an example of division as repeated subtraction or quotitioning. It can be difficult to remember the distinction between quotitioning and partitioning but it helps to note that quotitioning is the situation where the 'quota' is known – in this example we know the required number, the quota, of pencils per box, but not how many boxes are needed (notice again, that in talking of pencils per case there is a ratio at work here).

Again, the t-table provides support for strategic approaches to finding a solution if the division calculation is not immediately obvious:

Boxes	Pencils
1	15
?	90
2	30
4	60
6	90

The last line here being completed by recognising that adding the number of pencils in two boxes to the number in four boxes makes up the total of 90.

What if the unknown is in a different place in the table?

Boxes	Pencils
1	?
6	90

This time we know the number pencils and the number of boxes, but not how many pencils could be placed, equally, in each case – division as partitioning.

> *If I have 90 pencils to put into six boxes and I want to put the same number of pencils in each box, how many would that be?*

In the quotitioning (repeated subtraction) instance we knew how many pencils to put into each box, but not how many boxes would be needed. Here we already know how many boxes we want to fill, but not how many pencils to put in each box. Division as partitioning is the situation where we know the number of groups to divide between, but not the number needed in each group.

A solution strategy using the t-table for a pupil who cannot do the division might look like:

Boxes	Pencils
1	?
6	90
3	45
1	15

Getting pupils to set out the information in a problem in the form of a t-table can help them become clear about what they have to calculate, and it can also help them appreciate the connections and relationships between multiplication and division. Again there is a double pair of objects of learning in play here – the direct object of learning of how the t-table provides a model for working out a specific answer and the indirect object of learning of strengthening awareness of the relationship between multiplication and division.

Strategic approaches to fluency in multiplication and division facts

While some pupils benefit from learning the multiplication tables, it is important that they can deal flexibly with the information in the tables. For example, the child that knows that $6 \times 5 = 30$, should also be able to figure out from this that

$$5 \times 6 = 30$$
$$30 \div 5 = 6$$
$$30 \div 6 = 5$$

Unfortunately, for many pupils, too much emphasis on chanting the tables can lead to 5×6 and 6×5 being seen as completely separate facts, each to be committed separately to memory, and any connection to the division facts being hidden.

Instead, pupils need to be secure in knowing triples – 5, 6, 30 – the sets of three numbers that are multiplicatively linked together. To help build up a sound knowledge of the triples the multiplication facts can be worked on strategically, similar to the way that the addition facts to 20 can be worked on strategically, through working on:

- commutativity;
- doubling and repeated doubling;
- multiplying by 10 and halving;
- the pattern of nines;
- counting in threes.

Commutativity

The fact that multiplication is commutative (the order of the numbers leaves the answer unchanged, for example, $5 \times 6 = 6 \times 5$) immediately reduces by half the number of multiplication facts to commit to memory. As I have already argued, the use of arrays provides a strong visual image of this relationship.

Doubling

Being able to double gives the two times table.

Doubling, and then doubling again, provides a strategic approach to multiplying by four. And doubling three times means multiplying by eight.

A common misunderstanding here is that doubling three times is equivalent to multiplying by six. Again the array helps clear this up, as shown in Figure 6.20.

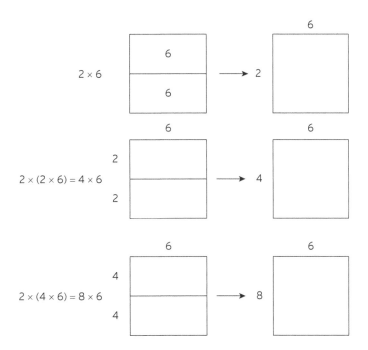

Figure 6.20

An advantage to these strategic (as opposed to memory-based) approaches is that they can be applied to numbers beyond the 'tables': 4 × 17 – easy, that's 34 (double once), 68 (double twice); 8 × 14? That's 28, 56, 112.

Multiplying by 10 and halving

Pupils should know rapidly how to multiply a single digit by ten. Rather than this being a symbolic rule of 'adding a zero' it is better to work on the idea that multiplying by ten makes everything ten times bigger and so the digits then each move up a column in the place value table.

Multiplying by ten and halving means you have multiplied by five. Again this can be applied to larger numbers than those in the tables: 5 × 26, well 10 × 26 = 260, so five times is 130.

The patterns of nines

One way of exploring the multiples of nine is to multiply by ten and subtract the number being multiplied. So 7 × 9 is 70 – 7 = 63 ; 8 × 9 = 80 – 8 = 72. The distributive rule is in play here: 7 × 9 = 7 × (10 – 1) = (7 × 10) – (7 × 1) = 70 – 7 = 63.

The pattern of the digital roots of multiples of nine provides a useful check that the answer obtained really is a multiple of nine. The digital root of a multi-digit number is the separate digits added, repeated if necessary, until the answer is a single digit. For example, the digital root of 489 is 3 (4 + 8 + 9 = 21 and 2 + 1 = 3). The digital roots of multiples of nine display a simple pattern:

9		9
18	1 + 8	9
27	2 + 7	9
36	3 + 6	9
...		
81	8 + 1	9

Counting in threes

There are no short cuts that I know of to learning the pattern of multiples of three, although again, it is helpful to examine the pattern that the multiples of three make and the digit roots:

3		3
6		6
9		9
12	1 + 2	3
15	1 + 5	6
...		
27	2+7	9

If you know the three times facts, then the six times facts can be got by doubling. Six eights: three eights are 24, double that is 48.

The tables

With these principles in place, the times tables can easily be strategically reconstructed if pupils forget them or have difficulty committing them to memory:

× 2   double
× 4   double and double again
× 8   double three times

× 10   place value
× 5   multiply by ten and half
× 9   pattern of nines
× 3   counting in threes
× 6   multiply by three and double.
× 11   the pattern in the answers
× 12   combine × 10 with × 2

What about the seven times table? If pupils know that multiplication is commutative, then most of the seven times tables can be derived from the others. So 7 × 8 becomes 8 × 7, and doubling seven three times gives 14, 28, 56. Only 7 × 7 is not in any of the other tables, and working on square numbers can address that.

Helping pupils with long division

A reminder of what the long division algorithm looks like:

```
       59 r 6
   28)1658
      140
      258
      252
        6
```

Although getting to grips with long division ultimately relies on quite a bit of practice, there are ways we can help pupils understand it a bit better.

Use extended notation

The concise nature of the recording in long division is what makes it effective, but it also hides a lot of what is going on, making it appear, for some learners, to be about the meaningless manipulation of symbols. A more extended form of notation can help here.

```
       59 r 6
   28)1658
      1400    (50 × 28)
      258
      252     (9 × 28)
        6
```

Put the calculation into context

If, say, 28 lottery winners are sharing out £1658 then, rather than handing out the prize a pound at a time to each member of the syndicate, it's helpful to think about giving a large amount of cash to each winner and then sorting out what is left over. In this case we can give everyone £50, that's £1400 given out, leaving £258 over to sort out, which is an easier calculation to do if you notice that this is close to £280.

Make sure learners have good multiplication skills

When it comes to long division, pupils' confidence with multiplication has to go beyond the times tables. They must feel comfortable enough to play around and generate multiples of two-digit numbers that have not been committed to memory – such as 50 × 28.

An idea from the Dutch helps here – they encourage pupils, before they start a long division calculation, to jot down easily calculated multiples of the divisor in a list at the side of the page. So, in our example (1658 ÷ 28), we can quickly and confidently generate some 'easy' multiples of 28:

28
56   (× 2 by doubling)
112   (× 4 by doubling again)
224   (× 8 another double)
280   (× 10)
140   (× 5 by halving the multiple of 10)

The point is not to generate a full list of the '28 times table' but to jot down those multiples which can quickly be derived through the mental strategies of doubling (repeatedly), multiplying by ten, and halving. Long division carries a high cognitive load – there is a lot to hold in your short-term memory and several things have to be manipulated at once – jotting down a list of multiples like this reduces this cognitive load.

Sandwiching the answer

This involves performing a check that helps pupils see if their answers are reasonable. The check is to 'sandwich' the answer between two multiples of the divisor (they can do this before they carry out the calculation so they know if they are working along the right lines).

For $1658 \div 28$: $100 \times 28 = 2800$ and $50 \times 28 = 1400$, so the answer must be between 50 and 100 (although in this case, I would note that since 1658 is closer to 1400 than to 2800, the answer is going to be closer to 50 than to 100).

Progression in multiplication and division

As argued earlier, rather than starting off with an abstract calculation like 4×5 and then setting up a physical model or diagram to represent it, we are better off teaching multiplication and division by starting with simple contexts that can be talked about, acted out and modelled through objects or diagrams and only finally represented by a multiplication sentence.

It is helpful to choose contexts that lend themselves to being modelled as arrays, such as rows of chairs, square tiles on a floor, windows made up of small panes, pies on trays. A search on the Internet can produce suitable images that, when displayed and talked about one at a time over a series of days, will provoke rich conversations about 'short cuts' to counting the total number of items, allowing the teacher to 'drip-feed' the notation of multiplication as representing arrays. *Counting arrays* sets out an extended direct teaching task around these ideas.

Introducing multiplication through simple contexts also helps pupils understand the close connection between multiplication and division, as any multiplication calculation can give rise to essentially two different types of division problems. As we have seen in the discussion about the t-table problems about putting, say, pencils into boxes can be adapted so that the number of pencils in each box is already known, creating a division as repeated subtraction (or quotitioning) problem. Alternatively the number of boxes may be known but we don't know the number of pencils to put into each box creates an example of division as sharing or partitioning. *At the bakery* sets out how to use these ideas as a foundational inquiry to introduce learners to both types of division problems.

As well as developing understanding of multiplicative reasoning pupils also need to develop fluency in recall of the multiplication bonds from 1×1 to 12×12 and they need to practise recall of the bonds in contexts that do not rely on going through the tables to arrive at a particular number bond. *Progressive noughts and crosses* takes this familiar game and uses it to practise the multiplication bonds. It is a frame game – the structure presented here can be used to practise many other facts that need to be committed to memory, for example, properties of shapes or Roman numerals.

Reasoning chains provides a foundational inquiry task to support learners moving into multiplying a two-digit number by a single digit. Like *Progressive noughts and crosses* this is a frame task – it can be adapted to explore other aspects of calculating, for example, equivalent multiplications could be explored through:

6×8
12×4
24×2

With a sound understanding of multiplication and division developed through the use of arrays and t-tables, pupils in Upper Key Stage 2 can deepen their understanding through inquiries and investigations that go beyond simply finding answers to calculations. *Release the prisoners* is a classic extension challenge that not only involves pupils in thinking about and working with multiples, but also involves thinking about the factors of square numbers.

Multiplying fractions is designed to help pupils further appreciate the power of arrays – the intention here is not that everyone becomes confident in multiplying fractions, but that through representing such calculations on an array pupils deepen their understanding of multiplication.

COUNTING ARRAYS

Foundational inquiry.

Stages

Key Stage 1.

Direct object of learning

Calculate totals in arrays and making connections between arrays and count in twos, fives, and tens.

Indirect object of learning

Reasoning: use and understand the language of rows and columns.

Tools

Images of arrays: these can easily be sourced from the Internet or created by cutting and repeatedly pasting images. The arrays should have either the number of rows or columns to be two, five or ten, for example a 2 × 6, 3 × 5, 4 × 2 array and so forth. You need a selection of these to display on the IWB and some simple ones printed off – two different sheets of arrays are needed for pupils to work with in pairs. Counters or cubes.

Task

Public talk

Project up on the IWB an image of an array of objects, for example a three by four array.

Ask the pupils to decide how many objects are in the array and to turn to their neighbour and see if they agree on the number. How can they be sure that they have counted correctly?

Invite pupils to say how many objects they think are in the array. Check if there is more than one answer – treat all suggestions equally, not indicating whether or not you agree or if they are correct but simply noting the suggestions on the board.

Invite pupils to say how they counted the number of objects. While many are likely to have counted the objects in ones, look out for anyone who, say, saw the number of objects in one row, or one column, and could use this to figure out the total without counting every object individually.

As the pupils describe how they found the total, introduce into the conversation the language of 'rows' and 'columns' to help the description.

After looking at and totalling up two or three such arrays, give out the sheets of arrays. The task for pairs is for one person to describe one of the arrays on their sheet (they should not show their partner the sheet). As they describe the array, their partner uses counters or cubes to recreate it. When the array has been completed they look at it alongside the image and check that it is correct. They then figure out how many objects are in the array and record the total on the sheet.

Assessment

- Can the pupils describe the arrays using the language of rows and columns?
- Do pupils use effective counting strategies for finding the total number of objects, for example, counting in twos or fives?

Private conversation

As the pupils are working on describing and constructing the arrays, talk to them about the patterns of twos, fives or tens in the arrays. Get them to run their fingers along the images or the counters to trace out the rows or the columns, using the language along the lines of, 'There are one, two, three rows with five spots in each row'. Or, 'There are one, two, three, four, five columns with three spots in each column'.

Public talk

Bring everyone together and display another array. Can the pupils describe this array in a variety of ways?

Variations

The arrays can be made up of separate items, or of items joined together. Over a series of such experiences in describing and counting objects organised in an array, start to introduce the arrays by only revealing a part at a time – as you show the number of items in one row and then in one column, can anyone figure out how many items there are altogether?

Source

Adapted from ideas developed in *Young Mathematicians at Work, Constructing Multiplication and Division* (Fosnot & Dolk, 2001a).

AT THE BAKERY

Foundational inquiry.

Stages

Key Stage 1.

Direct object of learning

Solve problems involving division.

Indirect object of learning

Reasoning: understand how contexts relate to division as both grouping and sharing.

Tools

Counters or cubes in at least six different colours. Large squared paper.

Task

Public talk

Orally set up two problems. Explain that you were chatting to the woman who runs a local bakery. It was early in the morning and a big tray of bread buns had just arrived that the owner was putting out. The buns were laid out on the tray in rows of five. (Put a quick sketch up on the board so that the pupils have a clear image of the layout of the buns on part of the tray, see Figure 6.21.)

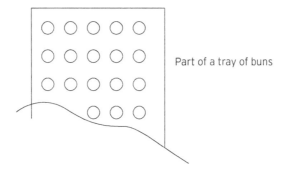

Part of a tray of buns

Figure 6.21

'That's a lot of bread buns,' you said to the lady, and she said, 'Yes, we get 75 on a tray.' Explain to the pupils that you were buying a bag of 5 bread buns and so wondered how many bags of 5 the tray of 75 could be used to fill?

Before setting the class off to explore this problem, offer the second problem.

In the window of the bakery, next to the tray of bread buns was a tray of muffins. You noticed that there were five different flavours of muffins: chocolate, raspberry, blueberry, orange and poppy seed. (Again, put up a sketch to show the arrangement of the muffins, making it clear that each flavour is in a separate column, see Figure 6. 22.)

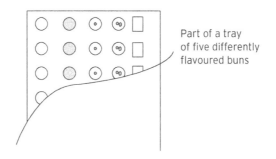

Part of a tray
of five differently
flavoured buns

Figure 6.22

'And that's a lot of muffins' you said. 'Yes,' came the reply. 'We get 75 of those in every day.'

So that got you wondering – how many muffins were there in each flavour?

Recap the two problems:

If there were 75 bread buns on the tray, how many bags of 5 buns would the tray fill?

If there are 75 muffins on the tray, in five different flavours, how many of each flavour are there?

Tell the pupils they can solve the problems in either order and find the answer using whatever method they like – setting up a model with counters or cubes, drawing a picture or whatever they think will help.

Private conversation

Although each problem is essentially 75 ÷ 5, it is likely that many pupils will not immediately see this underlying connection and solve each problem separately. Help them draw images of arrays (or construct these from interlocking cubes) – these images will help them understand the connection between the two problems. If the buns are in rows of five, the solution to the first problem is found through finding the total number of rows. If there are five columns of different flavoured muffins, the second problem is found by counting the number of items in each column. These are essentially two different ways of describing the same array but focusing on it in different ways – the first attending to the number of rows, the second attending to the number in the columns.

At this stage do not worry if the pupils are not using the formal notation of division.

As these are challenging problems, it might be helpful to bring the class together after a few minutes to share some of the strategies the pupils are using before setting them off again in their pairs.

Assessment

- Do pupils treat these as two distinct problems or can they see any connections between them?
- Are pupils able to create representations of the problems that effectively help them to find solutions?

Select two or three pairs to share their solutions with the class – these need not be the most sophisticated solutions but should be chosen in the expectation that they will prompt a discussion about the links between the two problems. Alert your chosen pairs to the fact that they will be sharing their methods so that they can be prepared for this.

Public talk

As the pupils share their solutions, use the array images to draw the class's attention to the links between the two problems. Did anyone spot that they could use the solution to one problem to find the answer to the other?

Talk about how one problem was a grouping problem – the 75 bread buns were being put into groups of 5 – and how the other was a sharing problem – the 75 muffins were being shared into five equal sized groups, each group being one flavour.

Show how both of these problems can be represented with the mathematical sentence:

$$75 \div 5 = 15.$$

Variations

The choice of context here is not arbitrary – the items are ones that are laid out in arrays to encourage the use of the array model in setting up solutions. Pupils will need a lot of experience of work on problems that are either grouping or sharing before they get a sound sense of these being two models underlying division. Other contexts could be things like vegetable patches with equal rows of plants; seats put out for a concert; stamps or stickers on a page; tiles on the floor or wall.

Source

Adapted from the *Young Mathematicians at Work*: *Working with the Array*, grades 3–5 materials on developing models of division (Hersch, Fosnot, & Cameron, 2004).

PROGRESSIVE NOUGHTS AND CROSSES

Practice and consolidation.

Stages

Lower Key Stage 2.
Adaptable for Upper Key Stage 2.

Direct object of learning

Learn multiplication and division facts for the three, four and eight multiplication tables.

Indirect object of learning

Fluency: recall multiplication facts.

Preparation

Prepare a sheet with 12 boxes on it, each containing a multiplication tables 'fact' but not the answer. These could be all the 12 facts for one table, or a 'mixed bag' of facts. Each pair of pupils will need one such sheet, that they will eventually cut up to create 12 'cards'.

Tools

Doubling as a strategy for linking the two, four and eight times tables.

Task

Public talk

The first part of the activity provides you and the pupils with initial information on which of these calculations the pupils already know, so that they can see if playing the game develops their fluency.

Give everyone paper and set them up for answering, individually, 12 questions.

Read out, in a random order, the 12 multiplication facts from the prepared sheet of cards. Pupils individually write down each calculation and their answer.

In pairs learners share their answers and try to agree on the correct ones.

Pairs note any questions and answers they are not completely certain of.

Go over the answers. Learners individually note their scores and calculate a paired score by adding their two individual scores. They note this score for later.

Give each pair a copy of the sheet: learners write the correct answer under the questions on their sheet. They cut up this sheet to make 12 cards to use to play *Progressive noughts and crosses*.

Private conversation

Explain the rules of *Progressive noughts and crosses*.

1   Players draw up a 3×3 board.
2   They mix the question cards and place them face down.
3   Player 1 turns over the top card and reads the calculation to player 2.
4   If player 2 answers the calculation correctly, they put their initials in one of the spaces. The question card is set aside and it is player 1's turn.
5   If player 2 gets the question wrong, they record nothing and that card is set aside. It is player 1's turn to answer a question.
6   To put their initials in a second square, players in their turn then have to answer two questions correctly, then three questions for the third square and so on. When they get a question wrong, it is their partner's turn.
7   Before their turn, a player may ask for five questions - if they get all five correct they can remove one of their opponent's set of initials from the board.
8   If the cards are all used up, shuffle them and start with a new stack.
9   Play continues until one person has a line of three sets of initials (vertically, horizontally or diagonally) or the game is a draw.

The pairs play the game. They continue to play until they are confident in answering all 12 questions.

Assessment

* Can pupils recall the multiplication facts without having to build up to them from 'one times'?
* For multiplication facts that pupils do know, ask them related division facts. For example, if a pupil knows that $9 \times 4 = 36$, can they say what $36 \div 9$ is?

Public talk

Go through the 12 questions again – learners note their scores and as before calculate a paired score by adding up the two individual scores. Does this beat the previous paired score?

Discuss with the learners what strategies they used for helping remember the answers to the questions.

What can they do to help them remember these facts in a month's time?

Variations

The possibilities for variation here are endless – any set of questions with unambiguous answers can be used.

Source

The basic frame game was developed by Dr Sivasailam 'Thiagi' Thiagarajan. Although a trainer and games developer, not a mathematics educator, many of his games can be adapted for the mathematics classroom and there are over 400 on his website: www.thiagi.com.

REASONING CHAINS

Foundational inquiry.

Stages

Lower Key Stage 2.
Adaptable to Upper Key Stage 2.

Direct object of learning

Solve problems involving multiplying and adding, including using the distributive law to multiply two-digit numbers by one-digit.

Indirect object of learning

Reasoning: understand, informally, the distributive law.

Tools

Arrays.

Task

Public talk

Put this calculation on the board:

4×3

Learners should just figure this out as they want – they put a thumb up against their chest to indicate when they have arrived at an answer. Take suggestions for the answer from the class – if more than one answer is suggested, just accept that – do not indicate which is the correct answer, simply note that answer on the board alongside any others offered. If there is more than one suggested answer, ask pupils to talk in pairs and decide on which they think is correct. Invite pupils to explain how they got to the answer, including the incorrect ones. Discuss the various explanations until there is consensus over the correct answer.

Set up a 4 × 3 array. Depending on how experienced the learners are in working with arrays, this may be a closed or open array. Closed it will show all the squares in an array of squares that is four rows of three squares. Open, the array would simply be a hollow rectangle labelled 4 along the side and 3 across the top with the product 12 written inside (see Figure 6. 23).

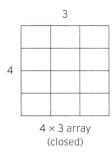 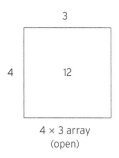

Figure 6.23

Record the product: 4 × 3 = 12
Now write up:

4 × 10

As before, learners indicate when they have an answer by quietly putting a thumb up on their chest, near their shoulder. Take the range of answers, and if need be reach agreement on the correct answer in the fashion described previously. If everyone is content that the answer is 40 there is no need to labour how they got that answer, just accept it and move on. Again set up an open or closed array (as in Figure 6.24) and record the product.

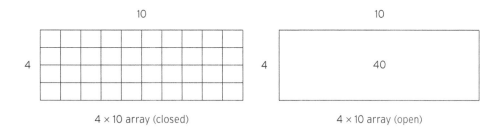

Figure 6.24

4 × 10 = 40

Next write up:

4 × 13

Go through the same routine of thumbs up to show an answer is arrived at and seeing if there is consensus on the answer. Irrespective of whether or not a range of answers was provided, invite suggestions from the learners as to how they got to the answer. Some may have known that 4 × 12 = 48 and added four more. Some may have doubled 13 and then doubled 26. Did anyone use the answers that were already on the board to figure out the answer to this calculation?

Model how the two arrays can be joined together (Figure 6.25 shows this for the open arrays) to give the answer and record the calculation in extended form.

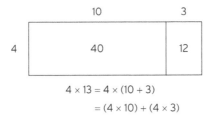

$$4 \times 13 = 4 \times (10 + 3)$$
$$= (4 \times 10) + (4 \times 3)$$

Figure 6.25

Repeat this routine with another reasoning chain:

5×4
5×10
5×14

Private conversation

Set the pupils a similar challenge:

Work with your partner to create two calculations that you can add to give the answer to with the same product as:

7×16

Work together to draw the arrays to show why your two calculations added together will have the same answer.

Assessment

- Do pupils use the arrays to help them justify their answers?
- Are pupils confident that other partitionings of the arrays, for example, $(3 \times 16) + (4 \times 16)$ will give the same answer?

Public talk

Invite one or two pairs to share what they have come up with.
    Can they convince everyone using arrays?

Variations

This task is a frame that can be varied and used often. Try to establish 'over to you ...' as a routine - a point of 'handover' to the students to have to come up with something themselves.

Source

Adapted from *Young Mathematicians at Work Professional Development Materials: Working with the Array, Grades 3-5* (Hersch, Fosnot, & Cameron, 2005).

RELEASE THE PRISONERS

Extension challenge.

Stages

Upper Key Stage 2.

Direct object of learning

Identify multiples and factors, including finding all factor pairs of a number.

Indirect object of learning

Reasoning: explore when a number has an odd or even number of factors.

Tools

A hundred square helps to keep track of things.

Task

Public talk

This is a classic problem that comes in various guises: a Christmas version has 100 reindeer and 100 gnomes. The version here is one of the original versions about prisoners and warders.

The problem is best set up by acting it out with some pupils, so invite around ten pupils to come up and be prisoners. They need to be able to show whether their prison door is open or closed – a strong visual way of doing this is to have the prisoners start off sitting on chairs. If they are sitting down, their cell door is locked, standing up it is open.

Other pupils come up one at a time to be warders.

Set up the context and the story for the problem:

There are 100 prisoners in 100 cells. Explain that the pupils at the front represent the first few prisoners – the learners will have to imagine the rest. At the beginning of the evening, all 100 prison cell doors are locked (so all the pupil prisoners start by sitting down).

Warder 1 goes to every cell and unlocks the door. What do they know about the cell doors now? Yes they are all open. (So everyone stands up.)

Warder 2 goes to every second door and locks it – the prisoners in places two, four, six . . . sit down.

Explain that from now on, every time a warder goes to a door they change that door's state – if the door was open they lock it and if it was locked they open it.

Warder 3 goes to every third door. Door 3 is open (the prisoner is standing) so warder 3 locks it (prisoner sits down), door 6 is locked (prisoner is sitting) so warder 3 opens it (prisoner stands up) and so forth.

In a similar fashion, warder 4 goes to doors 4, 8, 12, . . . and changes them from open to closed or closed to open.

Take questions from the class about the way the warders are acting. What will the 15th warder do? They will go to doors 15, 30, 45 . . . and change the state of them.

Suppose there are 100 warders. The question then is – which prisoners will escape? In other words, once warder 100 has gone past, which doors will be open?

Ask the learners to momentarily turn to the person next to them and talk about which number doors they think might be open after the 100th warder has gone past.

Take some suggestions and put these on the board for later.

Private conversation

Learners work in pairs on the problem. Although it initially sounds quite complicated, provided they go about recording the changes systematically they should be able to find the solution. If pupils need help in recording the problem work with them to develop a system like the one illustrated but give them time first to try and develop their own way of recording:

	Prisoner				
Warder	1	2	3	4	
	C	C	C	C	C – door closed
1	O	O	O	O	O – door open
2		C	O	C	
3			C	C	
4				O	

After a few minutes, encourage pairs to join up with another pair and to share what they have been doing. Have they noticed any patterns begin to emerge?

Back in their pairs they continue to work on a solution.

Assessment

- Are pupils recording their workings systematically?
- Are pupils displaying perseverance in looking for patterns and explanations?

Public talk

What have they found out? It should become clear that it is the doors with square numbers on them that are left open. Why is that?

Work with the class on looking at the factors of some numbers, one a square and the other not, say 12 and 9. Establish that the factors of 12 are 1, 2, 3, 4, 6 and 12.

How are these connected to the warders in the problem?

It is these that are the numbers of the warders who will alter the state of door 12. Warder 1 opens it, warder 2 locks it, warder 3 opens it, warder 4 locks it, warder 6 opens it, warder 12 locks it.

For door 9, the factors are 1, 3, 9.

Warder 1 opens door 9, warder 3 locks it, warder 9 opens it.

So why is door 12 locked and door 9 open?

Work with the pupils on the awareness that it depends on whether or not a door number has an odd or even number of factors – 12 has an even number of factors and this is made clear by matching up the factors in pairs: 1, 12; 2, 6; 3, 4.

But 9 has an odd number of factors 1, 3, 9. That's because 3 matches up with itself to make a factor pair $1 \times 9 = 9$; $3 \times 3 = 9$. And that happens with all the square numbers.

Variations

Pupils can explore prime numbers and the Sieve of Eratosthenes on the Internet. They can produce factor trees of numbers – exploring how different branches always finally end up with the same prime numbers at the tips – why is that so?

Source

A classic problem.

MULTIPLYING FRACTIONS

Foundational inquiry.

Stages

Upper Key Stage 2.

Direct object of learning

Multiply simple pairs of proper fractions, writing the answer in its simplest form.

Indirect object of learning

Reasoning: multiplying fractions through the use of the array.

Tools

Arrays.

Task

Public talk

Ask a learner to come to the board and draw a 3 × 4 array.

Does everyone agree with what has been drawn? Make sure there is agreement that 'three by four' is three rows by four columns.

Repeat this for 6 × 2.

Pose this problem:

> I have a painting that I want to varnish. The painting is 1/2 m × 2/3 m. If varnish comes in tins to cover 1/4 m², 1/2 m² or 1 m² what is the smallest size tin I could buy?

Working in pairs, ask the learners to talk about, and draw a representation of the size of the painting. Look out for anyone that has some sense that this might be done by starting with a larger 1 m × 1 m array and dividing in half one way and in thirds the other way – help them refine their image.

Work with the class on setting up an array to model 1/2 × 1/3. Draw a square open array, establish that this is representing 1 × 1 and halve it horizontally, labelling it as in Figure 6.26.

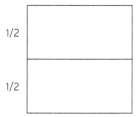

Figure 6.26

Pointing to the upper half, talk about it being 1/2 × 1 (the full width of the array). Can anyone suggest how the array could be adapted to show 1/2 × 1/3?

Divide the array into thirds vertically, labelling these as in Figure 6.27.

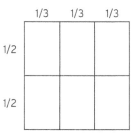

Figure 6.27

'Turn and talk. Which part of the array could I shade in to show 1/2 × 1/3?'

Establish that the top left hand corner could be 1/2 × 1/3 and shade it in (Figure 6.28).

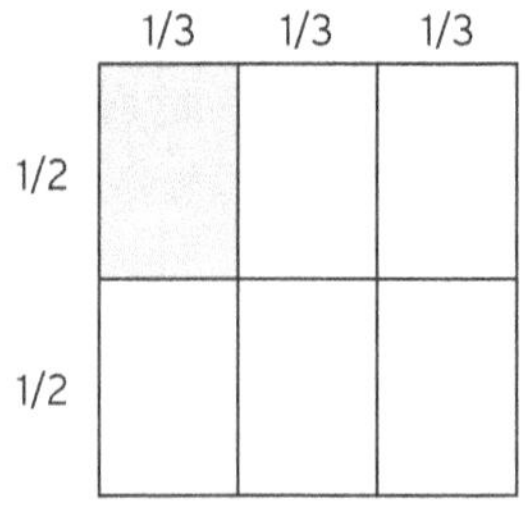

1/3   1/3   1/3

1/2

1/2

Figure 6.28

'Turn and talk. What fraction of the whole array is the shaded piece?'
Does everyone agree that the array has been sliced up into sixths, so the answer to 1/2 × 1/3 × is 1/6?

Private conversation

Ask the learners to work in pairs and draw the array to show 1/2 × 2/3.

Is everyone clear that the answer is 2/6 or 1/3? So what size tin of varnish will be needed? Explore how 1/2 of 2/3 is another way to talk about this multiplication and a half of 2/3 is going to be 1/3.

Set the pairs off to use arrays to find solutions to calculations like:

1/4 × 1/3
2/3 × 1/3
5/6 × 1/2

Public talk

Go over the solutions to the calculations.

Leave the solutions on the board set out:

1/4 × 1/3 = 1/12
2/3 × 1/3 = 2/6
5/6 × 1/2 = 5/12

Set up the calculation 3/4 × 2/3. The array model looks like that shown in Figure 6.29.

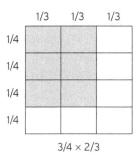

1/3   1/3   1/3

1/4

1/4

1/4

1/4

3/4 × 2/3

Figure 6.29

From this we can see that the overall array has been divided into 12 smaller parts, hence each subdivision is 1/12. And the shaded part is 3 × 2 = 6. So the answer is 6/12 and 3/4 × 2/3 = 6/12.

'Turn and talk. Do you notice any patterns in the products and answers?'

Steer the pupils to observing that multiplying the numerators and the denominator appears to give the answers. Can they justify this using the array?

Variations

If pupils are confident with this, they can work with more difficult fractions.

7   Geometry

Teaching geometry largely falls into two aspects of learning and inquiry:

*   the properties of two-dimensional and three-dimensional shapes;
*   position and movement.

While these two aspects can be treated separately they are connected. For example, pupils need to understand that a shape remains being, say, a square, irrespective of how it is positioned or moved in space. A square does not suddenly become a diamond simply because it is rotated through 45°! So although these two aspects are dealt with separately here, keep in mind the possible links.

When teaching geometry we also need to be aware of another, subtle, distinction; the distinction between the physical, real world of three- and two-dimensional objects and the theoretical world of mathematical ideas. When we work with images of, say, a circle, there are the physical representations (on paper, screen or cut out of card) of circles and the mathematical concept of a circle (as the points that are all a fixed distance from a given point). However accurately drawn, a physical circle can never be as perfect as the mathematical concept. A circle cut out of paper or card is, strictly speaking, a three-dimensional object – a cylinder, albeit a very short one. As teachers, we need to be clear about this distinction between the imperfect real and the perfect imagined, even if it is not always made explicit to pupils.

Big ideas

*   The Big Idea of invariance lies at the heart of geometry – what can be changed and what needs to stay the same for shapes to be well-defined. For example, having four right angles is an invariant property of rectangles, whereas their size can vary.
*   Shapes can be considered to be alike in two ways. Shapes that are alike in that they match each other in every way mathematically, both in terms of properties of shape and in terms of size, are described as congruent (non-mathematical properties like colour do not count). Shapes which are alike because they share the same geometrical properties and are not the same size but are scaled versions of each other are known as similar shapes. For example, all equilateral triangles have three equal sides and three equal angles, irrespective of how large or small they are, so all equilateral triangles are similar. But only two equilateral triangles of exactly the same size are congruent. And while all rectangles have four right angles, they are not all similar to each other as the proportions of the sides can vary.
*   Geometrical properties are independent of measures. A quadrilateral is a square if it has four equal sides and four equal angles. The fact that the angles are measured to be right angles is not the determining property of 'squareness', it is the fact that the angles all have to be equal. And the actual lengths of the sides have no impact on a quadrilateral being a square, just that the lengths all need to be equal.

Making connections

*   Pupils need to make connections between imagining and visualising, shapes in their minds, and the examples of shapes that they experience in the real world.

- The classification of shapes tells us more than just the name of a shape. For example, knowing that a shape is an isosceles triangle not only tells us that it has two equal sides, but also that it must have two equal angles and only one line of symmetry.

Progression in understanding properties of shapes

Often shape is treated as though it were less important than number (it certainly gets less teaching time). In the previous chapters on number, I have suggested that there is a strong spatial element to learning about number. Position and movement on number lines, or comparing arrays and how much space they cover, are just two aspects of foundational ideas in number that are linked to space, and our bodies and movement in space. So while there are aspects of the geometry curriculum that are distinct from the number curriculum, number and geometry are two connected, complementary ways of thinking.

Pupils start school with many experiences of working with three-dimensional objects – balls, bricks, Lego and Duplo, wheels, coins, counters and so forth. Building on these early experiences means that concepts of shape can be grounded in familiar experiences. The development of mathematical language associated with shapes is a key aspect to work on and initially the use of ordinary English words like box instead of cuboid is fine, as long as pupils eventually come to know that 'square boxes' or cubes are also cuboids.

Teaching geometry often focuses mainly on declarative ideas – identifying and naming shapes – but it can do much more than that; geometry can engage pupils in reasoning and problem solving and in considering how to engage pupils in thinking about geometry Duval's (1998) distinction of three types of thinking processes is helpful:

- visualisation processes
- construction processes
- reasoning processes.

Visualisation processes

Although we talk about teaching pupils to visualise, this is a far from straightforward task. Visualising is something that only happens inside the head and we can never know what anyone else is 'internally' seeing. All teachers can do is provide pupils with experiences that get them talking about shapes and describing what they can see (or feel) and hope that this leads to the development of some internal visualising processes. Having shapes on view may help develop the language of description, although working with hidden shapes may bring the processes of visualising into play and in Key Stage 1, working with 'feely bags' introduces hidden shapes. Having shapes in a bag that the learners can feel but cannot see not only gets them to describe the shapes but also encourages them to conjure up a mental image of the shape. Hide a 3D shape in a bag. Pass it round – everyone feels the shape and says something about it – but they cannot say what they think the shape is. For example, 'I can feel a square face' is ok, but, 'I can feel a cube' is not. Stress that it is okay to repeat what someone else has said. Help the pupils refine their language of description – for example, if they talk about feeling a 'side', use another shape that everyone can see to find out if they are using 'side' to refer to face ('a side of a cube') or an edge ('a side of a square') and to refine their description appropriately. When everyone has said something about the shape, get pupils to speculate what it is. Can the pupils identify the shape from the description given? Take it from the bag to check and continue to talk about its properties. (Depending on the age and level of attainment of the pupils you might have a set of all the shapes on the table labelled with their correct names for them to refer to as they hear the description.)

An alternative to having shapes in feely bags is to set things up in such a way that one pupil can see a shape but the rest of the group cannot: *Behind the wall* provides an extended description of such a task. One definition of spatial or geometrical reasoning is that it is 'the set of cognitive processes by which mental representations for spatial objects, relationships, and transformations are constructed and manipulated' (Clements & Battista, 1992, p. 420). Tasks like these where objects are present, but out of sight, prompt the mental activities of such reasoning.

Asked what the object in Figure 7.1 is, most people will answer 'cube'.

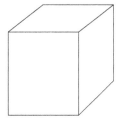

Figure 7.1

However, this is not a cube, but a stylised mathematical representation of a cube: no cube actually looks like that. Just as pupils have to learn to read meaning into the symbols of arithmetic, so too they need to learn to read meaning into the representations of shapes. This is best done through problems that challenge pupils either to make their own representations or to make sense of other people's representations. *Shape treasure hunt* provides both these challenges.

One representation of a right angle is created by a double fold on a piece of paper (see *Right angle everywhere*) – with their own right angle 'tester' pupils can visualise right angles in the environment and then see if they were reasonably accurate in identifying them.

Construction processes

Involving pupils in construction helps to deepen their understanding of geometry. Problems to encourage this can also build on visualising processes. For example, 'feely bags' tasks can be further developed by providing pupils with an object in a bag made up of, say, five interlocking cubes. The bag could be passed around a group, with each person feeling the object and describing it to everyone. Once they have all described the object, each person in the group takes five cubes and builds what they think is a duplicate of the object in the bag, before removing it to check. Or pupils might work with this in pairs: one puts her hand in the bag and describes the object to her partner who has to build a replica from this description.

Other construction activities can engage pupils in moving from two-dimensional representations of shapes to three-dimensional models. For example, the four images in Figure 7.2 show what a building made up of cubes looks like from each of four different directions. Working together, can the pupils use cubes to make a model of the building? Having made a model, is it possible to create it with fewer cubes? (It can be made with as few as six cubes!)

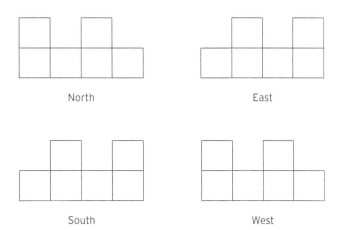

Figure 7.2

Something else to focus on is not just what can be constructed but what are the constraints on constructions, what conditions prevent something from being possible? *Can you make? . . .* provides opportunities for pupils to make two-dimensional shapes from a loop of string and to explore what is then possible or not. For example, an equilateral triangle is very stable in the sense that it cannot be transformed in the plane to create another shape, whereas a square can be transformed to create a (non-square) rhombus.

Reasoning processes

Visualising and constructing come together when pupils reason about results and ask the question 'why?' For example, pupils may observe that the opposite sides of a parallelogram are always the same length and simply take that as a given. Reasoning means asking why that might be so. The writer David Fielker (1983) suggests that properties like this can be explored through pupils drawing a pair of parallel lines on a sheet of paper and creating another pair of parallel lines (a different distance apart as the first pair) on an over-head transparency or sheet of tracing paper. Putting this second pair of lines over the first pair creates a parallelogram. Can the pupils position the paper in such a way that the parallelogram created does not have opposite sides equal? It cannot be done, and although this does not constitute a mathematical proof of the impossibility of a parallelogram not having two pairs of equal sides, it provides pupils with an informal sense of what is happening.

This example demonstrates the importance of exploring properties in a dynamic way. Simply looking at many representations of parallelograms may draw a pupil's attention to the fact that opposite sides are always equal in length, but it will not help her develop a sense of why that is so in the way that playing around with pairs of parallel lines can. Working dynamically is also important in helping pupils understand which properties uniquely define a shape and which properties are a consequence of that definition. A parallelogram, for example, is a quadrilateral with two pairs of parallel sides. We do not need to define it as 'a quadrilateral with two pairs of parallel sides, and opposite sides equal' – the equality of the sides is not an additional requirement, it is a consequence of the sides being parallel. Similarly, a rectangle is not 'a quadrilateral with two pairs of equal sides and four right angles', it is simply a quadrilateral with four right angles (try making a quadrilateral with four right angles that does *not* have two pairs of equal sides). *All kinds of quadrilaterals* is an extension challenge that leads to reasoning about the links between various properties of quadrilaterals. For example, trying to construct a quadrilateral with exactly one pair of parallel sides and two pairs of equal sides turns out to be an impossible task. Pupils can then explore, informally, what it is about the interaction of these two properties that makes this impossible.

Tree sorts is another construction challenge that engages pupils in reasoning. The naming of different types of quadrilaterals has a certain logic to it (although it is not entirely unambiguous) – this challenge gets pupils reasoning about the names of quadrilaterals and sorting them into various categories.

BEHIND THE WALL

Foundational inquiry.

Level

Key Stage 1.

Direct object of learning

Recognise and name common 2D and 3D shapes.

Indirect object of learning

Reasoning: understand properties of shapes and how rectangles, triangles, cuboids and pyramids are not always similar to each other.

Tools

A collection of two-dimensional shapes cut out from thin card. Include a variety of triangles and rectangles, some of which are similar to each other, and some of which are not. A screen of some sort to hide the shapes behind, for example a flip chart stand. A collection of three-dimensional shapes including cuboids and pyramids that are not similar to each other (have different proportions of lengths). A sturdy opaque bag to put the shapes in.

Task

Public talk

Hold one of the 2D shapes behind the screen. Reveal part of the shape – what do the pupils think the shape might be? Hide the shape again and reveal a different part. Continue until the pupils are confident that they know what the shape is. Remove it from behind the wall – were they correct?

   As the shapes are revealed, leave them on view. When the pupils think a shape of the same type has been hidden, talk about whether or not they think it 'matches' any of the shapes on display. When the shape is revealed, hold it up alongside a shape of the same type. Talk about what is the same and what is different about the shapes. An informal sense of the idea of shapes being similar can be introduced by getting two pupils to stand up and each hold one of the shapes. A third pupil stands where they can see both shapes lined up in their vision. If the shapes are similar, then the two pupils holding them can be positioned so that it looks like one shape exactly fits onto the other – can this be done? Invite pupils up one at a time to check if they think the shapes can be made to fit in this way. Introduce the language of shapes being similar.

Private conversation

Pupils play a hidden object game in pairs.

   Pupils make a wall between them with a book – one pupil can see a shape and their partner has to find out what it is by asking questions about the shape. As they get good at this, challenge the pupils to put two or three two-dimensional shapes down on their side of the wall, again through asking questions their partner has gather enough information to be able to draw the shapes and position them relative to each other. With 3D shapes, one partner builds a simple construction. From a collection of shapes that include copies of the hidden shapes, the other partner has to ask questions to enable them to create a duplicate construction.

Assessment

- Are pupils using 'guessing' questions ('Is it a square?') or are they using 'property' questions ('Are all the sides the same length?')?
- Can pupils use the vocabulary of shapes and their properties accurately?

Public talk

Keep a collection of 2D and 3D shapes on display and frequently play 'What's my shape?' One pupil secretly thinks of one of the shapes, their peers have to find out what it is by asking questions.

Variations

The range and types shapes can be added to over time.

SHAPE TREASURE HUNT

Foundational inquiry.

Level

Key Stage 1.

Direct object of learning

Compare common 2D and 3D shapes and everyday objects.

Indirect object of learning

Problem solving: use the vocabulary of position.

Tools

Everyday classroom objects. Mathematical vocabulary.

Prepare a collection of slips of paper each bearing the name of a 2D or 3D object and an image of that shape. Make sure there are examples of these shapes around the class, either in the form of everyday items or geometrical shapes placed around the room. There needs to be at least three examples of each shape in the room, for example, three square-based pyramids.

Prepare a pupil record sheet with space at the top for their name and room to paste one of the slips of paper with a shape name and image. The bulk of the record sheet has a two by three table:

Where I found my object	Where I found my object	Where I found my object
I think the object is	I think the object is	I think the object is

Task

Public talk

Discuss with the pupils what they know about how to describe the position of things – write up terms and phrases on the board, such as; in front of, behind, next to, under, on top of, beside, and so forth.

Explain what the task is:

Everyone will be given a slip of paper with the name of a shape on it, and an image of the shape. They are to stick this to the top of their record sheet. They have to find three objects in the classroom that they think are examples of their shape. On their record sheet, they describe where they found their object and write instructions for finding each on in the box labeled 'where I found my object'. They do not fill in the name of the object.

Model this by taking, for example, circle as the shape, and choosing the class clock as an object with this shape. Work with the pupils on writing a description of where the clock is, without naming it. For example: it is high up on the wall, to the left of the whiteboard.

When they have found three objects and described the whereabouts of each one, they will swap their sheet with a partner. They then go off and try to find the objects recorded by their partner on the sheet they have just been given. When they think they have found each object, they write its name in the box below the description of its whereabouts. Getting back together with their partner, they check to see if they had identified the same objects.

Private conversation

As the pupils are looking for objects, check that they are correctly identifying the shape they were given.

Help them refine their descriptions of the objects' locations.

Assessment

- Can pupils recognise two-dimensional shapes when they are embedded within three-dimensional objects; for example, seeing a circle as the bottom of a cup?
- Can they use the language of position to help others find their shape; for example, on top of the bookshelf, next to the pens?

Public talk

Put the pupils into new pairs. Ask them to 'think-pair-share' and talk about:

'What was the easiest object to find? Why was it easy?'

'What was the hardest object to find? Why was it hard?'

Get some pupils to share what they were discussing with the class.

Variations

The range of shapes to look for can be varied, or made more specific, for example, an equilateral triangle or a 'long thin rectangle'.

Source

Based on an activity from Gilpin. S. (2002), *Shapes, Shapes Everywhere. A Second Grade Geometry Unit Aligned with Mathematics Standards and Content Knowledge: A Compendium of Standards and Benchmarks for K-12 Education* (3rd ed.).

CAN YOU MAKE . . . ?

Foundational inquiry.

Level

Lower Key Stage 2 but adaptable to Upper Key Stage 2.

Direct object of learning

Compare and classify geometric shapes, including quadrilaterals and triangles, based on their properties and sizes.

Indirect object of learning

Reasoning: justify and explain findings about properties of two-dimensional shapes, including when conditions are impossible.

Tools

Lengths of string (around 2m) knotted to form a loop.

Task

Public talk

Both parts of this task need to be done in a space where pupils have plenty of room to move about.

Ask the pupils to wander around. Call out a number – they have to move quietly into groups of that size (it does not matter if one or two groups have one more or one fewer members). Then call out the name of a 2D shape – the group has to use bodies to show that shape. After they have made their shapes and you've invited one or two groups to remain in position while the other pupils look at them and see how they made the shape. They go wandering again before you call out a different size grouping and new shape. Keep the match between the group size and the shape a less than obvious one, for example, ask groups of four to create a pentagon or groups of five to create an isosceles triangle.

Private conversation

Finish with the pupils in groups of four. Each group collects a loop of string. They have to make various shapes with their string – the instructions can either be given orally or put up on the board.

- Make a shape with three equal sides.
- Without measuring, make the sides as accurately equal as you can. Keeping the sides equal, can you transform it into a different shape?
- What is the name of your shape?
- Make an isosceles triangle. Make it as accurately as you can.
- How can you convince someone that your triangle has two equal sides?
- Make a shape with four equal sides.
- Make the sides as equal as possible.
- Keeping the sides equal, can you transform it?
- Make a shape with four equal angles.

- Keeping the angles equal, can you transform it?
- Make a shape with exactly one right angle.
- Make a shape with exactly two right angles.
- Make a shape with exactly three right angles.
- Can you make a quadrilateral with exactly one line of symmetry?
- How can you convince someone that your shape has just one line of symmetry?
- Is there any other quadrilateral you can make with exactly one line of symmetry?
- What about a quadrilateral with exactly two lines of symmetry?
- Three lines of symmetry?
- Exactly four lines of symmetry?

Assessment

- How do pupils go about making the sides of their shapes as equal as possible? Can they find a way to divide the loop of string equally into thirds?
- As they transform their shapes, what do pupils notice stays the same? What do they notice changes?

Public talk

Look at some of the shapes that were created. Were any challenges impossible? How do they know they were impossible?

Variations

Pupils could work in pairs with small loops of cotton or fine string and make written records of the shapes they create. They could also work with straws and pipe cleaners or geostrips to create shapes.

Source

Adapted from Nrich's 'Stringy Quads', available online at http://nrich.mathematics.org/2913.

RIGHT ANGLES EVERYWHERE

Practice and consolidation.

Level

Lower Key Stage 2.

Direct object of learning

Identify right angles, recognise that two right angles make a half turn, three make three quarters of a turn and four a complete turn; identify whether angles are greater than or less than a right angle.

Indirect object of learning

Fluency: identify right angles and use the language of acute and obtuse for angles greater or lesser than a right angle.

Tools

Scrap A4 paper.

Task

Public talk

Make sure everyone has enough space to move about in.

With all pupils standing and facing front, check that everyone is clear about which direction they need to turn if you ask them to turn to their right or left. Also if you ask them to turn clockwise or anticlockwise that they are clear about this distinction. Establish that making a quarter turn is the same as being asked to turn through a right angle. And that a half turn is equivalent to turning through two quarter turns or two right angles and so forth.

Give a variety of turning instructions involving one, two, three or four right angles and a mix of instructions to turn left or right, clockwise or anticlockwise. For example:

Make a quarter turn to your left.

Turn through two right angles in a clockwise direction.

Turn anticlockwise through three right angles.

As the pupils become confident in this, ask them, before making a turn, to point and predict the direction they will end up facing.

Then challenge them to tell you what instruction would bring them back to facing the front. Can anyone come up with a different instruction that will also bring everyone back facing the front?

Make a quarter turn to the left.

'What instruction will bring us all back facing front?'

'Yes, turn through three right angles to the left.'

'Another?'

'Ok, make a quarter turn to the right?'

And so on.

Give everyone a piece of used A4 paper and show them how to a make a right angle tester. First they fold the paper in half – any fold line will do. Then they fold that crease back to meet itself – the corner formed is a right angle (see Figure 7.3).

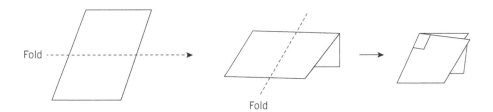

Figure 7.3

Private conversation

Send the pupils off in pairs to find and list various angles around the room: at least five should be very close to being right angles, at least five should be angles less than a right angle and at least five should be greater than a right angle.

As the pupils are looking for and listing their angles, go round and introduce the language of acute and obtuse angles appropriately.

Assessment

- Can pupils talk about the connection between finding right angles and quarter turns?
- Can they use the language of acute and obtuse to describe angles less than or greater than a right angle?

Public talk

Can pupils help each other see the angles they found by describing where they are but not revealing the actual object?

Variation

Show pupils how to make an angle indicator. Take two circles of thin card in two different colours. Cut one radius on each card and slot them together. By turning the circles different angles can be shown (see Figure 7. 4).

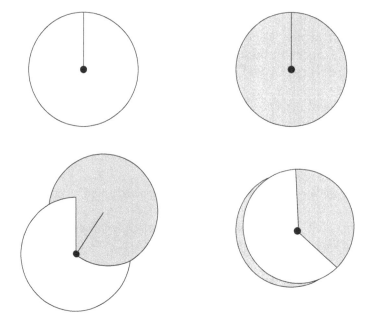

Figure 7.4

ALL KINDS OF QUADRILATERALS

Extension challenge.

Level

Upper Key Stage 2.

Direct object of learning

Distinguish between regular and irregular polygons based on reasoning about equal sides and angles.

Indirect object of learning

Reasoning: identify properties of quadrilaterals and which properties are dependent on others.

Tools

Thin card, rulers, pens, scissors.

Preparation

Groups each need a large (on A2 sized paper) copy of a grid like this one, for all kinds of quadrilaterals:

Pairs of parallel sides	Pairs of equal sides		
	0	1	2
0			
1			
2			

Task

Public talk

Go over how the grid has to be interpreted. Point out that it is 'pairs' of equal sides; so one pair of equal sides means exactly that: two equal sides, no more or less. Similarly, a shape with one pair of parallel sides cannot have two pairs of parallel sides.

Talk about the properties that a shape will have in some of the cells in the grid – for example the shapes in the middle of the grid (1, 1) have to have exactly one pair of equal sides and one pair of parallel sides (this does not have to be the same pair of sides).

The challenge is for groups to create as many different quadrilaterals as they can to go in the nine cells of the grid. If a cell can contain more than one type of quadrilateral, then they should make more than one. Not every cell has a possible quadrilateral, but do not tell the pupils this in advance.

Private conversation

Working in small groups, give pupils a large version of the grid and materials from which to construct quadrilaterals.

As the pupils are creating quadrilaterals, are they able to name them?

Are there any cells that pupils think can contain more than one type of quadrilateral?

This question focuses the pupils' attention on the fact that some quadrilaterals that we give different names to can still share common properties. For example a non-rectangular parallelogram and a rectangle both satisfy the condition of two pairs of parallel sides and two pairs of equal sides.

What about a square? Does that count as having two pairs of equal sides, given that all four sides are equal?

Are any of the cells impossible?

When pupils begin to think some cells have no solutions they usually want confirmation that they are right in this conjecture. Resist telling them whether they are correct or not but bring the class together to share their results and discuss the reasons for why they think quadrilaterals cannot be created for some cells.

The main point with this task is not so much the creating of the shapes as working with the pupils on developing the quality of their arguments for why certain shapes belong in particular cells and why some are impossible to find.

Assessment

- Can pupils accurately name the shapes they have created?
- Can pupils explain why they think some combinations are impossible?

Public talk

Put a large version of the grid up on the board. Pupils offer quadrilaterals to put in the cells. How many names can they give to each quadrilateral?

What about the empty cells? Can anyone convince the class as to why these cannot be made?

Variations

An extension of this activity is to replace the label 'pairs of parallel sides' with 'numbers of right angles' (that is, shapes with precisely no, one or two right angles). The basic structure of a 3 × 3 grid can be adapted to other contexts – for example putting properties of numbers along the axes – a multiple of three, less than 100, odd – along one axis. A multiple of five, prime, two-digit – along the other axis.

Source

This activity comes from Fielker (1983) *Removing the Shackles of Euclid.*

TREE SORTS

Extension challenge.

Level

Upper Key Stage 2.

Direct object of learning

Compare and classify geometric shapes based on their properties.

Indirect object of learning

Reasoning: explore the naming of shapes and how these names are based on properties of lines and angles.

Tools

A selection of 2D shapes.

Task

Public talk

Introduce the idea of tree sorts by inviting four pupils to the front to play 'Guess who'. Tell the pupils that you are secretly thinking of one of these four volunteers at the front and the class have to ask questions with 'yes' or 'no' answers to find out whom you are thinking of.

For example, 'Are they wearing trainers?' Or, 'Do they wear glasses?' Talk about what a good question is, looking for those that separate the group of four into two groups of two and then split the pairs.

Using appropriate questions draw a tree sorting diagram on the board and then invite pupils to take turns in secretly thinking of one of the four and have questions directed to them to find out who their mystery person is (see Figure 7.5).

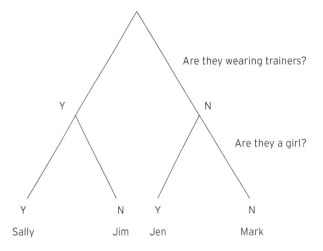

Figure 7.5

Private conversation

Working in pairs or small groups, give the pupils a collection of two-dimensional shapes to create their own tree sorting diagrams. Eight or sixteen shapes are a good number to start with as pupils can try to think of questions that repeatedly halve the collection.

They draw up their tree diagrams on a large sheet of paper and take it in turns to secretly think of a shape and check that their sorting diagram works by getting other pupils to work through the questions.

Assessment

- Can pupils pose questions that involve the properties of shapes, not just their names?
- Can pupils pose questions that separate their shapes into relatively equal groups, rather than just separating off one or two shapes?

Public talk

Display one or two of the pupils' sorting diagrams on the board. Check that they 'work' by inviting individuals to secretly think of one of the shapes and others to use the questions on the tree diagram to find out what the shape is.

Discuss what the pupils think are good questions – questions that help split groups of shapes. How do these questions relate to the naming of shapes?

Variations

One obvious variation is to work with three-dimensional shapes. The basic idea of a tree sort can be used with other mathematical objects, such as a collection of numbers. It can also be used across the curriculum to sort and classify objects, for example, leaves or insects. Basic yes/no questioning is at the heart of all modern technology – computers work on logic of on/off – pupils could explore this on the Internet.

Progression in position and movement

Learning about geometrical properties involves looking at shapes, comparing them with other shapes and identifying and describing key features. Understanding position of shapes in space is about the placing of shapes relative to something else. In *Shape treasure hunt*, pupils work on this with the everyday language of 'behind', 'above', 'next to' and so forth. But mathematical conventions have been developed to make the describing of position more precise, with the coordinate grid as the main convention that pupils meet in primary school. *Place the cubes* introduces pupils to using a simple grid: putting coloured cubes in squares and describing their position helps young learners to embody the idea of describing position in terms of along and up and link this to everyday language such as 'in front of', 'next to', 'behind'. The game helps pupils to observe, visualise and describe positions.

The task *Be seated* extends this into a more formal introduction to coordinates. By the end of primary school pupils are expected to be working with coordinates in the four quadrant grid that includes positive and negative numbers: *Plot the quadrilateral* provides an inquiry into this.

One of the challenges in coming to understand position and movement is how to capture something that is transitory – for example the movement of a shape in space – through the static medium of marks on paper. *Clap and tap* presents pupils with such a challenge: can they find a way to record a rhythmic pattern in such a way that someone else can produce it?

Angles can be thought about in two ways – as an object – this is what a right angle looks like – and as a process – a right angle is the result of an amount of turn that is equivalent to a quarter of a full turn. Pupils explore this connection through dynamically making angles in *Turn about*.

As pupils move into the later primary years they can begin to identify, describe and represent the positions of a shape following reflections, as suggested in *Mirror, mirror*.

PLACE THE CUBES

Foundational inquiry.

Stages

Key Stage 1.

Direct object of learning

Describe position, direction and movement.

Indirect object of learning

Problem solving: describe and communicate position.

Tools

Grids.

Task

Public talk

Explain to the class how the game is played modelling it through playing a sample round with a pupil.

Playing in pairs, each pupil needs a 3 × 3 grid (of squares, each about 5 cm × 5 cm). The top of the grid needs to be marked with a symbol so that they know which way to orientate the grid. Each pupil has four different coloured cubes (matched to their partner's cubes). The pair also needs a book to stand up as a screen so that they cannot see each other's grid.

The player to go first places her cubes on four different squares of the grid. Her partner then asks where to put cubes on his grid so that the arrangement matches. The pupil who put the cubes out describes where to place the cubes of particular colours. The players check to see if their completed grids match and then swap roles.

Private conversation

Once the learners are more confident suggest to them that they play the game on a 6 × 6 grid. This makes it more difficult to specify different positions on the grid without some system. Encourage the pupils to develop a way of labeling the squares, perhaps with colours along one side and letters or numbers on the other.

Assessment

- Can pupils follow instructions you give them for placing a cube on the grid?
- Do pupils use language such as 'along', 'up', 'next to' and so forth appropriately?

Public talk

Discuss with the class the different systems that pairs came up with to describe the position of the cubes on the grid. Work with a particular system, say, letters along the horizontal axis and numbers up the vertical axis. Introduce and work with the convention of always saying the letter (the horizontal axis) followed by the number (the vertical axis).

Variations

Learners can play a simple version of battleships - placing their four cubes on the grid and taking it in turns to guess where their partner's cubes are positioned - an answer of green means they have found a cube (and it is removed from the grid). Yellow means the square named has a side adjacent to a square with a cube in it.

Source

Adapted from an activity in Van de Walle (2007), *Elementary and Middle School Mathematics: Teaching Developmentally* (6th ed.).

CLAP AND TAP

Foundational inquiry.

Stages

Key Stage 1.

Direct object of learning

Order and arrange combinations of mathematical objects in patterns and sequences.

Indirect object of learning

Problem solving: devise notational systems.

Tools

Coloured cubes or different shapes such as polydron. Coloured pens and large sheets of paper.

Task

Public talk

Start a simple rhythm using claps and taps (both hands on your knees), such as 'clap, clap, tap, clap, clap, tap, clap, clap, tap . . . '

Invite the class to join in. When everyone has got the pattern, stop and set the challenge: can the learners go off and find a way to record the pattern so that someone else would be able to make it? Tell them they can use paper and pens to record it in some way or if they prefer that there are objects they could use.

Bring the class back together to look at the various ways the pupils solved the problem. Which representations do the class think were particularly helpful?

Set the further challenge of pairs going off and making up a new pattern of their own. They have to record their pattern and then swap with another pair to see if their recording works. Can the other pair make the same pattern from the representation they are given?

Private conversation

As pupils are working on the problem, those who have found a solution could be asked to include a new sound or action, such as a stamp. Can they extend their method of recording to include this new third sound?

Assessment

- Can pupils describe the rule behind their pattern?
- Can they predict what will be, say, the 20th sound or action in their pattern?

Public talk

Put some of the learners' records up on the board. Can the class follow the instructions thus presented for creating a sound pattern?

Create a sound pattern with a repeat of five, such as 'clap, clap, tap, stamp, stamp, clap, clap, tap, stamp, stamp, clap, clap, tap, stamp, stamp . . . '

After the class has joined in and got a good sense of rhythm, number the elements in the pattern, so that the 1st is a clap, the 2nd a clap, the 3rd a tap and so forth. Can the pupils say what sound the 10th will be? What about the 30th, the 39th? The 100th, 101st?

Variations

Learners could produce a visual pattern of images or objects and then make up a sound pattern to go with it. In what ways are the different sound patterns made up from the same visual pattern alike? In what ways are they different?

Source

Adapted from an activity in *Mathematics Their Way* by Mary Baratta-Lorton (1976).

TURN ABOUT

Practice and consolidation.

Stages

Lower Key Stage 2.

Direct object of learning

Recognise angles as a description of a turn.

Indirect object of learning

Fluency: describe angles using the language of right angle, acute, obtuse and reflex.

Tools

Angle measurers made out of strips of card, about 2-3 cm wide, fixed together at one end with a split pin - learners can make these themselves. Although usually made with two strips of card the same length, this can lead pupils to thinking that angles always have to be represented with lines of equal length and that the length of these lines has something to do with the size of the angle, so make the arms of the angle strips different lengths (see Figure 7. 6).

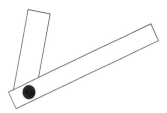

Figure 7.6

Preparation

Images of a number of angles to display on the whiteboard. Sets of four cards labelled obtuse, acute, reflex and right angle (learners could make these themselves).

Task

Public talk

Ask the pupils to stand up. Get them to physically model turning a certain amount of degrees by following your instructions.

Turn three right angles anticlockwise.

Rotate 90° to your left.

Introduce or recap on the terms obtuse, acute, reflex and right angle.

Private conversation

Pairs of pupils share an angle strip: they take it in turns to create an angle and their partner has to select the correct card to label it as obtuse, acute, reflex or right angle. The learners then find examples of each type of these angles around the classroom.

Public talk

Project up on the board images of angles - learners have to hold up the card indicating what type of angle it is.

Variations

Introduce the idea of a right angle being 90° and of half of this being 45°. Pupils make angles as before but have to decide what number of right angles (to the nearest half right angle) they think the angle is, and work out how many degrees this would be.

Source

Adapted from www.bbc.co.uk/schools/teachers/ks2_lessonplans/mathematics/angles.shtml.

BE SEATED

Foundational inquiry.

Stages

Lower Key Stage 2.

Direct object of learning

Describe positions on a 2D grid as coordinates in the first quadrant.

Indirect object of learning

Fluency: read, write and use pairs of coordinates, for example (2, 5).

Tools

Space for an embodied experience.

Task

Public talk

Arrange 16 chairs in four rows, a short distance apart, all facing towards the class.

Establish which one of the chairs is designated as being in the first row and the first column, and so referred to as the chair in position 'one, one'.

Which chair do the pupils think you are referring to when talking of the one in position 'three, two' - is this the chair in row three, column two or the one in column three, row two?

Establish the convention that the position is described by going along first to find the column that the chair is in and then 'up' that column to the row specified by the second number. Don't expect the pupils to immediately be correct in their use of language here - it is confusing that you need to go along the first row to find out which column you are in!

Ask four or five pupils to take up seats. In turns, can they and the 'observers' work out which column and row their particular chair is in and describe their position using this ordered pair of numbers (you'll need to judge when you think it is appropriate to introduce the language of coordinates)?

Invite other pupils to take up a chair by giving them appropriate instructions. For example:

'Joao, please go and sit in the chair in column four, row two.'

'Robyn, will you go and sit in chair three, four?'

Pupils not yet sitting can give similar instructions to others to take up seats. When most of the seats are full, give various instructions to carry out. For example,

- 'Pupils sitting in 2, 2 and 4, 3 please stand up and swap places.'
- 'Everyone in row three please stand up.'

Again, once the idea of this is clear, pupils can give the instructions.

When certain pupils have been asked to stand, for example everyone in column two, ask them, in turn to say their individual position (coordinates).

Jot these down on the board. What do the pupils notice that they all had in common (in this case a first coordinate of 2)? Can anyone explain why this has happened?

Pose challenges such as:

- Which pupils need to stand up so that their second coordinate is 4?
- Which pupils need to stand up so that both their coordinates are the same?
- Which pupils need to stand up so that their second coordinate is larger than their first?

Private conversation

In pairs, pupils play a treasure hunt game: Each player has a 10 × 10 grid – they label this with horizontal and vertical axes, the squares being numbered in each direction from 1 to 10. Working so that their partner cannot see where they are playing them, each player 'hides' eight pieces of treasure on their grid by marking eight squares. They take it in turns to guess where their partner's treasures are positioned – an answer of green means they have found a treasure (and scored a point). Yellow means the square named has a side adjacent to a square with treasure in it. Orange means the squared named shares a corner with a square containing treasure. Red means the square named is not near one with treasure in it.

Public talk

Put a large 'treasure map' on the board, overlaid with a coordinate system. Invite pupils to identify various locations on the map using the coordinate system.

Variations

Once learners are confident, they can label the grid lines instead of the squares, thus meeting the idea of the 'origin' at (0, 0).

Source

Adapted from an activity in Van de Walle (2007), *Elementary and Middle School Mathematics: Teaching Developmentally* (6th ed.).

MIRROR, MIRROR

Extension challenge.

Stages

Upper Key Stage 2.

Direct object of learning

Identify, describe and represent the position of a shape following a reflection.

Indirect object of learning

Reasoning: use a 2D grid and coordinates in the first quadrant to locate a shape following a reflection parallel to an axis.

Tools

Large grid paper, cubes (with sides the same size as the grid squares), mirrors, cardboard 'frames' – card rectangles about the same size as the mirrors with the middle cut out to leave a frame to look through, paper clips.

Task

Public talk

Explain the challenge. Working in pairs pupils take it in turns to set up a challenge for their partner: this involves first of all deciding where the mirror is going to be placed on the grid – the positioning has to be parallel either to the x- or y-axis. As the mirror is going to be moved in and out of position, the placing of it is marked with paperclips on the edge of the grid.

The same person places some cubes on the grid between the mirror line and the axis it is parallel to. (The cubes are placed singly on the grid – not stacked on each other, see Figure 7.7.)

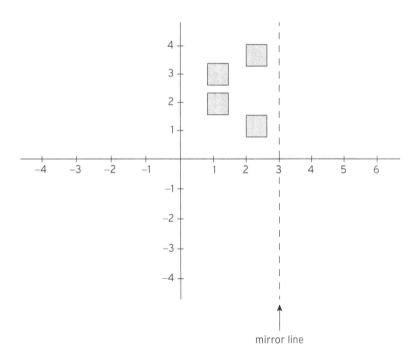

Figure 7.7

Their partner places the frame along the mirror line – they hold the frame in position, upright along the mirror line and looking from the side of the frame that has the cubes on it places cubes on the other side of the frame in the position they would expect to see them in the mirror. When they are confident that the cubes have been placed in the right position, they replace the frame with the mirror, lifting it in and out of position to check if the cubes are correctly placed and moving them if not.

Pairs swap over and create a new set up.

Private conversation

As the learners become confident in setting up a situation and accurately positioning the cubes in the reflected position, ask them to record the coordinates of the cubes and the positions of each reflected cube.

Assessment

- Do pupils notice any patterns in the coordinates recorded? Can they describe these?
- Are they able to predict any of the coordinates of the reflected cubes?

Public talk

Put up a coordinate grid on the board and draw in a mirror line parallel to the y-axis.

Mark up three or squares between the axis and mirror line. Invite learners to come up and write down the coordinates of each of these marked squares.

Can anyone predict what the coordinate of the one of the squares reflected in the mirror line is going to be? Can they explain how they think they know what the coordinates are going to be?

Work on where the reflected squares need to be located and check if any of the predictions about the coordinates are correct. Repeat this with a mirror line parallel to the x-axis.

Variations

Learners work with grids and shading in squares, marking a mirror line (always parallel to one of the axes). Before shading in the reflection of these squares, they write down the coordinates of the squares they shaded and their predictions for the coordinates of the reflections.

PLOT THE QUADRILATERAL

Extension challenge.

Stages

Upper Key Stage 2.

Direct object of learning

Describe positions on the full coordinate grid (all four quadrants).

Indirect object of learning

Reasoning: explore the effect of translating simple shapes on the coordinate plane and reflecting them in the axes.

Tools

Squared paper.

Task

Public talk

This sequence of activities develops from creating and using coordinates through to exploring translations, reflections and rotations involving all four quadrants.

Explain the first part of the task:

Using only the digits −5, −2, 1 and 3 the pupils, in pairs, list all the possible coordinate pairs that can be made (there are 16 in all, including (1, 1), (−2, −2) and so forth and the reversed pairs such as (3, −5) and (−5, 3).

Private conversation

As the pupils are working on this, if any of them are unconfident of working with negative numbers, make all the digits positive.

Public talk

Set up this challenge:

Selecting only from the coordinates just created, can the pupils choose sets of four that when plotted on a coordinate grid and joined produce these quadrilaterals:

- square
- rectangle (that is not a square)
- parallelogram (that is not a rectangle)
- rhombus (that is not a square)
- trapezium.

They record the coordinates for each of their quadrilaterals.

Private conversation

As the pupils are working on this, talk about whether they can predict any of the coordinates of a shape, given only two or three of the coordinates. For example, if (2, 5) and (6, 1) are the coordinates of diagonally opposite corners of a square, what are the other two coordinates?

Assessment

- Do the pupils notice any relationships in the coordinates of any particular shape?
- Do any pupils realise that shapes might be made that do not have sides parallel to the axes of the coordinate grid?

What do the pupils notice about the coordinates of, say, squares? If (2, 3) is one corner of a square and the square has a length of side of five units, what is the coordinate of the diagonally opposite vertex ((7, 8))? If you think the learners can deal with it, these could be expressed algebraically for example, if (a, b) is one corner of a square with side length d, then (a + d, b + d) is the coordinate of the opposite vertex.

Starting with a simple translation ask learners to explore the effect of this on the coordinates of their quadrilaterals. For example, you might give them the translation, 'Move five squares to the left and three squares up'. They apply this to one or two of their quadrilaterals, writing down the original coordinates and then the coordinates after the translation.

Can they identify a relationship between the coordinates before and after the translation? Can they then predict what the coordinates of a quadrilateral will be before carrying out the translation, checking their prediction by performing the translation?

Private conversation

Working together, can the pupils come up with a statement that expresses in general terms the effect of the translation on the coordinates? For example:

'Moving five squares left means subtracting 5 from the first coordinate and moving three squares up means adding 3 to the second coordinate.'

Pupils make up their own rules for translations, try these out and see if they can express the general rules. As they are doing this, watch out for pupils who seem ready to use the language of x-coordinate and y-coordinate instead of first and second.

Public talk

Talk about the rule that the learners have found for translations. These could be expressed algebraically for example, translating vertex (*a*, *b*) to (*a* – 3, *b* + 4).

Variations

Simple reflections – reflecting in the y-axis or reflecting in the x-axis – can be similarly explored.

Finally the pupils can play with what happens with rotations about the origin, clockwise and anticlockwise through 90° or 180°.

8 Measures

This chapter explores how to help pupils develop a sound understanding of measuring, with a particular focus on length, mass (weight) and volume and capacity as these measures are all based in the metric system and so also help develop understanding of number and place value. Some ideas on teaching about time are also included at the end of the chapter.

Big ideas

- Measuring is a way of making continuous quantities 'countable'.
- Measuring involves repeatedly using a unit.
- Benchmark measures provide a way of estimating quantities and checking whether or not measures are reasonable.

Making connections

- We can make measurements more accurate by creating smaller units – in our system this leads to decimals.
- Using a unit that is longer than the object being measured connects to understanding fractions.
- Using scales helps to develop understanding of multiplicative reasoning.

Aspects of measurement

Comparison is at the heart of measuring. Knowing that a bowl of flour weighs 150 g, or that a jug contains 50 ml of milk, are not, in themselves, useful pieces of knowledge, but if you are hoping that your muffins will compare favourably to the ones your mother makes, then your quantities have to measure up to the ones she uses. Based on the big idea of comparing then learning about the common measures involves similar stages:

- direct comparing;
- indirect comparing with informal units, such as sticks, shells or egg cups;
- indirect comparing using formal units, such as metres, kilograms or litres.

For example a sequence of teaching about measuring length in Key Stage 1 might include directly comparing the lengths, indirectly comparing two lengths and indirectly comparing using informal units.

Directly comparing the lengths of objects

Directly comparing the lengths of objects – ribbons, books, pencils, children's heights – establishes the language of longer than, shorter than, about the same length and so forth. Although pupils come to school with some informal understanding of such comparisons, there is evidence that they initially find it easier to talk about something being longer rather than shorter, possibly because the comparisons they will have met at home tend to focus more on the greater – who has the most sweets, who ran further, who is the tallest in the family and so forth. Pupils need plenty of experience so that they can talk about the opposite comparisons of less than and shorter.

At the time of writing, the new National Curriculum in England has introduced the use of the symbols ‹ and ›
as well as the equals sign. Evidence from countries that introduce these symbols early in the mathematics
curriculum suggests that young learners do not experience difficulty working with all three symbols. It makes
sense to use all three as we meet inequalities far more often than we meet equalities (a statement that itself
expresses an inequality!). The idea of equality then becomes a particular case on the continuous scale of
something going from being less than something else to being greater than it. For example, with a piece of
elastic that is shorter than a length of ribbon pupils can explore when the elastic is shorter than the ribbon,
when it is stretched to become longer than the ribbon and the one, unique, moment when the length of the
elastic and the ribbon are equal. Measures provide the ideal context for linking these three symbols to the
actions of comparing.

Indirectly comparing two lengths

Once learners are confident in the language arising out of direct comparisons they need problems comparing
two objects that cannot be placed side-by-side, by asking, for example, is the gap on the display board long
enough for a painting on paper to fit in? Can pupils decide without picking up the paper and positioning it on
the board? What could they use to make the comparison? Or, if we move the bookcase would it fit between
the two tables opposite? Such comparisons are best experienced using a unit that is longer than either object
(in the way that many of us will have used a length of string or dressing gown cord to decide if a wardrobe will
fit in an alcove or some similar problem) before moving on to using smaller units, either informal ones such
as cubes or the formal ones of centimetres and millimetres.

Setting up two towers (made, say, out of cardboard tubes covered in foil) and placing them on classroom
surfaces at different heights (on the floor and on a desk, for example) provides the opportunity not only for
dialogue about which is the taller tower, but also how this idea relates to being higher or lower – the top of
one tower may be higher than the top of the other but that does not necessarily mean it is the taller tower.
A metre stick (used simply as a stick) can help pupils find out which is taller. Setting the stick alongside one
tower and marking the height by putting a sticker there or wrapping an elastic band is better than trying to
keep a finger and thumb in place and then comparing this to when the stick is set against the other tower lays
the foundation for reading scales.

Indirectly comparing using informal units

Which is longer – the length of the classroom or the width? Unless a very long piece of string is available, a
question like that means repeatedly using a unit. As the question is which is longer, not how much longer, the
unit can be informal: pencils, shoes, cubes. Offering the learners a range of possible units like this (rather than
simply giving them one to use) provokes a conversation about choosing appropriately – cubes might be useful for
comparing the height of the two towers, but may not be the best unit for measuring the length of the classroom.

Recording the number of units provides the ground for an informal conversation about inverse proportion –
how was it that the classroom was 24 shoes long but only eight sticks long? Of course, the classic story of the
Emperor's new bed has to be told (Google it if you do not know the story).

Restricting the number of units available – providing, say, only three metre sticks – leads into the idea of
having to repeat the use of a single unit. How many metres long is the hall? Providing three metre rulers takes
away the difficulty of marking the end of each unit when measuring with only one ruler.

As metres are quite long and centimetres rather short, pupils can make their own informal 'unit cube' rulers. Joining ten interlocking cubes (of sides about 2.5 cm) together, they cut a strip of card to this length and
use it to measure and compare various things around the classroom.

Using formal units

Understanding how formal units work, and in particular the importance of lining up the zero on a ruler (and
ignoring the 'dead-end' if there is one), can be deepened by giving pupils broken rulers to work with. These
can be actual rulers with the end cut off or card images like the one in Figure 8.1. Realising that measuring
lengths by finding the difference between two numbers on the scales reinforces the ideas that simply looking
at the number on the ruler at one end of the thing being measure is not always sufficient.

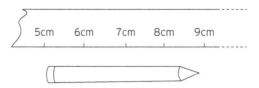

Figure 8.1

Although I have presented these ideas as a neat sequence of progression, the reality is that some pupils will come to class knowing about centimetres and metres, and with some sense of how to use formal tools. Rather than asking these learners to work only with informal units, I suggest making use of their knowledge. There is no harm in having some learners using formal units alongside others using informal ones – they bounce ideas off each other and everyone gains.

Progression in length, area and perimeter

Some ideas that we take for granted as adults are not intuitively obvious to young learners. One such idea is that a measure of height does not necessarily have to be done with a person standing up – measuring the length of your body lying down will produce the same (or very close to) the same result. *Standing up and lying down* addresses this idea.

In moving away from direct and indirect comparison towards the use of units, it is common practice to introduce children to units that are shorter than the object being measured: cubes for the length of a ribbon or hand spans for the length of the mat. As noted earlier, learners' understanding of the need to measure using tools is developed when they begin by using units that are longer than the thing being measured. *Secret ribbons* provides such a challenge.

Most arithmetical relationships that primary pupils encounter obey simple direct or indirect rules: for example, the larger the number you add, the larger the total (a direct relationship), or the smaller the unit of measure, the greater the number of units needed (an indirect relationship). The relationship between perimeter and area is probably the first connection that pupils meet where the 'rules' are not simple. While it is often the case that, as the areas of shapes increase, so too do the perimeters, this is not universally true. Similarly increasing the perimeter does not necessarily lead to a greater area. Pupils' 'common sense' will lead them to expect that the rule 'make one bigger and the other will always be bigger' will hold with respect to area and perimeter. Finding the perimeters of shapes in isolation can reinforce the erroneous idea that shapes with larger areas always have larger perimeters, so rather than introduce finding perimeters in isolation I suggest using tasks that link area and perimeter from the beginning – *Ideal gnome homes* provides such a task. Pupils need time, experience and lots of talk about measuring shapes to work through to understanding that there is no simple relationship between area and perimeter. *Down on the farm* challenges pupils to investigate the relationship between area and perimeter further, and the task also provides consolidation in calculating areas and perimeters, as well as working systematically.

When learning about area, pupils usually start with counting: initially covering surfaces with unit squares and then creating areas on squared paper. However, the move to finding areas of rectangles using the formula has a problematic connection to counting squares.

Consider the rectangle shown in Figure 8.2.

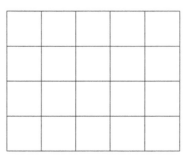

Figure 8.2

Counting the squares is straightforward and talking about there being four rows of five or five columns of four can make some links to multiplication. But compare this with the version of the rectangle shown in Figure 8.3.

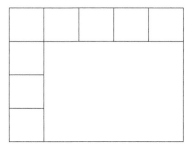

Figure 8.3

In moving from counting all the squares to using the limited information provided in the diagram, a shift has to occur in relation to attending to the square in the top left hand corner. When counting all the squares to find the area, this corner square must be counted once and once only, but in moving to use multiplication to find the area, this square must be counted twice: once to determine the number of squares in length of the rectangle and once again to find the number in the width. *Ripped and torn* is an activity that can help children move away from counting every square, while still supporting the underlying idea of area being about covering a surface with squares and supporting the shift in understanding from thinking of squares to considering lengths of sides.

Given that calculating the area of rectangles is, once understood, relatively easy to do, it is sensible to find ways of using rectangles to calculate the areas of non-rectilinear shapes. *Into rectangles* explores ways of doing this.

STANDING UP AND LYING DOWN

Foundational inquiry.

Stages

Key Stage 1.

Direct object of learning

Compare, describe and solve practical problems involving lengths and heights.

Indirect object of learning

Reasoning: understand that quantity is conserved when switching being between measuring height and length.

Tools

Long strips of paper around 5 cm wide (till-rolls are ideal). Chalk or post-its to mark positions on the wall or floor. Blu-tak.

Task

Public talk

Show how, working in pairs, pupils can measure each other's heights: one learner stands against the wall and their partner marks their height with a book or ruler. The first learner steps away and their height is recorded with a chalk line or a post-it with an arrow on it. They swap roles and record their partner's height.

Private conversation

As the pupils are finding and marking each other's heights, engage them in conversation using appropriate language such as taller than, shorter than. Help them cut paper strips that match their heights – they label these in whatever way they wish.

Get pairs then to find out how 'long' they each are when lying down: feet against the wall, they mark where their heads end on the floor. They check, using their height strips, how their lying down 'lengths' compare with their heights. If there is any difference, talk about why this might be so (and so in a simple way introduce the idea that measuring can involve errors).

Assessment

- Can pupils explain the relationship between how tall they are and the length of the paper strips they cut?
- Can they use the paper strips to put three or more pupils in height order and then check if they were correct by pupils lining up?

Public talk

Have a dialogue about what the pupils noticed. Why is their height the same as their length when lying down?

Get around six children to bring up their height strips – can the class help them to sort their strips into order, shortest to longest? Attach the strips to the wall with the bottom end of each on the ground. Get the children to line up in the same order as the strips – are they in height order? Why is that so?

Variation

Pupils cut strips the same length as, say, their foot or the distance from their middle finger tip to their elbow. They find objects around the room that are longer than or shorter than this strip, recording these appropriately.

Source

Adapted from an activity in Biggs and Shaw (1995) *Mathematics Alive!*

SECRET RIBBONS

Foundational inquiry.

Stages

Key Stage 1.

Direct object of learning

Choose and use appropriate standard units to estimate, measure, compare and order lengths.

Indirect object of learning

Reasoning: appreciate the need for standard units of measurement.

Tools

Metre rulers, elastic bands.

Task

As a lead into the main activity, set up some simple activities involving direct comparison, for example comparing two shoelaces.

Experience of comparisons that cannot be done directly also help, for example, pupils can draw around their foot and their closed hand, and are asked:

'If an ant crawled around the edge of your foot and another ant crawled around the outline of your hand, which ant would crawl further?'

Pupils can cut lengths of thick cotton (or fine string), dampened to help it stay in place, matching the distances around each outline and so find which is the longer by comparing the two lengths of cotton.

Public talk

Set up two 'secret' ribbons in boxes on opposite sides of the classroom. Tell the pupils that there are two ribbons, one in each box and, without moving the ribbon away from where it is in the room, they have to find out which hidden ribbon is the longer.

Private conversation

If the ribbons are close enough in length for the difference not to be discerned simply by looking, pupils can be introduced to the use of a tool that is longer than each ribbon: a metre ruler (pupils who have not been formally introduced to the standard metre ruler can ignore the marks). They also need elastic bands. Lining up one of the ribbons along the stick they mark the length of it by rolling an elastic band onto the ruler and matching it up with the end of the ribbon, repeating this with the other ribbon. The two elastic bands provide the visual evidence for the longer ribbon but are the basis of beginning to work with and understand scales.

Assessment

- Do the pupils measure from the same end of the ruler each time?
- Does anyone know anything about the numbers on the ruler?

Public talk

Look at the metre rulers and discuss how the pupils decided which ribbon was the longer.

Draw their attention to the centimetre markings on the ruler. Have a dialogue about whether they could use these markings to compare the two ribbons if they did not have any elastic bands to mark the lengths.

Talk about whether it makes any difference which end of the ruler they measure from.

Set the pupils off to use the rulers to see which was the longer – the length of cotton that was the distance around their hand or the one around their foot and to record what they find in some way.

Variation

Similar challenges could involve finding the taller of two towers of bricks, one on the floor and one on a table.

IDEAL GNOME HOMES

Foundational inquiry.

Stages

Lower Key Stage 2.

Direct object of learning

Measure the perimeter of simple 2D shapes.

Indirect object of learning

Reasoning: explore how the perimeter of a 2D shape can change while the area stays constant.

Tools

Plastic or strong cardboard squares around 3 cm square.

Task

Public talk

Set up the problem – it is a fantasy context where pupils are asked to imagine that gnomes all like their houses to be the same size (in terms of the area they cover) but also like them to look different.

Introduce the problem:

> *A community of gnomes are building houses to live in. Each house has a 'footprint' made up by fitting four small square tiles together and then building walls around the space enclosed.*

The challenge is to investigate the different houses that can be made from putting together four tiles and whether they all need the same amount of material for building walls. All buildings are one storey high.

Model how the tiles can be arranged in different configurations (the tiles need to be arranged so that their sides lines up, as shown in Figure 8.4) and how the side of one tile is the 'unit' to be used for measuring the distance around the outside. If anyone introduces the term perimeter then pick up and use it; otherwise, the term can be introduced at the end of the lesson when having a dialogue about what the learners have found.

This is OK   This is not OK

Figure 8.4

Private conversation

Set the pupils off in pairs to work on the challenge – they can draw around the different arrangements of the four tiles and record the amount of walling needed in whatever fashion they choose.

As the pupils are working, look to see who is working systematically to make sure they have found all the different arrangements of the four tiles – prepare these pupils for sharing what they did with the rest of the class. Excluding rotations and reflections there are essentially four different possible arrangements.

Assessment

- Do pupils think that the different arrangements of four tiles all provide the same amount of space to live in? Can they explain why?
- Can they suggest any ways to check that they have found all possible arrangements of the four tiles?

Public talk

Invite pupils to share what they have found. Is anyone confident that they found all the different ways to arrange the four squares? Introduce into the conversation, if not already present, the language of perimeter.

What can the pupils say about the perimeters of the different shapes?

Variation

Extend to five squares.

Provide centimetre squared paper and get pupils to create their initials (or a short name) out of exactly ten squares for each letter. What is the perimeter of each letter?

RIPPED AND TORN

Foundational inquiry.

Stages

Lower Key Stage 2.

Direct object of learning

Find the area of rectilinear shapes by counting squares.

Indirect object of learning

Reasoning: find areas when not all squares are visible.

Tools

Squared paper.

Task

Public talk

Have prepared some demonstration rectangles made up of, say, 4 cm × 4 cm squares. Hold these up (or display on the IWB) long enough for children to be able to count the number of squares in each row and column, but not long enough for them to be able to count every individual square.

Encourage pupils to use the language of multiplication in sharing their answers with the class:

'I could see that it was 6 squares across and 5 down, so there must have been 6 times 5 squares. That's 30 squares altogether.'

Have some rectangles prepared with a corner torn off. Hold them up or display them one at a time and invite pupils to talk in pairs and decide how many squares were in the rectangle before it got torn (see Figure 8.5).

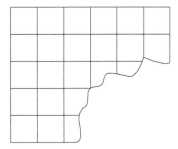

Figure 8.5

Have prepared some rectangles with more than one piece torn off where it is not immediately obvious how many squares there are in each row and column (see Figure 8.6).

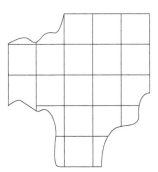

Figure 8.6

How do the pupils now figure out how any squares there were originally?

Also have some rectangles where so much has been torn off that finding a unique answer is not possible (see Figure 8.7).

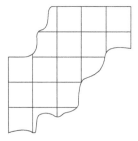

Figure 8.7

What are some possible answers?

Private conversation

Working in pairs or small groups have the learners prepare *Ripped and torn* puzzles for each other to solve. They cut out rectangles from squared paper, note down the dimensions of the rectangle (say, 4 × 7) and the area (28 square units). They rip pieces from the rectangle and swap with a partner. Can their partner write down the dimensions and find the area of the original rectangle?

Assessment

- Can anyone see a relationship between the lengths and breadths recorded and the area of each rectangle?
- Were any of the puzzles created impossible to solve? Why?

Public talk

Bringing the class back together, put up a selection of the data in a table and discuss the relationship between the numbers

Side 1 (squares)	Side 2 (squares)	Area (square units)
2	6	12
5	5	25
3	8	24

Work on articulating the rule for finding the area given the lengths of two sides.

Variation

Provide learners with simple shapes on squared paper made up of two rectilinear shapes joined along a common edge (see Figure 8.8). They find the area of the overall shape.

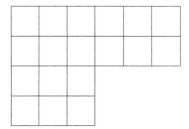

Figure 8.8

DOWN ON THE FARM

Foundational inquiry.

Stages

Upper Key Stage 2.

Direct object of learning

Measure and calculate the perimeter of composite rectilinear shapes and calculating the area of rectangles (including squares).

Indirect object of learning

Reasoning: explore the relationship between perimeter and area.

Tools

Alongside pencils and rulers (including some metre rules), centimetre squared paper is the only thing needed, although some pupils may benefit from having square tiles to move around.

Task

Public talk

Set up the context by talking about farms and how some have an enclosure (pen) where children can go and see animals close up. Talk about a farmer, Jenny say, who was setting up such pens and she wanted each pen to have a total area of 16 square metres. Use metre rules to mark out a square metre on the floor and talk about what a total of 16 of these might look like.

   (As my work is usually in urban schools I set the context of the lesson within a city farm. Obviously children in rural schools will be more familiar with farms proper.)

   Jenny thinks it would be interesting to have the animals' pens different shapes. She wants each one to be a rectangle but was wondering if 16 square metres can be arranged to create different rectangles. Turn to your partner. How could 16 squares be arranged to create a rectangle?

Take suggestions from the pupils and note these on the board. Invite pupils up to make quick sketch of each suggestion to check that it does have an area of 16 squares. Discuss whether, say, a rectangle 8 squares long and 2 squares wide is different from one that is 2 long by 8 wide. Establish that these are essentially the same rectangle. Work on listing all the solutions (there are only three) in an organised fashion.

   1×16
   2×8
   4×4

Explain that as well as wanting to build some pens with an area of 16 square.metres, Jenny also wanted to have some with areas of 24 square metres. Working in pairs, can the pupils find all the different arrangements of 24 squares to make rectangular shaped pens?

Private conversation

As the pupils begin to generate examples, direct their attention back to the board. Explain that Jenny is going to put a wire fence around the outside of the pens and wants to know how many metres of fencing will be needed for each pen.

> *Look again at these three pens that all have an area of 16 square metres. Talk to your partner. Will Jenny use the same length of chicken wire for putting a fence up around each one?*

Discuss whether the pupils think the 16 square metre pens will all need the same length of fencing or whether different pens require different lengths. Work on finding the perimeter of the 1 × 16 and 4 × 4, recording the lengths of all four sides to make the overall calculation clear.

Pupils continue to look at the possible rectangles with an area of 24 square metres and also the perimeters of these.

Assessment

- Are pupils being systematic in listing all the possible rectangles?
- Can pupils calculate the areas of the pens they create or are they still counting squares?

Public talk

At the end of the lesson gather all the information and order it into a table:

Rectangle	Area in square metres	Perimeter in metres
1 × 24	24	50
2 × 12	24	28
3 × 8	24	22
4 × 6	24	20

What do you notice about the areas of all the rectangles? What about the perimeters? Why does the 4 × 6 rectangle need so much less fencing than the 1 × 24? Talk to your partner.

Discuss the fact that it is possible for shapes to have the same area but to have different perimeters.

Variation

Change the problem to areas with a fixed perimeter:

> *Jenny has been given some rolls of chicken wire. Each roll is 12 m long so she has decided to make some rectangular pens that need exactly 12 m of chicken wire to fence them in. Talk to your partner and see if you can suggest a rectangle that Jenny can make.*

Into rectangles

Extension challenge.

Stages

Upper Key Stage 2.

Direct object of learning

Recognise that shapes with the same areas can have different perimeters and calculate the area of parallelograms.

Indirect object of learning

Reasoning: relate areas of simple non-rectilinear shapes to areas of rectangles.

Tools

Centimetre dot squared paper, rulers.

Task

Public talk

Model how to put two rectangles together to create a new shape that is not a rectangle. The new shape has to have at least part of a side of each rectangle fitted together for a whole number of squares: Figure 8.9 shows examples of what is acceptable and what is not.

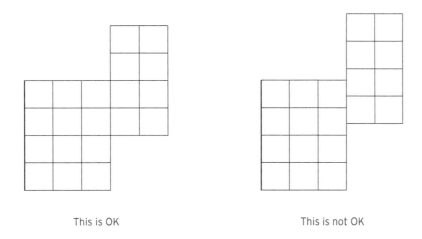

This is OK   This is not OK

Figure 8.9

Private conversation

Working in pairs, each pupil cuts out a rectangle from squared paper. They can choose the dimensions, but to make things manageable you might want to specify that each side of the rectangle should be no longer than ten units.

They put their two rectangles together to create a non-rectangular shape like the ones they have just seen modelled.

Pairs record the shape on centimetre squared or dot squared paper, only drawing the outline and not indicating where the two rectangles are joined. They swap this with another pair. They find the area of the shape they have been given by dividing it up into rectangles. Can they do this in at least two different ways? (Even though the shape they were given was originally made from two rectangles, they can divide it up into three or more.)

Public talk

Share some examples with the class.

Private conversation

Working in pairs, learners draw a parallelogram on the centimetre dot paper – the corners of the parallelogram have to be at dots on the paper. They find, using whatever method they like, the area of the parallelogram.

They cut out the parallelogram and decide how and where to cut it, with a single cut, so that the two pieces can be put back together to create a rectangle. They record the dimensions of the parallelogram (lengths of sides, area) and the related rectangle (lengths of sides, area). They do this for two or three different parallelograms.

Assessment

- Can pupils explain why the area of a parallelogram can be made equal to the area of a rectangle?
- Can they say what they need to know about the parallelogram in order to be able to find the lengths of the sides of the rectangle with the same area?

Public talk

Talk about what they did and noticed.

Draw up a table of results of the inquiry into parallelograms and turning these into rectangles. Are there any patterns that the learners notice? Once you have established that the areas of the parallelograms and the rectangles are the same, look at the dimensions of the rectangle and how these relate to that of the parallelogram. Explore how making a vertical cut across the parallelogram means you can always make a rectangle with one side the same length as the original parallelogram and the other side the height of the parallelogram (see Figure 8.10). Can learners use this construction to express a rule for finding the area of a parallelogram without actually doing the cutting?

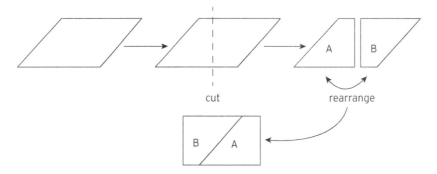

Figure 8.10

Variations

Work on finding areas of triangles in a similar way. In this case, rather than cutting up triangles and trying to rearrange them to make rectangles, work on enclosing the triangle in a 'snug' rectangle. What is the relationship between the area of the rectangle and the area of the triangle? What do they need to know about the triangle in order to be able to find the lengths of the sides of the rectangle?

PROGRESSION IN MEASURING MASS AND WEIGHT

A note on terminology: mass or weight?

Mass is the measure of the amount of 'matter' in an object, whereas weight is a measure of the effect of gravity on an object. A 1 kg weight, on the moon, will no longer 'weigh' 1 kg although its mass will be unaltered. Some purists argue that we are really teaching about mass. I don't think the more everyday language of weight lays down any problems for later understanding of this distinction and would use the terms interchangeably, as I do in the following.

Directly comparing weight

Lengths can be compared directly simply by putting things side-by-side: pupils have little difficulty knowing who is the taller of a pair of children or which is the longer ribbon, as they can see the difference. Comparing masses is more challenging, in that bodily sensations arising from the actions of informal comparing can be misleading. Judging which is the heavier by looking at the size of objects, or being a human 'balance' and comparing the 'feel' of an object in each hand does not always lead to a correct comparison. The large parcel might look as though it should be heavier than the small one, but place one on each of your upturned hands, and the pressure in the palm of your hand from the small parcel may make if feel heavier than the large one. Only balance scales can really tell us which perception is correct, so these need to be around in the classroom to supplement bodily experiences. It is helpful to have a collection of sealed, wrapped, identically sized containers with different amounts of clay or dried beans in them, so that pupils can act as human balance scales to decide which of a pair of these containers they think is heavier before testing out their choice on balance scales.

Balance scales can only compare the weight of objects pair wise: ordering five or six objects by 'feel' of weight and then checking the order using the scales is a challenging problem to solve. *Heavier or lighter* provides a practical context for exploring this.

Indirectly comparing weight

Using non-standard units to measure the weight of objects requires multiple units to be used, which is subtly different from what happens when measuring length. I can find the length of, say, a rug by repeatedly using only one pencil. I cannot, however, weigh a box using only one pebble or a single 20 g weight – I must have several. Although ultimately having an extensive collection of weights is replaced by using scales, weighing tools with vertical or circular scales provide no visible sense of the 'weights' making up the measure. Understanding here is helped by getting pupils to make an elastic band (spring) weighing 'machine'. Cutting about 12 cm off the bottom of a juice carton provides a suitable 'pan': punch a hole midway along each side, thread four knotted strings through and join them together about 20 cm above the pan. This can then be attached to a large rubber band or length of elastic and suspended from a hook, in front of a sheet of paper. Learners mark the position of the empty pan – either its top or bottom edge and its position with objects placed in the pan (making sure that they are consistent in where they are measuring from) to create a spring balance scale.

Using formal units

Given plenty of experience of non-formal units and creating scales to measure weight, pupils will come to understand that measurement is approximate, even when using formal units. As they seek out smaller units to make their measures more accurate it is helpful to discuss that although the measuring becomes more precise even at the level of grams it can never be completely accurate: however small our unit, there is always a possible error of half a unit either under or over.

Being able to read scales with increasing accuracy is an important skill but it needs to be supplemented with good estimation skills. Pupils often come to believe, largely through their experiences in school, that estimating is of lesser importance than actually measuring, yet in our daily lives we estimate quantities far more often than we measure them. *Weight scavenger hunt* introduces the idea of using benchmark masses to make reasonable estimates. Share with the pupils typical benchmarks such as a 250 g pack of butter, 1 kg bag of sugar. Encourage the children to look out for other everyday objects that can be added to a poster of favourite benchmark quantities.

Make weights provides a foundational inquiry for exploring how sets of weights for balance pans are constructed. Converting between the different metric weights is put in the context of problem solving in *Victoria's sponge*, which is a classic problem where the unknown (the weight of one egg) is at the start of the problem, rather than at the end. So you have to flip things and work backwards from the known end result (the weight of one pan of cake mixture) reversing the steps (doubling that to get the weight of the total mix, and so on). The power of working on such problems is not so much in finding the solution but drawing pupils' attention to the strategy of working backwards.

Exploring the connection between metric measures and imperial measures is dealt with in *Vegetable market*. Some learners will find pleasure in investigating the links between the different metric measures – how in the metric system a cubic centimetre of water has a mass of 1 g (at a particular temperature and pressure). They could research the 'neatness' of the metric system compared to the imperial system of pints and fluid ounces and pounds and ounces.

Finally *Strong as an ant* brings multiplicative reasoning into focus through an intriguing context that extends understanding of mass.

HEAVIER OR LIGHTER?

Foundational inquiry.

Stage

Key Stage 1.

Direct object of learning

Compare, describe and solve practical problems for mass/weight and use the language of heavy/light, heavier than, lighter than.

Indirect object of learning

Problem solving: solve practical problems.

Tools

A collection of sealed, wrapped containers or boxes of different dimensions containing different amounts of clay or dried beans. Balance scales.

Task

Public talk

Take a pair of the wrapped containers, show them to the class and invite the pupils to say which they think is going to be the heavier. Pass the containers round the class, Which one of the pair do pupils now think is the heavier? Invite learners to share with the class why they think one is heavier than the other. Did anyone change her or his mind after holding the packages? Why?

Use a pair of balance scales to check which is the heavier object.

Private conversation

From the collection of containers label one as the 'target' weight: groups sort the collection into two sets, those containers they think are heavier than the target and those they think are lighter. They do this by using only their bodies to decide – they do not use balance scales to check. They record this sorting in whatever way they choose.

They then re-sort the objects by using scales and comparing each object to the 'target' mass. How does this fit with their first sorting?

They collect objects from around the room that they think are either lighter or heavier than the target object. Do they get better with practice?

Assessment

- When comparing the mass of objects only using their bodies, do pupils take into consideration how an object 'feels' as well as how it looks?
- If pupils can use the balance scales to compare two objects, can they use the scales to put three objects in order from heaviest to lightest?

Public talk

Talk about what the pupils did. Were there any objects that were tricky to decide if they were heavier or lighter? What made them tricky?

Variation

Provide learners with a 1 kg or 500 g weight as the object to make the comparison against.

WEIGHT SCAVENGER HUNT

Practice and consolidation.

Stages

Key Stage 1.

Direct object of learning

Use appropriate standard units to estimate and measure mass (kg/g) and compare and order mass.

Indirect object of learning

Reasoning: develop a sense of 'benchmark' weights.

Tools

A selection of everyday items that can act as 'benchmark' weights: a 500 g bag of pasta, a 250 g tub of spread (use a recycled tub filled with rice or plasticene to make the weight up to 250 g), a 1 kg bag of sugar. Standard 250 g, 500 g and 1 kg weights. Balance and kitchen scales.

Task

Public talk

Introduce the pupils to the idea of having 'benchmark' items: items that help you make an estimate about the weight of things when you cannot actually weigh them. Pass around the 1 kg bag of sugar and the 1 kg weight and discuss whether these feel the same weight. It is quite likely that some pupils think they do not – the smaller, more compact 1 kg can feel heavier because it applies more pressure to the hand. Use the balance scales to check that they do weigh the same. Repeat this with the 500 g object and weight and the 250 g pair.

Private conversation

Set the pupils off to find, in pairs, collections of sets of three objects for each of the 1 kg, 500 g and 250 g weights: something they think is a little bit lighter than the weight, something they think weighs almost exactly the same and something they think is a bit heavier.

 Once they have collected their nine objects, they use balance scales to check if they were correct. They devise a way to record their findings.

Assessment

- Do pupils use a range of information – both size and 'feel' – to find their objects?
- Are they prepared to risk being wrong by choosing objects that feel close to the benchmark weights or do they play safe and choose objects that are much heavier or lighter?

Public talk

Have some pupils share their findings. How good were they at estimating whether something weighed almost 500 g or 1 kg? Get pupils to show how they used the balance scales to check.

 Use the kitchen scales to weigh and record the masses of some of the items the pupils had collected. Over the remainder of the day send pupils off to use the scales to find the weights of their items and to add this to their records.

Variations

Learners can use rice or small pasta to weigh out 250 g and 500 g and other amounts that you specify.

Extension challenge.

Stages

Lower Key Stage 2.

Direct object of learning

Measure, compare, add and subtract mass.

Indirect object of learning

Problem solving: solve practical problems.

Tools

Plasticene or similar dough/clay material. Balance scales, weights totalling 400 g. Rice or small pasta.

Task

Public talk

Set up the challenge:

Explain that pairs are going to be given weights that total 400 g. They are to use this and the balance scale to measure out a 400 g ball of plasticene. They will then return the 400 g weight(s) as they will not use them again.

   The challenge is to use their 400 g ball of plasticene to create balls of other weights: 200 g, 100 g, 50 g and 25 g.

   Once they have made these different weights you will put a list up on the board of various masses. The learners have to use the weights that they created to measure out those masses of rice (or whatever material you have made available).

Private conversation

Watch as the learners set about creating a set of weights – they need to use the scales to halve the various masses. Encourage them to be as accurate as possible when halving the quantities.
   Put the following list of quantities on the board:

   75 g
   175 g
   225 g
   350 g

Get the pupils to use their plasticene weights to measure out these quantities. They choose how they are going to record what they did. Can they find a different way to measure out the same quantity?

Assessment

- Do pupils realise that they might put plasticene weights on each side of the balance pan?
- Can they list three other masses that they could measure out using their weights?

Public talk

Invite pupils to share their recordings of how they measured out the various amounts. What different methods were used?

Variation

Learners could investigate the system of measures used in pounds and ounces: 1 oz, 2 oz, 4 oz, 8 oz, 16 oz. How did these weights allow every amount from 1 oz to 31 oz to be measured out? They could make a similar set of weights by sealing marbles into small plastic bags, one-marble bag, two-marble bag, four-marble bag and so forth.

VICTORIA'S SPONGE

Extension challenge.

Stages

Lower Key Stage 2.

Direct object of learning

Convert between different units of measure, between grams and kilograms.

Indirect object of learning

Problem solving: work backwards.

Tools

Some children may find balance scales, weights and plasticene helpful. Others may be confident enough to simply work with the numbers.

Task

Public talk

Set up the challenge. Explain that the following recipe was passed down by Grandmother Victoria and it is how she was able to bake a sponge cake without using any formal weights. You (or someone you know) tried it and it worked.

Here is how she did it:

- Place two large eggs in one of the pans on a balance scale.
- Measure out into the other pan an amount of sugar that exactly balances the weight of the eggs.
- Also weigh out the same amounts (that is, two eggs' weight) of (soft) butter and the same of flour.
- Beat the sugar and butter together until light and fluffy. Gradually beat in the eggs. Finally stir in the flour.
- Split the mixture between two cake tins and bake.

Explain how you tried this recipe and just before putting the tins in the oven you weighed the *contents* of *one* of the tins and it was a quarter of a kilogram.

Can the pupils use this information to figure out the weight of one egg?

Set the pupils off in pairs to investigate.

Private conversation

There is a lot of information here for the learners to make sense of, and it is likely that they may initially feel the problem is overwhelming. In that case, encourage them to represent the problem using a picture or diagram – they might use a bar to represent the weight of one egg. From there it should then be relatively easy to build up a diagrammatic representation of the problem and go on to find a solution (see Figure 8.11).

Figure 8.11

You may also need to remind the children that there are 1,000 grams in a kilogram.

Assessment

- If stuck, can pupils start with a trial and improvement approach by guessing the weight of one egg?
- Can they create models of the situation using physical materials or pictures or diagrams?

Public talk

Go over the various solutions with the class. Which solution method do the learners like best? Why?

Variation

A similar problem that involves working backwards is:

> *Tulela started to read a story book on Saturday and read 15 pages. She read twice that number of pages on Sunday. She finished the book on Monday by reading the last 28 pages. How many pages were there in the whole book?*

Source

Adapted from the Nrich problem 'Cherry Buns', available online at http://nrich.maths.org/2015.

VEGETABLE MARKET

Extension challenge.

Stages

Upper Key Stage 2.

Direct object of learning

Understand and use approximate equivalences between the metric units and common imperial units of kilograms and pounds.

Indirect object of learning

Reasoning: understand the relationship between different measuring scales.

Tools

Some learners may be helped by having some imperial and metric weights to handle and work with.

Task

Public talk

Talk about shopping for vegetables and the common amounts that people buy. For example, you might buy a 5 kg bag of potatoes, but would you buy that mass of, say, green beans? Elicit a list of common vegetables from the learners and record the typical weight of each that you might buy.

Talk about the imperial system of measures – what do the learners know about this? Introduce this approximate pair of conversion facts:

0.45 kg = 1 lb
2.20 lb = 1 kg

Talk about how, although they now have to sell things in grams and kilograms some people who run market stalls still think in terms of selling things in pounds (lbs). They can do this because they can calculate mentally what a mass in pound is in kilograms and vice versa.

Put up, or talk through this problem:

You get about 8 onions in a kilo.
So, approximately, what would 32 onions weigh in pounds (lbs)?

Give the pupils a little time to talk with a partner about what they think the answer is and why. Go over the solution on the board.

Private conversation

Put up these problems on the board for pupils to work on in pairs.

You get about three potatoes to the pound.
Roughly, how many potatoes might you get in a 5 kg bag?
About 8 beetroots weigh 1 kg.
About how many pounds would 28 beetroots weigh?
Medium carrots and parsnips weight about the same: you get around six carrots or six parsnips to 1 lb.
What would a bag of nine carrots and nine parsnips roughly weigh in kilograms?

As the pupils are working, note the different strategies they are using to solve the problem and select two or three pairs of learners to share what they have done with the rest of the class.

Learners who finish early can make up similar problems for others to solve.

Assessment

- Do the learners want to work with 'unit' weights (for example, finding the weight of one beetroot) or can they work with simple ratios?
- Are they using models like a t-table or double number line to help them find answers?

Public talk

Invite the pupils you identified to share their solution methods with the class.

Variation

Get children to investigate on the Internet the average weights of fruits and to create similar problems about fruits.

Source

Adapted from the Nrich problem 'Weighing Fruit', available online at http://nrich.mathematics.org/6055.

STRONG AS AN ANT?

Extension challenge.

Stages

Upper Key Stage 2.

Direct object of learning

Use and convert between standard units of mass from a smaller unit of measure to a larger unit and use decimal notation to up to three decimal places.

Indirect object of learning

Problem solving: connect different aspects of mathematics.

Tools

Calculators or spreadsheets.

Task

Public talk

Introduce the challenge by discussing the fact that ants are strong for their size. What would the pupils be able to lift if they were as strong as an ant? Give them a moment to chat with a partner and to come up with a list of things they think they would be able to lift if they had, relatively, the strength of an ant.

Then provide the following information:

An average ant weighs about 0.004 g.
An average ant can lift about 0.2 g.

Based on this information, do they want to change the list of things that they think they might be able to lift?

Write up on the board a list of some of the things the pupils think they would be able to lift if they were as strong as an ant.

Private conversation

Set the learners off to work in pairs and figure out what they would be able to lift if they were as strong as an average ant.

If some find this is too challenging, provide them with the information that some ants can carry 10 times their own body weight. It is even claimed that some ants can carry 50 times their own body weight.

Once the pupils have worked out the approximate weight that they could lift, they can use the Internet to investigate what sort of objects would weigh around that amount.

Assessment

- Can pupils work out the scale of the relationship between 0.004 g and 0.2 g?
- Are pupils clear that the relationship here is a multiplicative one – how many times more than bodyweight – rather than additive – how much more than bodyweight?

Public talk

Return to the list of objects that the pupils originally speculated that they might be able to lift if strong as an ant. Did they overestimate or underestimate what their strength would be?

Variation

What about jumping? If the average grasshopper is 2.5 cm long and can jump 50 cm, how far could the average child jump if they could jump as well as a grasshopper?

What other amazing feats can the children find out about minibeasts and convert to superhuman skills? Is what Spiderman purported to be able to do possible?

PROGRESSION IN MEASURING VOLUME OR CAPACITY

Capacity is the amount a container can hold, which is sometimes (confusingly) also referred to as the volume of the container. If a full bottle holds 250 ml of water, then the capacity of the bottle is 250 ml, and the volume of the water in the bottle is also 250 ml. The confusion comes from all solid objects having volume but not necessarily any capacity, so, strictly speaking the volume of a bottle is the amount of space occupied by the solid matter that makes up the bottle, rather than the amount that the bottle holds. And talk of the volume on the TV only makes things worse.

Direct comparison

A wide collection of empty plastic containers – drink and shampoo bottles, yogurt and cream cartons – provides most of the kit needed for direct comparison of capacity. As with mass, sight alone can be deceptive: which has the greater capacity, a tall thin bottle or a short, wide one may not be immediately obvious. Some 'flowing' material is needed to make the comparison – rice, dried beans or small pasta are less messy than sand or water. Cutting the top off a 2 l plastic drinks bottle and inverting it makes a funnel that can reduce spillages. Pupils can select a pair of containers, decide which they think has the greater capacity and check this. Do they fill what they think is the smaller bottle first, pour the contents into the larger and look for unfilled space, or vice versa and look for material left in the larger bottle?

Indirect comparison

In a sense, pupils are indirectly comparing capacities even when just ordering two containers as some sort of intermediate 'measure' that can be poured from container to container has to be introduced. Ordering three or more containers raises the level of challenge. Containers can only be compared in pairs so keeping track of the relationship between, say, four visually different bottles is far from trivial. It is interesting to simply pose this ordering as a challenge without any guidance as to how to do it and see what strategies pupils come up with.

Before introducing a smaller unit – egg-cups say – that needs to be counted to find the capacity, children benefit from pouring the contents of several different containers into larger, similar containers. A collection of 2-l plastic bottles, tops sliced off at the 'neck' provide a set of uniform containers that can be compared side-by-side. Pupils order a collection of different containers first by estimating what order they think they will go in and then filling each with dried goods (rice, sand or small pasta). Pouring the contents of each into several matching larger containers, pupils can then compare the level to which each is filled, thus setting the stage for reading scales on measuring jugs later.

When introducing the use of a repeated smaller unit, it is helpful to start off by filling up multiple copies of the unit, rather than having only one to fill and counting the number of times it is filled. Plastic egg cartons are perfect for this: cut one up to provide a collection of single 'units', and also have complete cartons to hand. Bottles can then be compared by filling them with rice, and then emptying the rice out by repeated filling a single 'egg-cup' unit and transferring each filled unit to a different section in a complete egg-tray. Pupils will then be able to see that, for example, one bottle held seven egg-cups, while the other held nine. *Five empty bottles* develops this task further.

Standard units

Make a measuring cylinder is a practical problem that helps learners to understand where the scale on a measuring cylinder comes from. *Litre box* takes this further and helps learners understand the relationship between cubic centimetres and millilitres.

Converting and using the relationship between millilitres and litres is explored through the problems presented in *Sports day*.

Imagining what very large volumes look like is not easy: *Olympic pool* provides a context for examining this. Finally, at the upper end of primary school, exploring the relationship between surface area and volume provides an opportunity to use spreadsheets to plot a graph and think about why it takes the shape that it does. There are also cross curricular links to be explored in terms of how animals' need to eat is related to their size: *Invasion of the giant ants* looks at this.

FIVE EMPTY BOTTLES

Foundational inquiry.

Stages

Key Stage 1.

Direct object of learning

Compare, describe and solve practical problems for capacity and volume.

Indirect object of learning

Reasoning: use a set amount to reason about the capacity of containers.

Tools

A collection of different empty bottles – soft drinks, washing-up liquid, shampoo and so forth. A small container to use as a non-standard unit, for example an egg-cup or small yogurt carton. Water (or rice or sand).

Task

Public talk

Display five empty bottles. Invite pupils to say which bottle they think would hold the most water. Which do they think would hold the least? What order between these two do they think the other bottles should be placed in? Label the bottles and record the order for later reference.

Private conversation

Working in pairs or small groups the pupils take turns to order the collection of five bottles. They do this in three ways. First, they agree on what order they think the bottles need to be placed in from the one holding the most to the one holding the least – this may be different from the order the class had decided upon. They record their chosen order.

They then fill each bottle with five units – say egg-cups – of rice. When each bottle has five units of rice in it, they check again to see if they still think the bottles are in order of capacity.

Finally, they empty the bottles and take it in turns to fill the bottles – one pupil uses the unit and repeatedly fills and pours rice in a bottle. Another pupil tallies the number of times the unit is filled. When the bottle is full, they count up and record the number of tallies. Everyone has a turn at filling and tallying.

Assessment

- Can pupils use appropriate language associated with capacity, for example, more than, less than, most, least?
- Are pupils thinking in three dimensions when deciding on the order of the bottles, not just looking at the height of them?

Public talk

Bring the class back together when every group has ordered the bottles. Was the original order that the class had agreed on correct? If it was, what had helped them to get the order correct? If it was not, why do they think they were originally wrong?

Variation

Have a selection of open topped cardboard boxes – make these 'sand-proof' by putting sticky time along all the edges. Using sand or rice to fill the measure, repeat the activity.

MAKE A MEASURING CYLINDER

Practice and consolidation.

Stages

Key Stage 1.

Direct object of learning

Choose and use appropriate standard units to estimate and measure capacity.

Indirect object of learning

Reasoning: create and use scales.

Tools

Empty 1 1/2 or 2 l drinks bottles: cut the top off just at the neck where the bottle narrows – keep the cut-off part to invert and create a funnel. Masking tape, 100 ml measures, water. A kitchen measuring jug or measuring cylinder. A collection of clean empty bottles.

Task

Public talk

With the class, look at and talk about the measuring jug. Has anyone seen one of these being used? What was it used for?

Explain that the pupils are going to make their own measuring jugs. Model sticking a strip of masking tape up the side of a top-cut-off drink bottle. Use the 100 ml measure to pour in 100 ml of water, marking and labelling the water level on the tape. Repeat, until nine units of 100 ml have been poured into the bottle. The last label was 900 ml – does anyone know what the next label will be?

Private conversation

The pupils should not need much guidance in creating their measuring cylinders. When they have completed them, ask them to use their measuring cylinders to find the capacity of some bottles.

Assessment

- Can the pupils use their measuring cylinders to decide which of two bottles holds the most?
- When the level of water in their measuring cylinder comes between two markers, can they make a reasonable estimate of the volume of water?

Public talk

Talk about how to read the scales on their measuring cylinders when the level of water does not exactly match a marker. Put a large version of the scale on the board and indicate various readings. What are sensible estimates?

Variation

Provide kitchen measuring jugs to measure various containers.

LITRE BOX

Practice and consolidation.

Stages

Lower Key Stage 2.

Direct object of learning

Measure, compare, add and subtract volume/capacity (l/ml).

Indirect object of learning

Problem solving: solve a practical problem and reason about relationships between measures.

Tools

Squared paper, rulers, scissors, tape, rice, sand or small pasta. Measuring cylinders or jugs. Centimetre cubes.

Task

Public talk

Set up the practical problem. Working in pairs the pupils are to make, from squared paper, an open-topped box that is 10 cm × 10 cm × 10 cm. Explain that the box needs to be strong enough to be filled with rice (or whatever dry pour material is to hand), so they will also have to decide how to make the box strong enough for that purpose.

Private conversation

As the pupils are working on constructing their boxes, ask them to think about how many centimetre cubes they think it will hold.

Public talk

Have to hand a measuring cylinder containing 1 l of rice.

Take one of the boxes made (a sturdy one!) and show this alongside the litre of rice. In their pairs, pupils decide whether they think the rice, when poured into the box, will be less than a full box, more or about the same. Record the numbers selecting each option. Pour the rice into the box – it should just about fill it.

Having thus established that the box has a capacity of 1 l, work on calculating the volume of the box in cubic centimetres (or centimetres cubed). You may need to model how there will be 100 cubic centimetres in one layer, so given that there are ten layers, the box must hold 1,000 cubic centimetres. What do the pupils know about the number of millilitres in a litre? What can they conclude about the relationship between millilitres and cubic centimetres?

Private talk

Put up a number of quantities on the board such as:

* 500 cubic centimetres
* 250 millilitres
* 1 1/4 litres.

Back in their pairs, pupils use their boxes to measure out these amounts of rice into other containers.

Assessment

* Can pupils confidently convert between cubic centimetres and millilitres?
* Can they use the relationship between litres and millilitres to convert fractions of litres to centimetres cubed?

Variations

Challenge pupils to make boxes that would hold 100 or 500 cubic centimetres.

SPORTS DAY

Practice and consolidation.

Stages

Lower Key Stage 2.

Direct object of learning

Convert between different units of measure, millilitres to litres and vice versa.

Indirect object of learning

Problem solving: relate volume and capacity to ideas of scale.

Tools

Measuring cylinders and empty containers.

Task

Public talk

Set up the context: the problems are about providing refreshments for sports day. Have these problems available to show on the IWB or on paper (if on paper provide these on separate slips, so that pupils can choose the order in which they want to do the problems).

> *To make up drinks for the school sports day, you mix 20 ml of squash for 180 ml of water. If a beaker holds 250 ml of drink, how many beakers can be filled from 1 l of squash? If you buy 5 l of squash, how many litres of drink will that make?*

> *A 1 l jug of water will serve eight cups of coffee. How many millilitres are in each cup of coffee? If people add 5 ml of milk to a cup of coffee, how many cups of coffee can be given milk from half a litre of milk?*

Private conversation

If pupils are having difficulty, encourage them to use practical equipment to try out some solution methods.

After they have had some time to work on the problems, get pairs to join up with other pairs and share what they have done so far.

Assessment

- Can learners scale up from finding the answer for, say 1 l, to finding it for 5 l?
- Can they record their working clearly enough for someone else to follow it?

Public talk

Invite selected pairs to share their solution methods with the class. Who can re-explain, in their own words, the method of solution that they have just heard?

Variation

Challenge the pupils to make up similar problems for others to work on.

OLYMPIC POOL

Extension challenge.

Stages

Upper Key Stage 2.

Direct object of learning

Estimate and calculate volume.

Indirect object of learning

Reasoning: make sense of a large volume and how measures given in metres can be converted to cubic metres and then into litres.

Tools

Internet access.

Task

Public talk

Talk about swimming pools. Does anyone know how long an Olympic pool is? How wide do they think it is? How deep is a swimming pool at the shallow end? At the deep end? Record the various estimates on the board and draw up a sketch of a pool, labelled with appropriate estimates.

How many litres of water do pupils estimate it would take to fill an Olympic swimming pool?

Note down the various suggestions and agree on the upper and lower bounds that the pupils think the answer is going to lie between.

Tell the pupils they are going to use the Internet to check the dimensions of an Olympic-size swimming pool and the relationship between cubic metres and litres. Once they have found this information they need to figure out the answer to the problem.

Private conversation

Part of the challenge here is that a swimming pool does not have a flat base. If some pupils are struggling to get started, suggest that they imagine that the swimming pool is, say, 2 m deep for its entire length.

There are at least two ways that pupils might deal with working with a sloped base. One is recognising that a pool is a very large prism, calculating the area of the vertical cross section (a trapezium) and then using that information to find the volume of the prism. Another approach is to look at a diagram of the cross section and think about how that could be theoretically cut up and rearranged to make the cross section a rectangle, and so making the pool equivalent to a cuboid (see Figure 8.12).

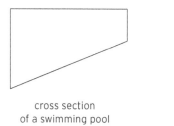
cross section
of a swimming pool

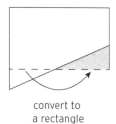
convert to
a rectangle

Figure 8.12

The answer that pupils are going to come up with is going to be in cubic metres, so the second challenge is how to convert that into litres. They might figure out how many litres are in a cubic metre, or they might convert cubic metres to cubic centimetres and use the fact that a cubic centimetre is equivalent to a millilitre.

The main teaching challenge here is to encourage the learners to persevere with the challenge and not provide too much guidance so that the thinking is taken away from the learners.

Assessment

* Can pupils set out their workings clearly so that someone else can follow them?
* Can they talk about the relationship between volume of water and the capacity of the pool?

As the pupils are working, select two or three pairs or groups who you will ask to share their workings with the class. These may not be the most sophisticated solutions, but ones that you think will provoke a rich mathematical conversation. Alert the pupils to the fact that you will be calling on them.

Public talk

Invite the pupils you had identified to share their working with the class.

Talk about the use of volume (of water) and capacity (of the pool). In what ways are these similar? In what ways are they different?

Variation

Pose some Fermi-type problems:

* If you were going to fill the pool one litre-jug of water at a time, walking to and from a tap, how long would it take to fill the pool?
* If you used the water in the pool to fill a household bath, and you bathe seven days a week, how long would the water in the pool provide baths?

Source

Adapted from an activity in Bobis, Mulligan and Lowrie (2013).

INVASION OF THE GIANT ANTS

Extension challenge.

Stages

Upper Key Stage 2.

Direct object of learning

Explore the relationship between volume and surface area.

Indirect object of learning

Reasoning: investigate the ratio of surface area to volume.

Tools

Interlocking cubes, spreadsheets.

Task

Public talk

Set the context of the giant bugs beloved of science fiction writers. Who has read books involving such creatures or seen movies with them in? Explain that by exploring the relationship between surface area and volume pupils are going to investigate whether such giant bugs could ever exist for real.

Private talk

Pupils need a number of cubes, preferably interlocking. Starting with a single cube, taking the length of its side as one unit they calculate the surface area and volume of the cube. They then construct a $2 \times 2 \times 2$ cube and find the same measures. They record the results in a table:

Length of side of cube	Surface area	Volume
1	6	1
2	24	8
3	54	27
4		

They can plot two graphs: one each the length of the side of the cube is along the x-axis and two different scales up the y-axis – one for the surface area and one for the volume. Doing this on a spreadsheet allows for playing with the data and including fractional lengths of sides. They then superimpose one graph on top of the other. Although these need two different scales on the y-axis – square units and cubed units – the same size divisions on the scale can be used for each. That is, a step of one unit squared can be the same as a step for one unit cubed.

Public talk

Talk about the graphs – for small cubes the number of units of surface area is greater than the number of units of volume but there comes a point where this crosses over and the number of units of volume is greater than the number of units of area.

What does this have to do with giant bugs? Small creatures can take in oxygen through their skin but for larger creatures the ratio of skin surface to volume is not great enough to let in sufficient oxygen. Hence the need for lungs. As insects have no lungs, those large sci-fi spiders would not take in enough oxygen to survive.

Variation

Pupils could investigate what this also has to do with small children needing to be wrapped up warmly in cold weather, and why mice need to eat almost constantly whereas elephants do not even need to eat every day.

Teaching time

There are two distinct aspects to learning about time: telling the time and elapsed time. Time is a measure but it is markedly different from those discussed earlier and although it is included in the mathematics curriculum, I think a cross-curricular approach to teaching time is best. History, science, PE and other parts of the curriculum present plenty of opportunities for exploring different aspects of time. Telling the time, in particular, I think, is a skill that we need to help pupils develop over time (sorry about the pun). The class clock is the best resource – referring to this across the days and weeks puts telling the time firmly into context. Worksheets on telling the time are really only exercises in reading dials and the fact that a clock showing ten past three can instantly turn into one showing five to six does not help pupils develop a sense of elapsed time. But for completion's sake, here are some tasks for teaching about time.

KEY STAGE 1 TASKS

Silly stories

Talking about and putting in order pictures of everyday activities provides pupils with the opportunity to develop the language associated with time.

Prepare some simple blank 'comic strips' of four or five boxes.

Talk with the children about everyday events such as what they do each evening when they get home from school or what they do on a Saturday morning. Pupils individually choose something that they regularly do that they record in a comic strip form. Help them to describe their event in four or five clear steps, for example, getting ready in the morning: getting out of bed, getting washed, getting dressed, eating breakfast. They draw the comic strip of their event.

When they have finished, the pupils cut up their comic strip into the separate boxes. Taking it in turns, they mix up the illustrations and, turning them over one at a time, tell the 'silly' version of their event: this morning I ate my breakfast, got washed, got dressed and then got out of bed. Everyone in the group helps put the pictures back in a suitable order, using the appropriate language of time: before, after, first, second, next and so forth.

My time line

Pupils can think about elapsed time over a longer period by making a time line showing their personal history.

In preparation for making the time lines, encourage pupils to bring in photographs of themselves and family events. Talk about what has happened in their lives since they were born and get them to draw pictures of those events that they don't have photos of.

Prepare strips of paper about 1 cm × 15 cm with a track of eight boxes (each about 12 cm × 12 cm) on it.

Work with the pupils on labeling the box at the far right with the current year and then working back to label the previous years. Which year were they born in? They put their picture of themselves in that box. What other events have happened? When did they start school? Who had a brother or sister born? How old were they when they learned to read? Help the children flesh out their time lines with details and to write these in or make illustrations.

LOWER KEY STAGE 2 TASKS

One hand clock

The two hands on the clock serve different purposes: the hour hand broadly indicates the approximate time and the minute hand adds precision. In introducing pupils to telling the time it helps to start with a clock with only the hour hand.

Remove the minute hand from a class demonstration clock and discuss telling the time with only the hour hand. As well as positioning the hand to point exactly to an hour, position it so that the pupils can talk about 'just before' and 'just after' the hour. What does it mean when the hour hand is about half way between the three and the four?

Get a cheap analogue clock with exposed hands and take (or break!) off the minute hand. Use this throughout the day to talk about the approximate time.

When the class are familiar with this, provide individual practice by preparing a page of clock faces with only the hour hand drawn in. They record the approximate times using appropriate terms.

Body clock

Use simple activities in PE to help pupils develop a sense of the duration of 30 seconds or a minute. For example, throwing in the air and catching a bean bag for a minute, running on the spot for 30 seconds.

You can also use this time to help pupils explore the beginning of inverse proportion. For example, stride swiftly across the hall and ask a learner to do it at the same time and to keep up with you so that you both start and finish together. Because the pupil will need to take more steps that you they may think that they were 'quicker' at crossing the hall than you were. Discuss how, since you started and ended together, you both took the same amount of time, but the shorter the size of a person's stride, the more steps they need to make to cover the same distance.

UPPER KEY STAGE 2 ACTIVITIES

Cooking problems

Prepare a series of problems involving time elapsed in cooking. Vary these between:

- problems where the elapsed time has to be found:

  Mike put a cake in the oven at 15.55 and took it out at 16.35. How long was the cake in the oven for?

- problems where the finished time has to be found:

  Helen puts a stew in the oven at 11.15. If it has to cook for 90 minutes, what time will she take it out?

- problems where the start time has to be found:

  Tim wants to have supper at 7.55. If he needs to cook a chicken for an hour and ten minutes, what time does Tim need to put it in the oven?

Rather than showing the pupils one way of calculating the answers to elapsed time problems, encourage them to sketch and use a 'empty time line' to figure out the answers.

Pair of timers

Provide pairs or groups of pupils with a three-minute and a five-minute sand timer. There are some times that can obviously be measured using these two, for example, six minutes, or eight minutes.

How can the pair of timers be used to measure four minutes? Or seven minutes?

Is there any number of minutes that cannot be measured out using this pair of timers?

9 Data handling and statistics

Traditionally, teaching about data handling and statistics has largely focused on getting pupils to create graphs. Now, however, few graphs are drawn by hand; they are more often created using technology such as spreadsheets. The ease with which graphs can be created means that they are used more frequently and so the emphasis in teaching now needs to focus more on reading and interpreting graphs. In fact, producing graphs is only one part of a five stage data handling cycle that comprises:

- identifying and refining a question or issue;
- deciding what data to collect and how to collect it;
- collecting the data;
- presenting the data;
- interpreting the data in the light of the original question.

Big ideas

- Learning about data handling and statistics means engaging with all the stages of the data handling cycle.
- Posing good questions is essential in deciding what data to collect.
- The same data can be presented in many different ways and different presentations highlight different aspects of the data.

Making connections

- Data handling and statistics connects to measures.
- Presenting data can help learners' understanding of scale.
- Data handling can provide pupils with experience of posing problems as well as solving them.

Progression in data handling and statistics

Although England's National Curriculum does not specifically include work on statistics in Year 1, as a prelude to work on bar charts and pictograms, children can be invited to solve problems that involve sorting them-selves in groups and so create 'human' bar graphs, as the task *Sort us out* demonstrates.

Through the use of pictograms, *What's in a name* introduces the big idea that one item (picture, symbol, block on a graph) in a mathematical representation can 'stand in for' more than one item in the real world.

Collecting data can often be time consuming and pupils' attention is more caught up in the collecting than in the subsequent presenting. The task *What's your score?* provides an example of a way of quickly collecting a range of data and representing it.

Too often data collection can become simply an end in itself, with pupils collecting and presenting data without any real questions that they are trying to answer. *Is it true that?* takes a claim - that three times the distance around your crown is about the same as your height - as an opportunity for pupils to use data they have gathered to check the veracity of something. Over and above this, it provides a practical, embodied introduction to the idea of the mean average.

The final two tasks take pupils into working with data that is broader than that which can simply be set up and collected within the classroom. The fantasy context of *How far could you get?* engages pupils in collecting data from the Internet and challenges them to set up some mathematical models to enable them to compare how far they could travel by different modes of transport in the same time.

The world wide web has extended the range of data that pupils can gain access to, including data about other schools and other learners. *Are you a bookworm?* involves pupils in interrogating a large data base and then gathering data to test out whether the pupils in their school are representative of what this large data set purports is typical.

SORT US OUT

Foundational inquiry.

Stages

Key Stage 1.

Direct object of learning

Introduce simple bar charts.

Indirect object of learning

Problem solving: create and interpret human bar charts.

Tools

Paper and coloured pencils.

Task

Public talk

Put the class into groups of about eight and ask each group to stand in a line facing the front of the class.

Ask, 'How quickly can you find the tallest person in your group and put everyone in order?'

Pupils sort themselves into a line with the smallest person at one end and the tallest at the other and in so doing will be engaged in a lot of comparing of heights.

Now ask them to sort themselves by the day of the month their birthday is on, or the number of buttons they can see on each other.

Private talk

Further challenges, like sorting by shoe size or numbers of brothers or sisters, are likely to mean that a single line is not possible (for example, three children might have the same shoe size), and so several children may have to stand together. Work on how they could form a 'human graph' by these sub-groups standing one behind the other. Pupils take a different coloured cube each and use these represent their orderings. These will go from putting the cubes out in one line, to piling some cubes up on top of others (three children have no brothers or sisters), thus producing instant mini-block graphs. Provide paper and coloured pencils and invite pupils to find some way of recording the ordering.

Assessment

- Can pupils suggest some criteria according to which they can sort themselves?
- Do pupils record their work in a simple graph-like format?

Public conversation

Bring the class together and invite pupils to go and stand in new groups, this time in response to questions with 'yes/no' answers:

- 'Do you like sprouts?'
- 'Do you walk to school?'
- 'Are you wearing trainers?'

Variations

An extension to this is to get the pupils to line up facing you. You decide on a 'secret' question (such as, 'Are you wearing a sweat shirt?'). Each pupil approaches and is directed to the left or right according to whether or not they fit your rule. Once the two groups have been established, can the learners figure out what your rule was? Pupils can take it in turns to think of a rule and sort everyone out.

An 'instant graph' chart can easily be set up and used almost every day to do some data handling (and a bit of calculating). All you need is a board about 1 m × 50 cm (strong cardboard will do), with a line drawn down the centre, lengthwise. Paper, a bulldog clip and a collection of spring clothes pegs complete the set up.

Each morning, before the pupils arrive, clip paper to the top of the board with a 'yes/no' question on it, such as, 'Do your shoes have laces?' or, 'Is 592 an even number?' Label the halves of the board 'yes' and 'no'. As they arrive, pupils collect a peg and clip it to the side of the board according to their answer to the question. An instant, visible representation of the data is created and you can discuss this as well as looking at the number of pegs on each side and the differences between these.

WHAT'S IN A NAME?

Practice and consolidation.

Stages

Key Stage 1.

Direct object of learning

Use information presented in scaled bar charts and pictograms and tables to answer questions.

Indirect object of learning

Problem solving: select and use appropriate calculation skills to solve problems involving data presented in a scaled fashion.

Tools

Class lists of names of children in various classes across the school.

Task

Public talk

Ask the pupils to write down their first name and to count the number of letters in it.

Who has the name with the most number of letters? Whose name has the least number of letters?

Say the range is from three ('May') to nine ('Christina') letters - write the numerals from '3' to '9' on the board.

Go round the class asking each pupil in turn for the number of letters in their name, tallying alongside the numbers and finally putting up the total.

Talk about creating a block graph for the data collected and explain that this will be in the form of a pictogram where an image will be used to represent every two people. Decide on a simple image to use and go through the totals working out with the class the number of symbols required for each number of letter names. Construct the graph either using post-its with one symbol on each or electronically. Label the axis, and put in the scales

Ask various questions about the graph such as:

- Which is the most common number of letters in our names?
- How many children have names with that number of letters?
- Which is the least common number of letters in our names?
- How many children have names with that number of letters?
- What is the difference in numbers of children between the most common and the least common?

Private conversation

Give pairs of children a class list. Working together they draw up a chart like the one on the board. One child counts the number of letters in the first names while the other tallies – they swap over about half way through. They complete a pictogram with a symbol representing two children. They pose and answer five questions about their graphs.

Assessment

- Can pupils pose questions that involve comparisons, for example, how many more pupils have names with six letters than names with five letters?
- Asked questions about their graphs, do pupils correctly the use the fact that each symbol stands for two pupils?

Public talk

Display some of the graphs produced and the questions the pupils asked about them.

Looking across a number of graphs are there any patterns in the data?

Draw up a chart to collate the data from five or six classes.

Back in their pairs, pupils produce a pictogram for this combined data but this time one picture represents every five pupils.

Variation

As pupils become confident, help them turn their pictogram graphs into bar charts with appropriate scales on the y-axis. There are many things that can be used for such surveys but choose data that is not going to embarrass any learner: favourite colour or flavours of crisp rather than, say, height or weight.

 ## WHAT'S YOUR SCORE?

Practice and consolidation.

Stage

Lower Key Stage 2.

Direct object of learning

Interpret and construct simple pictograms, tally charts, block diagrams and simple tables.

Indirect object of learning

Problem solving: interpret, collate, organise and compare information.

Tools

Semi-open number lines.

Task

Public talk

Demonstrate to the class how to draw a star by drawing a triangle and drawing a second one inverted over the other.

Let the pupils practise drawing these. Explain that they are going to have one minute to draw as many stars as they can. Emphasise that the point here is not to try and 'win' by drawing the most number of stars. They should draw the stars as quickly as they can but not sacrifice making them reasonably accurate for speed.

After the pupils have had a short time to practise, time them for exactly one minute. They count up the number of stars they completed.

Provide everyone with a 1–100 number line, the scale marking the multiples of five and ten. Also have one on the board to complete in the same way that the pupils will complete their individual ones. Go round the class asking each pupil to call out their score.

For each value an X is marked above that point on the number line – the pupils also write in the number below on their lines if it is not already there. For example, if a pupil drew 23 stars, everyone marks the point 23 on their lines, with the numeral 23 below the line and an X marked above it. If a score is called out again, a second X is marked above the X already there – so a form of block graph is built up.

Talk about the highest and lowest scores and get the pupils to figure out the difference between these two values. When the class has agreed on this value, talk about how this value is called the 'range' of the data.

Do any scores have more than one X on them? Is there a score that has more Xs than any other score? That is the mode value of the data.

Most likely the Xs will be spread out along the number line with gaps between them with several values having, at most, only have one or two Xs on above them. Discuss with the children how the Xs from an 'instant' graph, but that is it a bit 'spread-out' and rather 'flat'. Discuss how rather than recording the exact score of every child, the scores can be put into groups, say, scores between 20 and 24. Work with the class on agreeing on a set of groups that will reduce the data to around 6 or so groups. This will depend on the range of the scores. For example, if the scores have a range of around 50 (from say 25 to 76) then the groupings might be 20-29, 30-39, 40-49, 50-59, 60-69, 70-79. But if the range is smaller, say 20 (from 22 to 41) then the groups need to be smaller; 20-24, 25-29, 30-34, 35-39, 40-45.

Draw up a table for the groupings chosen and get the pupils to record their own.

Go round the class again with pupils calling out their scores once more. Now as scores are called out, everyone puts a tally into their chart to record which group the score goes in.

Private talk

The pupils can now create block graphs of the grouped data.

Assessment

- Do pupils display knowledge of the conventions of graphs: clear scales, labelling axes and so forth?
- Can they answer questions about their graphs such as, 'How many pupils scored more than 30?' or, 'Which did more pupils score in, between 10 and 19 or between 20 and 29?'

Public talk

Display the number line record and grouped data together and discuss why the same data looks different on each. What are the advantages and disadvantages of each representation?

Variation

A variety of tasks to be completed in a short period of time could be used. For example, the children could be asked to list multiples of five for one minute. How many were they able to write down?

IS IT TRUE THAT?

Extension challenge.

Stage

Lower Key Stage 2, but also suitable for older learners.

Direct object of learning

Interpret and present discrete and continuous data using appropriate graphical methods.

Indirect object of learning

Problem solving: collect data and use scales in their representations.

Tools

Tape measures.

Task

Public talk

Before setting off on the main inquiry, pupils can explore the idea of mean average from measuring their 'crowns'.

Provide each pupil with a strip of paper that is more than long enough to fit around his or her head and across the forehead (as if making a paper crown). Working in pairs the pupils fold the strip to create a reasonably accurate measure of their 'crown' (not allowing for any overlap – the ends of the strip should just meet). They cut or tear off the extra paper and discard this. Using rulers or tape measures, everyone measures and records the length of their 'crowns' – some may measure this in centimetres and millimetres, some you may direct to measure it to the nearest centimetre.

Private conversation

Working in groups of four or five, using their paper strips, can the children figure out what the average 'crown' is for their group? Discuss the idea of 'average' being what the measurement would be if everyone had the same size crown but the total of all the crowns together did not change. Pupils can tape all their paper strips together, end to end, and then fold the long strip into four or five equal parts depending on the number in the group. They measure the length of this 'average' that they have created. Using calculators and the lengths that they previously recorded can they check by calculating if their practical way of finding the average has worked?

Public talk

The children are now set up for the challenge. Explain that you heard someone say, *'Three times round your head is about the same as your height'*.

Discuss this statement. What would count as 'about'? Set the pupils off in groups to find out if the statement is true.

Private conversation

Provide the learners with paper strips, tape measures, calculators and, if they are familiar with them, the opportunity to use spreadsheets. But apart from that, leave it to the pupils to decide what data they are going to collect and how they will present it.

Groups have to prepare a presentation that they will give to the class on their conclusions about whether or not the claim is accurate.

Assessment

- Do the pupils use measuring tools accurately?
- Are they checking the relationship by multiplying (scaling up the lengths of their crowns by a factor of three) or by dividing (dividing their heights by three)?

Public talk

As it would take too long for everyone to present their findings to the class, you could divide the class up into two sets of the groups. So if, say, there were eight groups, four work together, each group presenting their findings to the other three groups in their half of the class.

Variation

There are other 'folk' claims about proportions of body parts that could be checked, for example:

- Holding your arms out wide, the distance from fingertip to fingertip (body span) is the same as your height.
- The length of your nose is the same as your ear's.

Source

A classic inquiry that I first met in around 1992 (Askew, Brown, Prestage, & Walsh, 1992) when developing materials to support the introduction of the National Curriculum.

HOW FAR COULD YOU GET?

Extension challenge.

Stage

Upper Key Stage 2.

Direct object of learning

Read and interpret information in timetables.

Indirect object of learning

Problem solving: decide how best to organise and present findings.

Tools

ICT.

Task

Public talk

Set up a fantasy scenario:

Aliens have announced that they are going to transport the school, its grounds and the surrounding area into space in two hours' time. The aliens have disabled all cars and motor cycles, but not public transport. Everyone is going to try and get as far away from the school as possible, either on foot, cycling or public transport.

Using one, some, or all of these modes of transport, what is the furthest the learners think that they could get away from the school? Take some suggestions of how far they think they could get – record these for later reference.

Private conversation

Pupils work in pairs or small groups. The problem is set up in such a way that they are going to have to either generate data (speed of walking) or search the Internet to find out things like average cycling speeds or local timetables for public transport.

Give the groups initially only around five minutes to talk together and plan what information they are going to seek out. Get groups to join up with other groups and share their ideas and plans.

Assessment

- Are the pupils prepared to pursue different lines of inquiry, for example comparing travelling by bus with cycling?
- Can they present their workings in ways that make clear to others the assumptions they are making about the models they create?

Public talk

Ask groups to share their plans for solving the challenge.

How do the solutions found compare with the suggestions made at the beginning of the lesson?

Which group thinks they have found the furthest that could be travelled? Can they convince everyone else of their findings?

Variation

Challenges of the 'would you rather' type provide contexts for setting up models and finding solutions:

- Would you rather have your weight in £1 coins, or your height as a stack of £2 coins?
- Would you rather have to copy out a chapter from a reading book or do 1000 long multiplications?

ARE YOU A BOOKWORM?

Extension challenge.

Stages

Upper Key Stage 2.

Direct object of learning

Interpret and construct pie charts and use these to solve problems.

Indirect object of learning

Reasoning: decide how best to organise and present findings and explain and justify reasons.

Tools

Calculators. Data from the Internet – see the 'Source' section at the end of this activity.

Use this data and a spreadsheet program such as Excel to produce two pie charts to display the reading preferences of males and females from a survey carried out in 2003:

	Male	Female
Adventure	2 274	2 007
Crime	1066	392
Factual	850	2 069
Fantasy	1087	589
Horror	1961	1754
Other	951	1775

(The data can be downloaded directly into excel from the link at the end of this activity. The original data had eight categories – here, some categories have been collapsed together to make the pie charts easier to compare.)

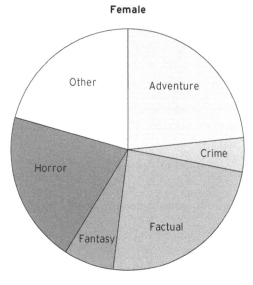

Task

Public talk

Display the two pie charts on the IWB, explaining what they represent.

In pairs, pupils spend a few minutes talking about what they can conclude about the reading preferences of males and females.

Discuss things like, which genre is most popular for each gender and whether there are any different preferences between the genders.

Talk about, say, the different regions showing a preference for fantasy books. Can we conclude from the pie charts that more boys than girls expressed a preference for fantasy?

Ask the learners to suppose the 500 males had answered the survey and 2,000 females. Could you conclude that more males expressed a preference for fantasy?

This is a key teaching point: pie charts only show the relative proportions. Without knowing the number of people in each sample, conclusions about absolute numbers in each category cannot be deduced.

Reveal that the total numbers of people sampled were:

Male: 8189
Female: 8586

Model on the board how to figure out an approximation for the actual numbers of people in each category by measuring one of the angles. Say it was 56° on the 'males' pie chart. Then as a proportion of the full turn, it is 56/360. So you need to find 56/360 of 8189. Take suggestions for how to do that. Go through finding 1/360 by dividing 8,189 by 360 and then multiplying that by 56.

Private conversation

Give pairs of children copies of the pie charts, protractors and calculators. Challenge the learners to use the protractors to measure the size of the angle of each piece of the pie chart and figure out an approximation of the number of people who gave that preference. Support those children who need further help either in measuring the angles or carrying out the calculation.

Assessment

- Are pupils able to use the protractors correctly and accurately?
- Can they use the calculators appropriately and make sense of the answers obtained?

Public talk

Go through the numbers the learners came up with – how close are they to the actual numbers in the survey? Why are they not exactly the same?

Put the class into groups of three or four and set the challenge of coming up with a survey to see if the children in the class have preferences that are similar to these.

Private conversation

Groups carry out the survey and use a spreadsheet to present their findings. They should present these as pie charts and choose one other form of representation that they think highlights something different from the pie chart.

Public talk

Look at and discuss the various ways the learners chose to present the data? What does each highlight?

Variations

The Census at School website (see next) has a wealth of data that learners can explore.

Source

The data provided here was sourced from censusatschool.org.uk – a great resource for data handling. This particular challenge was adapted from: www.censusatschool.org.uk/resources/data-handling/142-are-you-a-bookworm.

References

Alexander, R. (2006). *Education as dialogue: Moral and pedagogical choices for a runaway world.* Cambridge, UK: Dialogos.

Ashlock, R. B., Johnson, M. L., Wilson, J. W., & Jones, W. L. (1983). *Guiding each child's learning of mathematics: A diagnostic approach to instruction.* Columbus, OH: Charles E. Merrill Publishing Company.

Askew, M. (2012). *Transforming primary mathematics.* London and New York: Routledge.

Askew, M., Brown, M., Prestage, S., & Walsh, A. (1992). *Using and applying mathematics: Book A (notes for teachers at key stages 1-4).* York, UK: National Curriculum Council.

Ball, D. L. (1993). With an eye on the mathematical horizon: Dilemmas of teaching elementary school mathematics. *The Elementary School Journal, 93*(4), 373-397.

Baratta-Lorton, M. (1976). *Mathematics their way.* Menlo Park, CA: Addison-Wesley.

Biggs, E., & Shaw, K. (1995). *Mathematics alive!* London and New York: Cassell.

Bobis, J., Mulligan, J. T., & Lowrie, T. (2013). *Mathematics for children: Challenging children to think mathematically* (4th ed.). Sydney: Pearson Education Australia.

Bruner, J. (1960). *The process of education.* Cambridge, MA: Harvard University Press.

Cameron, A., Hersch, S. B., & Fosnot, C. T. (2004). *Young mathematicians at work. Professional development materials. Taking inventory, grades K-1.* Portsmouth, NH: Heinemann.

Carpenter, T., Fennema, E., Franke, M. L., Levi, L., & Empson, S. B. (1999). *Children's mathematics: Cognitively guided instruction.* Portsmouth, NH: Heinemann.

CensusAtSchool. Available online at www.censusatschool.org.uk.

Clements, D. H., & Battista, M. T. (1992). Geometry and spatial reasoning. In D. A. Grouws (Ed.), *Handbook of research on mathematics teaching and learning* (pp. 420-464). New York: Macmillan.

Department of Education and Early Childhood, Victoria. (n.d.). *Fractions and decimals; online interview classroom activities.* Available online at http://goo.gl/COwC90.

Duckworth, E. R. (2006). *"The having of wonderful ideas" and other essays on teaching and learning* (3rd ed.). New York, NY: Teachers College Press.

Duval, R. (1998). Geometry from a cogntive point of view. In V. V. C. Mammana (Ed.), *Perspectives on the teaching of geometry for the 21st century: An ICMI study* (pp. 37-52). Dordrecht: Kluwer.

Dweck, C. S. (2000). *Self-theories: Their role in motivation, personality, and development.* Philadelphia, PA: Psychology Press (Taylor and Francis Group).

Empson, S. B., & Jacobs, V. R. (2008). Learning to listen to children's mathematical thinking. In D. Tirosh & T. Wood (Eds.), *Volume 2: Tools and process in mathematics teacher education of the international handbook of mathematics teacher education* (pp. 257-281). Rotterdam/Taipei: Sense Publishers.

English, L., & Sriraman, B. (2010). Problem solving for the 21st century. In B. Sriraman & L. English (Eds.), *Theories of mathematics education* (pp. 263-290). Heidelberg: Springer.

Erickson, T. (1989). *Get it together.* EQUALS: University of California.

Ericsson, K. A., Krampe, R. T., & Tesch-Romer, C. (1993). The role of deliberate practice in the acquisition of expert performance. *Psychological Review, 100*(3), 363-406.

Fielker, D. (1983). *Removing the shackles of Euclid.* Derby, UK: Association of Teachers of Mathematics.

Fosnot, C. T., & Dolk, M. (2001a). *Young mathematicians at work: Constructing multiplication and division.* Portsmouth, NH: Heinemann.

Fosnot, C. T., & Dolk, M. (2001b). *Young mathematicians at work: Constructing number sense, addition and subtraction.* Portsmouth, NH: Heinemann.

Gilpin. S. (2002). *Shapes, shapes everywhere. A second grade geometry unit aligned with mathematics standards and content knowledge: A compendium of standards and benchmarks for k-12 education* (3rd ed.). Aurora, CO: Mid-continent Research for Education and Learning.

Gould, P. (1993). *Co-operative problem solving in mathematics.* Sydney: Mathematical Association of N.S.W. Australia.

Gravemeijer, K. (1997). Instructional design for reform in mathematics education. In *The role of contexts and models in the development of mathematical strategies and procedures* (pp. 13-34). Utrecht: Freudenthal Institute.

Gravemeijer, K. (1999). How emergent models may foster the constitution of formal mathematics. *Mathematical Thinking and Learning, 1*(2), 155-177.

Hersch, S. B., Fosnot, C. T., & Cameron, A. (2005). *Young mathematicians at work professional development materials: Working with the array, grades 3-5.* Portsmouth, NH.

Kilpatrick, J., Swafford, J., & Findell, B. (Eds.). (2001). *Adding it up: Helping children learn mathematics.* Washington, DC: National Academy Press.

Kirkby, D. (1992). *Games in the teaching of mathematics.* Cambridge, UK: Cambridge University Press.

Kutnick, P., Sebba, J., Blatchford, P., Galton, M., Thorp, J., MacIntyre, H., & Thorp, J. (2005). *The effects of pupil grouping: Literature review. Research Report 668.* London, UK: DfES publications.

Lakoff, G., & Johnson, M. (1980). *Metaphors we live by.* Chicago, IL: University of Chicago Press.

Lakoff, G., & Núñez, R. E. (2000). *Where mathematics comes from: How the embodied mind brings mathematics into being.* New York: Basic Books.

Langer, E. J. (1997). *The power of mindful learning.* Cambridge, MA: Da Capo Press.

Marton, F., Runesson, U., & Tsui, A. B. M. (2004). The space of learning. In Marton, F., & Tsui, A. B. M. (Eds.), *Classroom discourse and the space of learning.* Mahwah, NJ: Lawrence Erlbaum Associates, Inc., Publishers.

Marton, F., Tsui, A. B. M., with Chik, P. P. M., Ko, P. Y., Lo, M. L., Mok, I. A., Ng, D. F. P., Pang, M. F., Pong, W. Y., & Runesson, U. (2004). *Classroom discourse and the space of learning.* Mahwah, NJ: Lawrence Erlbaum Associates, Inc., Publishers.

Mason, J. (2002) *Researching your own practice: The discipline of noticing.* London, UK: RoutledgeFalmer.

Moschkovich, J. (2007). Bilingual mathematics learners: How views of language, bilingual learners, and mathematical communication affect instruction. In N. S. Nasir & P. Cobb (Eds.), *Improving acess to mathematics: Diversity and equity in the classroom* (pp. 89-104). New York and London: Teachers College Press.

Nunes, T., Bryant, P., Sylva, K., & Barros, R. (2009). Development of maths capabilities and confidence in primary school [Research report DCSF-RR118]. London: Department for Children, Schools and Families (DCSF).

Rinaldi, C. (2001). A pedagogy of listening. *Children in Europe, 1*(1), 2-5.

Siegler, R. S. (2010). Playing numerical board games improves number sense in children from low-income backgrounds. In *Understanding number development and difficulties, BJEP Monograph Series II* (pp. 15-29). Leicester: The British Psychological Society.

Siegler, R. S., & Ramani, G. B. (2009). Playing linear number board games - but not circular ones - improves low-income preschoolers' numerical understanding. *Journal of Educational Psychology, 101*(3), 545-560.

Van de Walle, J. A. (2007). *Elementary and middle school mathematics: Teaching developmentally* (6th ed.). Boston: Pearson Education.

Van Galen, F., Feijs, E., Figueiredo, N., Gravemeijer, K., van Herpen, E., & Keijzer, R. (2008). *Fractions, percentages, decimals and proportions.* Rotterdam/Taipei: Sense Publishers.

Vergnaud, G. (1983). Multiplicative structures. In R. Lesh & M. Landau (Eds.), *Acquisition of mathematics concepts and processes* (pp. 128-175). London: Academic Press.

Wright, R. J., Stanger, G., Stafford, A. K., & Martland, J. (2006). *Teaching number: advancing children's skills and strategies* (2nd ed.). London, UK; Thousand Oaks, CA: SAGE Publications Ltd.

Index

actions 12, 15-16, 17, 70
Adding and subtracting large numbers 70, 77-79
Adding It Up: Helping Children Learn Mathematics (National Research Council, 2001) 2
addition 56, 81; calculation methods 57; change situations 66; compare situations 67; compensation strategies 21; developing understanding of 60-62; number bonds 70; part-part-whole situations 66-67; place value 23, 33, 35; progress in 70; rounding 24; strategies 62-65
additive reasoning 56-80, 81; big ideas 56; calculation methods 56-57, 68-69; change situations 66, 68-69; compare situations 67, 68; developing understanding 60-62; key words 69; making connections 56; number bonds 57-60, 70; part-part-whole situations 66-67, 68, 71; place value 33; strategies 62-65; unknowns 68
Alexander, Robin 22
algebra 18, 86, 88, 129
algorithms 57, 87
All kinds of quadrilaterals 112, 118-119
All that I know 50-52
angles 109, 110, 111, 115, 116-118, 121, 124-125
Are you a book worm? 162, 168-171
area 132-133, 137-142, 152, 157, 158
arrays 12-13, 81, 83-89, 93, 96-100, 102-104, 107, 110
Askew, M. 167
assessment: additive reasoning 71-72, 73-74, 75, 76, 79, 80; counting and ordering 25, 26-27, 28, 29, 31-32; data handling and statistics 162-163, 164, 165, 167, 170; formative 20, 45; fractions 47, 48-49, 50, 51, 53, 54-55; geometry 113, 114, 116, 117, 119, 121, 123, 128, 129; measures 134, 136, 138, 140, 141-142, 144, 146, 148, 149, 150, 152-154, 155, 157; multiplicative reasoning 98, 100, 101-102, 104, 106; place value 36, 37-38, 39, 40, 41, 43
associative rule 86
attentive listening 19-21
averages 161, 166
At the bakery 96, 98-100

balance scales 142-143, 144, 145, 147
Ball, Deborah 86
bar charts 163, 164
bar diagrams 66-67, 70, 71
Baratta-Lorton, Mary 124
Barros, R. 3
Battista, M. T. 110
battleships 122
Be seated 121, 125-126
bead strings 57-58, 59-60, 70, 72-74
Behind the wall 110, 112-113
benchmark measures 130, 143, 145
Best at? 46, 53-55
Biggs, E. 134
Birthday presents 70-72

Bobis, J. 157
Body clock 160
Bohm, David 21
bottles 151, 152-153
'bridging through ten' 61, 62, 75
Brown, M. 167
Bruner, Jerome 17
Bryant, P. 3
Buying lunch 70, 75-76

calculation methods 56-57, 62-63, 64-65, 68-69
Cameron, A. 100
Can you make? 111, 115-116
capacity 151-157
Cartesian product of two measures 81, 82
Census at School 170-171
change situations 65, 68-69, 81
Chocolate boxes 9-10
Choral counting 24, 27-28
circles 109
Cities of the world 34, 42-43
Clap and tap 121, 123-124
Clements, D. H. 110
clocks 159-160
Closest to 24, 28-30
collections 15, 16, 36, 61; containers 151; number bonds 57
collective memory 10
column arithmetic 87-88
communicative resources 21
commutativity 62, 86, 93, 95
compare situations 61, 65, 67, 68, 81
comparison 130
compensation strategies 21, 24
complements 59, 62, 70, 74-75
conjecture 5, 18, 21
containers 151, 155
contexts 12-14, 17; additive reasoning 70; fractions 44; multiplicative reasoning 96; percentages 55
Cooking problems 160
coordinate grids 121, 122, 125-126, 127-128, 129
counting 23-28, 57-58; additive reasoning 72-73; *Say ten* 4-5; in threes 94, 95
Counting arrays 96, 97-98
cubes: additive reasoning 61, 71-72; counting 24-25; geometry 110-111, 121-122, 123, 127-128; unit cube rulers 131; volume 158
cuboids 110

data collection 161, 162, 167
data handling and statistics 161-171
Deal-em 8
decimals 23, 35, 50-52, 130
decomposition 61

deliberate practice 7
diagrams: additive reasoning 66-67, 69, 70, 71; measures 147-148
dialogue 21-22
dice 53, 58, 61
direct objects of learning 4, 21; additive reasoning 60; arrays 88; t-tables 92
distributive rule 86
division 23, 81, 98-100; contexts 12; *Deal-em* 8; fractions 45; link with multiplication 88, 92, 96; long division 4, 95-96; progression in 96-97; t-tables 91-92
Dolk, Maarten 63, 98
double number lines 46, 54, 81, 89-90, 149
doubling 85-86, 93-94, 101
Down on the farm 132, 139-140
Duckworth, Eleanor 19
Duval, R. 110
Dweck, Carole 7

Eating toast 44, 48-49
elastic bands 131, 135, 143
embodied learning 15
Empson, S. B. 20
end of term party 10
English, Lyn 6-7
equality 131
equations 15, 18
equilateral triangles 109, 111
Erickson, T. 76
Ericsson, K. A. 7
estimation 143, 145
Every day a shower! 8-9
Exploring temperatures 24, 30-32
extension challenges 8-10, 19

factor trees 106
'feely bags' 110, 111
Fermi problems 8-9, 157
Fielker, David 112, 119
Fill the wall 46, 52-53
fingers, counting with 57
Five empty bottles 151, 152-153
fluency 2, 3, 4, 11; additive reasoning 72; counting and ordering 24, 27; geometry 116, 124, 125; indirect objects of learning 4; multiplicative reasoning 92-93, 100; number bonds 57-60, 70; *Say ten* 4-5
formal units 130, 131, 132, 143
formative assessment 20, 45
Fosnot, Cathy 36, 63, 98, 100
foundational inquiries 3, 5-6, 8, 70
Four hungry children 6
fractions 6, 23, 43-55; arrays 89; contexts 13; measures 130; multiplicative reasoning 81; *Multiplying fractions* 97, 106-108; naming 7; as relationships 44
frame games 8, 24, 29-30, 32-33, 96, 101-102
Freudenthal Institute 63, 69

games 7-8, 58; *see also* frame games; tasks
gender issues 21-22
generalisations 5, 18
generative learning 20
geometry 109-129; big ideas 109; construction processes 111; making connections 109-110; position and movement 121-129; progression in understanding properties of shapes 110-121; reasoning processes 112; visualisation processes 110-111; *see also* shapes
Gilpin, S. 115
Gould, Peter 76

graphs 152, 158, 161, 162, 163-164, 165
Greater or smaller? 34, 38-39
grids 121, 122, 125-126, 127-128, 129
group work 19; data handling and statistics 166-167, 168, 170; fractions 51; geometry 115, 119, 120; measures 138, 152; place value 41

halving 85-86, 94
Heavier or lighter? 143-144
height 132, 133-134
Hersch, S. B. 100
hidden object games 110, 113
'horizontal mathematising' 69
How far could you get? 162, 167-168
How many at the party? 45, 46-47

Ideal gnome homes 132, 135-136
improper fractions 46, 52, 53
independent practice 19
indirect objects of learning 4-5, 11; additive reasoning 60; arrays 88; t-tables 92
inequality 131
informal units 130, 131, 132
initiation, response and evaluation (IRE) 19, 20
Internet 9, 106, 156; arrays 96, 97; *Cities of the world* 42, 43; data handling and statistics 162, 169, 170-171; geometry 121; temperatures 32; weights 149, 150
Into rectangles 133, 140-142
invariance 109
Invasion of the giant ants 152, 158-159
IRE *see* initiation, response and evaluation
Is it true that? 161, 166-167
isosceles triangles 110, 115

Jacobs, V. R. 20
jumping 62-63

Key Stage 1: additive reasoning 70-74; counting and ordering 24-27; data handling and statistics 162-164; fractions 46-49; geometry 110, 112-115, 121-124; measures 133-135, 143-145, 152-154; multiplicative reasoning 97-100; place value 33, 35-38; time 159
Key Stage 2: additive reasoning 70, 74-80; counting and ordering 24, 27-33; data handling and statistics 164-171; fractions 46, 49-55; geometry 115-121, 124-129; measures 135-142, 146-151, 154-159; multiplicative reasoning 97, 100-108; place value 34, 38-43; time 159-160
key words 69

Lakoff, G. 15-16
Langer, Ellen 21
laptops 20
large numbers 34, 40-42, 70, 77-79
learning: embodied 15; generative 20
length 130, 131, 132, 133-135, 142, 143
listening 19-21
Litre box 151, 154-155
long division 4, 95-96
long multiplication 4, 86, 87-88
Lowrie, T. 157

Make a measuring cylinder 151, 153-154
Make weights 143, 145-147
Market stalls 34, 37-38
Marton, Ference 4
Mason, John 18
mass 142-151

'mathematising' 14, 34, 66, 69
mean average 161, 166
meaning 14, 17, 67, 111
measures 4, 130-160; aspects of measurement 130-132; big
    ideas 130; data handling and statistics 161, 166; fractions
    23, 44-45; length, area and perimeter 132-142; making
    connections 130; measuring stick metaphor 16; shapes
    109; time 159-160; volume and capacity 151-159; weights
    142-151
metaphors 15-16
metre sticks 131, 135
metric and imperial measures 143, 148-149
Mirror, mirror 121, 126-128
mixed numbers 46
modelling 8-9; additive reasoning 56, 57; arrays 84, 85-86
models 12, 14-15, 17, 63-64
Moschkovich, Judit 20-21
movement 109, 110, 121, 128-129
moving along a path 16
Mulligan, J. T. 157
Multi-step problems 70, 79-80
multiple proportions 81, 82
multiplication 81; calculating area 137; *Deal-em* 8; link
    with division 88, 92, 96; long division 95-96; long
    multiplication 4, 86, 87-88; multiplying by ten 94;
    progression in 96-97; surface metaphor 16
multiplication tables 92-93, 94-95, 100-101
multiplicative reasoning 81-108; arrays 83-89; big ideas 81;
    double number lines 89-90; long division 95-96; making
    connections 81-82; mass 143, 150; place value 23, 33,
    34-35; progression in multiplication and division 96-97;
    scales 130; strategic approaches 92-94; t-tables 90-92;
    tables 94-95
Multiplying fractions 97, 106-108
My time line 159

National Curriculum 2, 131, 161
negative numbers 24, 30-32
nines 94, 95
notation: additive reasoning 67; decimal 150; fractional 6,
    44, 45, 48-49, 50; multiplicative reasoning 84, 95, 96;
    place value 34
number bonds 57-60, 70, 96
number lines 13, 14, 23-24, 26-27; additive reasoning
    58, 59, 60, 62-65, 73, 74-75, 77-78; fractions 46,
    51; geometry 110; multiplicative reasoning 81, 89-90;
    percentages 54; temperatures 32; weights 149
number system 23-55; big ideas 23; counting and ordering
    23-33; fractions 23, 43-55; links with geometry 110;
    making connections 23; place value 23, 33-43
number tracks 14, 23-24, 25, 58, 66-67
Nunes, T. 3
Núñez, R. E. 15-16

object collection 16; *see also* collections
object construction 16
objects of learning 4-5, 11, 21; additive reasoning 60; arrays
    88; t-tables 92
Olympic pool 152, 156-157
One hand clock 159-160
Order on the line 24, 26-27
Order, order 34, 39-40
ordering 23-24, 28-33, 39-40, 162

Pair of timers 160
pair work 5, 19; additive reasoning 70, 75, 77-80; counting
    and ordering 29, 30; data handling and statistics 168;
    fractions 47, 49-50, 53, 54-55; geometry 111, 114, 117,
    120, 122, 126, 127-128; measures 133-134, 138, 141, 146,

149, 150, 152; multiplicative reasoning 100, 101, 105-106,
    107; place value 36, 37, 38-39, 40, 41, 43
Pairs to 100 70, 74-75
parallelograms 112, 119, 129, 140, 141-142
part-part-whole situations 61, 65, 66-67, 68, 71, 81
party, end of term 10
percentages 46, 53-55
perimeter 132, 135-136
pictograms 161, 164
pie charts 168-171
Place the cubes 121-122
place value 23, 33-43, 95
plasticene 146, 147
Plot the quadrilateral 121, 128-129
position 109, 110, 114, 121-129
posters 41
practical problems 9
practice 7
Prestage, S. 167
prime numbers 106
private talk 18-19
problem solving 2, 3, 6-7, 11; choice of problems 5-6;
    data handling and statistics 161, 162, 163, 164, 166, 167;
    fractions 6, 49; geometry 114, 122, 123; indirect objects
    of learning 4; measures 144, 146, 147, 150, 154, 155; place
    value 34, 35, 41, 42; *Say ten* 4, 5; *see also* foundational
    inquiries; tasks
proficiencies 2-3, 11
Progressive noughts and crosses 96, 100-102
proportion 81, 82; inverse 131, 160; t-tables 91
protractors 170
pseudo-practical tasks 9
public conversation 19

quadrilaterals 109, 112, 116, 118-119, 128-129
quantity 13, 14, 16; measures 130, 146; place value 34
questioning 19, 20
quotitioning 92, 96

ratio 81, 82, 91
Realistic Mathematics Education 69
reasoning 2, 3, 11; additive reasoning 70; counting and
    ordering 26, 29, 30; data handling and statistics 168;
    fractions 44-45, 46, 48, 50, 52; geometry 110, 112,
    115, 118, 120, 127, 128; indirect objects of learning 4;
    measures 133-135, 137, 139-140, 145, 148, 152-153, 156,
    158; percentages 54; place value 37, 38, 39; *Say ten* 5;
    see also additive reasoning; multiplicative reasoning
reasoning chains 61
Reasoning chains 96, 102-104
rectangles 109, 112, 119, 129, 133, 137, 139, 140-142
relational listening 19-21
relationships, fractions as 44
Release the prisoners 97, 104-106
revoicing 20
rhombus 111, 129
Right angles everywhere 116-118
Rinaldi, C. 19
Ripped and torn 133, 136-138
rounding 21, 24, 32-33, 43
Rounding four in a row 32-33
Rounding up or down? 24
rulers 4, 131, 135, 139

'sandwiching' answers 96
Say ten 4-5
scales 130, 131; balance 142-143, 144, 145, 147; data handling
    and statistics 161; measuring cylinders 153-154
scaling down 35

scaling up 34-35
Secret ribbons 132, 134-135
Shape treasure hunt 111, 113-115, 121
shapes 109, 110-121; area and perimeter 132-133, 135-136, 137-142; translations 128-129
sharing 23, 45
Shaw, K. 134
Sieve of Eratosthenes 106
Silly stories 159
simple proportions 81, 82
Sleep tight 34, 40-42
small group work 19; data handling and statistics 166-167, 168, 170; fractions 51; geometry 119, 120; measures 138, 152; place value 41
Sort us out 161, 162-163
splitting 62-63
Sports day 152, 155-156
spreadsheets 152, 158, 161, 167, 169
square numbers 97
squares 109, 111, 129, 137-138
Standing up and lying down 132, 133-134
statistics *see* data handling and statistics
Stocktaking 34
Strong as an ant? 143, 150-151
subtraction 56, 81; calculation methods 56-57; change situations 66; compare situations 67; developing understanding of 60-62; number bonds 57, 59-60, 70; part-part-whole situations 66-67; progress in 70; rounding 24; strategies 62-65; *see also* additive reasoning
Sullivan, Peter 10
surfaces 16
swimming pools 156-157
Sylva, K. 3
symbols 12, 14, 15, 16-17; additive reasoning 61, 67, 70; measures 131
symmetry 110, 116

t-tables 81, 90-92, 149
tables 92-93, 94-95, 100-101
tablets 20
talk 1, 18-22
tasks 1, 2-11; *Adding and subtracting large numbers* 70, 77-79; *All kinds of quadrilaterals* 112, 118-119; *All that I know* 50-52; *Are you a book worm?* 162, 168-171; *At the bakery* 96, 98-100; *Be seated* 121, 125-126; *Behind the wall* 110, 112-113; *Best at?* 46, 53-55; *Birthday presents* 70-72; *Body clock* 160; *Buying lunch* 70, 75-76; *Can you make?* 111, 115-116; *Chocolate boxes* 9-10; choosing task with aims in mind 2-3; *Choral counting* 24, 27-28; *Cities of the world* 34, 42-43; *Clap and tap* 121, 123-124; *Closest to* 24, 28-30; *Cooking problems* 160; *Counting arrays* 96, 97-98; *Deal-em* 8; *Down on the farm* 132, 139-140; *Eating toast* 44, 48-49; *Every day a shower!* 8-9; *Exploring temperatures* 24, 30-32; *Fill the wall* 46, 52-53; *Five empty bottles* 151, 152-153; focus on fluency 4; focus on problem solving 3; focus on reasoning 3; *Four hungry children* 6; *Greater or smaller?* 34, 38-39; *Heavier or lighter?* 143-144; *How far could you get?* 162, 167-168; *How many at the party?* 45, 46-47; *Ideal gnome homes* 132, 135-136; *Into rectangles* 133, 140-142; *Invasion of the giant ants* 152, 158-159; *Is it true that?* 161, 166-167; *Litre box* 151, 154-155; *Make a measuring cylinder* 151, 153-154; *Make weights* 143, 145-147; *Market stalls* 34, 37-38; *Mirror, mirror* 121,

126-128; modelling 8-9; *Multi-step problems* 70, 79-80; *Multiplying fractions* 97, 106-108; *My time line* 159; objects of learning 4-5; *Olympic pool* 152, 156-157; *One hand clock* 159-160; *Order on the line* 24, 26-27; *Order, order* 34, 39-40; *Pair of timers* 160; *Pairs to 100* 70, 74-75; *Place the cubes* 121-122; *Plot the quadrilateral* 121, 128-129; practical problems 9; practice and consolidation 7-8; *Progressive noughts and crosses* 96, 100-102; *Reasoning chains* 96, 102-104; *Release the prisoners* 97, 104-106; *Right angles everywhere* 116-118; *Ripped and torn* 133, 136-138; *Rounding four in a row* 32-33; *Rounding up or down?* 24; *Say ten* 4-5; *Secret ribbons* 132, 134-135; *Shape treasure hunt* 111, 113-115, 121; *Silly stories* 159; *Sleep tight* 34, 40-42; *Sort us out* 161, 162-163; *Sports day* 152, 155-156; *Standing up and lying down* 132, 133-134; *Stocktaking* 34; *Strong as an ant?* 143, 150-151; tasks cycle 5; *Tree sorts* 112, 120-121; *Turn about* 121, 124-125; *20-bead string* 70, 72-74; *The twins' party* 45, 49-50; *Twos, fives, tens* 24-25; *Vegetable market* 143, 148-149; *Victoria's sponge* 143, 147-148; *Weight scavenger hunt* 143, 144-145; *What's in a name* 161, 163-164; *What's your score?* 161, 164-165; whole class challenges 9-10
technology 20
temperature 24, 30-32
Thiagarajan, Sivasailam 102
three-dimensional shapes 109, 110, 111, 114, 121
threes, counting in 94, 95
time 159-160
tools 1, 12-17
translations 128-129
trapezium 129, 157
treasure hunt game 126
Tree sorts 112, 120-121
triangles 109, 110, 111, 115, 142
triples 93
Turn about 121, 124-125
'turn and talk' 18
20-bead string 70, 72-74
The twins' party 45, 49-50
two-dimensional shapes 109, 111, 114, 115, 120, 135-136
Twos, fives, tens 24-25

unitising 23
unknowns 68

Van de Walle, J. A. 122, 126
variation theory 4, 60-61
Vegetable market 143, 148-149
Vergnaud, Gerard 81
'vertical mathematising' 69
Victoria's sponge 143, 147-148
visual, auditory or kinaesthetic learning 15
visualisation processes 110-111
volume 151-159

Walsh, A. 167
Weight scavenger hunt 143, 144-145
weights 142-151
What's in a name 161, 163-164
What's your score? 161, 164-165
whole class challenges 9-10
word problems 12, 70
Wright, Bob 28